(Re-)Mobilising Voters in Britain and the United States

(Re-)Mobilising Voters in Britain and the United States

Political Strategies from Parties and Grassroots Organisations (1867–2020)

Edited by
Véronique Molinari and Grégory Benedetti

DE GRUYTER
OLDENBOURG

ISBN 978-3-11-111030-1
e-ISBN (PDF) 978-3-11-071040-3
e-ISBN (ePUB) 978-3-11-071045-8

Library of Congress Control Number: 2020950239

Bibliographic Information published by the Deutsche Nationalbibliothek
The Deutsche Nationalbibliothek lists this publication in the Deutsche Nationalbibliografie;
detailed bibliographic data are available on the Internet at http://dnb.dnb.de.

© 2022 Walter de Gruyter GmbH, Berlin/Boston
This volume is text- and page-identical with the hardback published in 2021.
Cover image: Togapix / iStock / Getty Images Plus
Printing and binding: CPI books GmbH, Leck

www.degruyter.com

Table of Contents

Dr. Gregory Benedetti & Prof. Véronique Molinari
Introduction —— 1

Part 1: Empowering Racial Minorities: Legal Measures, Grassroots Mobilisation and Political Strategies

Olivier Richomme
1   **Empowering Minority Voters in the U.S.**
    The Paradoxes of Redistricting in the Age of Conjoined Polarisation —— 25

John A. Kirk
2   **From Representation by the Elite Few to the Mobilisation of the Masses**
    The Long Grassroots Struggle for Black Voting Rights in Arkansas since the 1860s —— 47

Sharon Baptiste
3   **Mobilising Black and Minority Ethnic (BME) Voters in the United Kingdom**
    The Political Strategies of Operation Black Vote (1996–2019) —— 77

Part 2: Mobilising Women: Grassroots Action and Political Discourse

Jean-Louis Marin-Lamellet
4   **Mobilising Agrarian Men and Women in the Late Nineteenth Century**
    The Case of Farmers' Alliances and the Populist Movement —— 109

Karine Rivière-De Franco
5   **Women Speaking to Women?**
    Margaret Thatcher, Theresa May and the Female Electorate —— 131

Part 3: Digital Mobilisation: Revolutionising Politics in the Twenty-first Century?

Géraldine Castel
6 **Digital Politics and Mobilisation in the UK**
The Elusive Silver Bullet —— 153

Marion Douzou
7 **Mobilising the Right(-wing) voters**
The Tea Party's Use of Technology —— 181

Part 4: When Grassroots and Party Mobilisation Interact: the Case of the Republican Party in the Twentieth Century

Robert Mason
8 **The Republican Minority and Voter Mobilisation**
The Pursuit of Grassroots Activism and the Politics of Conservatism and Moderation in the United States, 1933–1964 —— 201

List of contributors —— 225

Index —— 227

Dr. Gregory Benedetti & Prof. Véronique Molinari
Introduction

In 2020, in the midst of the Covid-19 pandemic and protests for racial justice and equality,[1] the presidential (and congressional) elections in the United States took on a particular importance as to the decisive impact they might have on the future of U.S. politics. Following the unpredictable victory of Donald Trump in 2016, and in a country that has become increasingly ideologically, politically, racially and socially polarised over the last decades, the question of voters' mobilisation appears to have been at the core of many debates, both among the two major parties – Republicans and Democrats – and grassroots organisations. In the United Kingdom, the last elections, in December 2019, were also held against a background of concern over the national fragmentation of the country that is said to have been both revealed and intensified by the 2016 Brexit vote and has been epitomised by the phrase "divided Britain" conveyed over the past three years by politicians, the press and even literature. While political disaffection had become a major concern among both observers and political elites as turnout had fallen below 60 percent at the 2001 general election, the political turbulence of the last three years (including the 2017 elections, the change in premiership in 2019 and new elections in 2019) appear to have led to the political engagement of previously disaffected groups, especially young people.[2]

Political mobilisation, as defined by Rosenstone and Hansen, is "the process by which candidates, parties, activists and groups induce other people to participate."[3] It can be direct and include door-to-door canvassing, phone calls, mail solicitations, and targeted ads, or indirect, through the identification of leaders who will, in turn, mobilise people in their individual networks. While mobilisation by political parties and its impact are the object of an important literature, less studied are the efforts undertaken by civil rights organisations, popular and grassroots movements to mobilise and re-mobilise various groups of voters. Be-

---

[1] On May 25, 2020, an African-American man, George Floyd, died after being arrested by the police of Minneapolis, Minnesota. Dereck Chauvin, a police officer, knelt on George Floyd's neck for more than eight minutes leading to the death of the suspect. In the aftermath of the murder, protests and demonstrations occurred across the United States and around the world to denounce police brutality, in particular, and racism in general against ethno-racial minorities.
[2] Sarah Birch, "Our new voters: Brexit, political mobilisation and the emerging electoral cleavage," *IPPR Progressive Review* 23, no. 2 (2016).
[3] Steven J. Rosenstone and John Mark Hansen, *Mobilisation, Participation, and Democracy in America* (Macmillan, 1993), 25.

https://doi.org/10.1515/9783110710403-001

yond the simple desire to make voters position themselves in favour of one party or another, these organisations have intended to shed light on the right to vote and on political participation as a way of helping these minorities get heard. In the past, these strategies may have been synonymous with mobilising new voters, as was the case with feminist movements in the United States and the United Kingdom, or African Americans in the early twentieth century when organisations like the NAACP, under the impulse of black leaders like W.E.B. Du Bois, for instance, raised the voting right issue as a symbol of racial progress and integration. The question is still being raised today, however, as ethno-racial minorities are often disinterested and even disenfranchised sometimes in some states of the United States when it comes to political participation. This has led organisations like the National Council for La Raza or *Voto Latino* in the United States to try to get Hispanics to vote, generating potentially major changes in future elections, whether it be at the local or at the federal level. More recently, the movement "Black Lives Matter" has endeavoured to mobilise according to an intersectional[4] strategy which encompasses other marginalised minorities in a larger activist and political approach. Operation Black Vote in Britain is another example of a non-partisan, non-governmental political organisation aiming at encouraging members of the BME (Black and Minority Ethnic) population to participate in the electoral process at both local and national levels. The women's vote has also regularly drawn people's attention on both sides of the Atlantic Ocean and led to mobilising efforts on the part of long-established organisations like the League of Women Voters, National Organization for Women, or the Fawcett Society, as well as of newly emerging organisations that have chosen to focus on some specific groups according to age, marital status or ethnic origins (Moms4Bush and Granny Voter in 2004, Moms4Trump in 2016, Higher Heights of America and *Mujeres Latinas en Accion*, among others in the United States).[5]

The enfranchisement process throughout the English-speaking world has all but been a simultaneous one. In addition to the repeal of religious bans in the early nineteenth century, no less than six electoral reforms (Representation of

---

[4] The concept of intersectionality was coined by American civil rights activist and legal scholar Kimberlé Crenshaw in 1989. It contends that social categorisations such as race, class and gender are interconnected, leading to overlapping and interdependent systems of discrimination. The movement Black Lives Matter seems to symbolise the fact that different forms of oppression may be taken into consideration when trying to mobilise voters to fight for several policy issues.

[5] See Véronique Molinari, "Mobilisation des électrices et instrumentalisation de la différence: les campagnes électorales de 2004 et 2005 en Grande-Bretagne et aux États-Unis", dans Renée Dickason, David Haigron and Karine Rivière-De Franco (dir.), *Stratégies et campagnes électorales en Grande-Bretagne et aux Etats-Unis* (L'Harmattan, 2009), 85–106.

the People Acts) were passed by the British Parliament between the mid-nineteenth century and the late 1960s, first enlarging the electorate on a property basis – yet still within the confines of an exclusively male electorate – then extending the right to vote to women in two stages (1918 for women over 30 and 1928 on equal terms with men) and finally lowering the voting age to 18 at the end of the 1960s. In the United States, the history of voting rights offers an even more fragmented picture with – in addition to the extension of the franchise to the same categories following a similar timetable at federal level – the inclusion or exclusion of voters from the registers on the basis of ethnicity and race through the vote of a dozen Acts between 1790 and 1965. African Americans who obtained the right to vote with the 15th Amendment in the aftermath of the Civil War thus had to keep fighting throughout the first half of the twentieth century to actually enjoy the franchise. Nowadays, the question remains a potent issue in the Southern States where some legal measures, such as gerrymandering, redistricting and the use of voter ID, tend to restrict the right to vote by disproportionately excluding minorities, especially people who have been convicted, even in the case of minor crimes or misdemeanours. These practices naturally target people of colour in the United States where African Americans, for instance, represent 40 per cent of the total prison population, while accounting for less than 15 per cent of the whole population. This step-by-step enfranchisement based on property, sex, ethnicity and age quite naturally engendered fears or expectations among the main political parties and occasionally led in turn to forceful attempts to attract each new – and potentially still free of allegiance – group of voters.

Concurrently and subsequently to some of these changes, British and American politics experienced periods of dealignment and realignment, when weakening or changing partisan ties seemed to threaten existing structures. The first major episode of realignment in Britain[6] occurred in the wake of the First World War, as the electorate rocketed from 28 per cent to 78 per cent of the adult population between 1910 and 1919 and the Labour party began to displace the Liberals as the major party of the left.[7] Another instance was the early 1970s, when the two elections of 1974 marked the end of what Ivor Crewe defined as an

---

[6] This study will focus on Britain only as Northern Irish politics have been centred on different socio-economic issues, led by different political parties and using a different electoral system.
[7] After some 20 years of a three-party system, marked by coalition and minority governments, the Liberals were finally displaced by Labour at the end of the 1930s and, by the end of World War II, the country had reverted to a two-party system ; Hugh W. Stephens, "Party Realignment in Britain, 1900–1925: A Preliminary Analysis." *Social Science History* 6, no. 1 (1982): 35–66, www.jstor.org/stable/1170846, accessed March 22, 2020.

era of "stable two party voting"[8] and the combined vote for the Conservatives and Labour fell from 96 per cent in 1951 to 77 per cent.[9] Finally, the surge of support for the Liberal Democrats on the occasion of the 2010 general elections provided another episode of realignment, leading to the first coalition government since the Second World War. While the change was gradual in the first two instances, and could correspond to what has been called "secular realignment", the 2010 general elections corresponded to a more abrupt change among the electorate, directly linked with dissatisfaction with the two major parties, but short-lived (the term "critical realignment," or "critical election" coined by V. O. Key, cannot apply here, however, as critical elections were for him a realignment within the electorate "both sharp and durable").[10] Partisan switching has also happened a handful of times in the United States. One such moment that has been identified is the 1860 elections, when the Republican victory brought to an end some 40 years of Democrats' control of both Congress and the Oval Office. Another major period of realignment then came in 1932, when the election of Franklin D. Roosevelt during the Great Depression ushered in an era of Democrats' control that would, here again, last for decades. Using empirical evidence, Key went on to identify a number of elections which he termed as "critical," or "realigning" which resulted in American voters changing their political party affiliations. As in the case of the United Kingdom, although with a couple of years' lag, the U.S. presidential elections from 1964 to 1972 have been regarded as heralding a period of fundamental political realignment, during which civil rights became as important a cleavage as economic rights.[11] In the late 1970s to the early 1980s, while the United States witnessed a shift away from the consensus politics of Eisenhower's Modern Republicanism towards the "Reagan Revolution", Britain saw its own so-called post-war consensus come to an

---

8 Bo Sarlvik and Ivor Crewe, *Decade of Dealignment: The Conservative Victory of 1979 and Electoral Trends in the 1970s* (New York: Cambridge University Press, 1983), 183. 1945–1970 had been a period of relative electoral stability dominated by the two major political parties, the Conservative Party and the Labour Party, and characterised by "votes cast primarily along class lines, limited regional differences in party support and consistent ideological differences". Between 1945 and 1970 the Conservatives and the Labour Party regularly gained approximately 90 per cent of the votes cast in general elections and few voters switched their party allegiance between general elections.
9 Ivor Crewe, B. Särlvik, and J. Alt, "Partisan Dealignment in Britain 1964–1974", *British Journal of Political Science* 7, no. 2 (1977): 129–190, 130.
10 V.O. Key, Jr, "A Theory of Critical Elections", *The Journal of Politics* 17, no. 1 (1955): 11, https://www.jstor.org/stable/2126401, accessed March 22, 2020.
11 Norman Schofield, Gary Miller and Andrew Martin. "Critical Elections and Political Realignments in the USA: 1860–2000". *Political Studies* 51, no. 2 (2003): 217–240.

end, to be replaced by a widening gap between the two major parties and the "Thatcher Revolution". One year after Margaret Thatcher's election, the 1980 presidential election was thus another critical election, when Republican challenger Ronald Reagan defeated the Democratic incumbent Jimmy Carter by 489 to 49 Electoral Votes. More recently, Trump's 2016 victory has also raised the issue of a "critical election" as the Republican underdog disrupted the established political order by defeating Hillary Clinton who, pundits believed, should have capitalised on her long and rich experience as a former First Lady, New York Senator and Secretary of State in the Obama Administration. After a new election cycle in 2020, the question of a potential realignment embodied and symbolised by Donald Trump's presidency remains an open question when looking at the voters who contributed to the success of the businessman turned politician, despite his failure to secure a second term in office.[12] However, more presidential elections will need to take place before the affirmation of political realignment within the Republican Party can be ascertained, especially since realignments may be triggered by the rise of a political figure but are rarely candidate-specific but characteristic of a larger ideological shift within a party.

Next to periods of realignment, the second half of the twentieth century has witnessed an increase in the number of floating voters and a general decline in voting participation common to the United States and Britain, beginning in the 1960s and continuing up to this day.[13] This phenomenon of dealignment[14] has been identified as coinciding with voters "growing increasingly critical of the performance of governments."[15] Many political observers thus attribute what they see as a "crisis in democracy" or a "crisis of political participation" to the "erosion of confidence in the institutions of representative democracy" taking place in Western countries.[16] This declining participation in formal politics, whether it is due to voter apathy or political alienation, has led to a growing

---

[12] First of all, it is important to mention that Donald Trump did not win the popular vote in 2016 (62,980,160 votes for Trump, against 65,845,063 for Clinton). Secondly, statistics demonstrate that Donald Trump built his success thanks to the mobilisation of core Republican voters: whites, men, people over 50 and non-graduates.

[13] Richard Brody, "The puzzle of political participation in America", *The New American political system* (Washington: American Enterprise Institute for Public Policy Research, 1978), 287–324; Ruy A. Teixeira, *Why Americans don't vote: turnout decline in the United States, 1960–1984* (New York: Greenwood Press, 1987).

[14] Unlike realignment, dealignment is said to occur when people leave the party with which they were affiliated, but do not affiliate with any other party.

[15] Paul Whiteley, *Political Participation in Britain* (London: Palgrave Macmillan), 6.

[16] Pippa Norris, *Critical Citizens: Global Support for Democratic Government* (Oxford: OUP, 1999), 257.

gap between political institutions and the people that they are supposed to represent. This, as shown by Miller,[17] has resulted in three clear trends:
- First, a decline in electoral turnout: the average turnout at general elections in Britain fell from highs of over 82 per cent at the two elections of 1950 and 1951 to between 71 and 78 per cent thereafter, with an all-time low of 59.4 per cent in the 2001 elections; in the United States, while voter turnout in the presidential elections has historically been better than for midterm elections (in recent elections, about 40 percent of the voting eligible population votes during midterm elections), it has also been much lower, starting from a 60.6 per cent of the voting age population in the 1956 elections to 55.7 per cent in the 2016 elections.[18]
- Second, a decline in party membership. While in the 1950s, Conservative Party membership peaked at three million and Labour at one million, these figures had dropped to around 190,000 for Labour and 150,000 the Conservatives in 2013.[19] The situation is slightly different in the United States where a stagnation in terms of party membership has been observed over the last 10 years. However, what is worth noticing is that in 2020, for the first time in U.S. history, the number of registered independents outnumbered the number of registered Republicans (it will take several election cycles however to determine whether this is revelatory of a new trend or just one of the many consequences the Republican Party has had to handle since Donald Trump's victory in 2016).[20]
- Finally, and maybe most importantly, a growing lack of trust in politicians on the part of the public. In 2015 an Ipsos MORI poll revealed that just 21 per cent of Britons trusted politicians to tell the truth compared with 25 per cent trusting journalists and estate agents or bankers (37 percent). The trend is not as recent as it might seem (at no point since 1983 have more than a quarter of the public ever trusted politicians to tell the truth)[21]; it

---

[17] Car Miller, "We are living through a radical shift in the nature of political engagement...", *The Rise of Digital Politics*, Demos, 2016.
[18] https://www.presidency.ucsb.edu/statistics/data/voter-turnout-in-presidential-elections, accessed March 19, 2020.
[19] Ibid., 15. Miller notes that despite recent surges in membership for Labour, the SNP, UKIP and the Green Party, the broader trend is "a clear, deep decline in the proportion of the electorate who are members of any party involved in formal politics".
[20] http://ballot-access.org/2020/03/27/march-2020-ballot-access-news-print-edition/#ref, accessed June 22, 2020.
[21] "Politicians are still trusted less than estate agents, journalists and bankers", Ipsos-Mori, January 22, 2016, Trust in Professions, https://www.ipsos.com/ipsos-mori/en-uk/politicians-are-still-trusted-less-estate-agents-journalists-and-bankers, accessed March 2, 2020.

is, however, in marked contrast with the early 1970s, when four in 10 people in Britain trusted governments to put the needs of the nation above those of their political party (only one in five still did so 30 years later).[22] In the United States, according to recent studies by the Pew Research Center, public distrust in federal and local government has increased over the last 20 years. Three-quarters of U.S. citizens are convinced that their fellow citizens' trust in federal government has been shrinking dramatically. This perception of the federal government also reveals the deep polarisation of U.S. politics as Democrats and Republicans are strongly divided over the question of whether the federal government does too much (according to Republicans) or not enough (according to Democrats) for people. What is also worth noticing is that this low level of trust is disproportionate among non-white, poorer and less-educated individuals. This low level of trust among more marginalised citizens is to be linked with their broader lack of trust in institutions such as the justice system or the police, which in the current context is even more acute.[23] In 2016, the victory of a political outsider like Donald Trump may be said to have epitomised this phenomenon. One of the consequences of this growing cynicism, Norris suggests, has been a decline in "conventional participation: discouraging electoral turnout, political activism, and civic engagement".[24]

While realignment tends to be particularly worrying for the main political parties, which must strive to win back their electorate, dealignment can in turn be a concern for civic associations, all the more so as these trends are particularly marked in some sections of the population, such as young people and BME voters. In the context of the fight for racial justice and equality in the United States, it is interesting to notice that all civic organisations fight to mobilise or re-mobilise citizens, even marginalised ones, insisting on the fact that voting remains one of the main options to advance policies that may reform society and lead to more social justice. Black Lives Matter organisers, members and followers have, for instance, launched registration campaigns all across the United States to encourage people to make their voice heard. As a result, the Democratic

---

[22] Catherine Bromley, John Curtice and Ben Seyd, "Is Britain Facing a Crisis of Democracy?", The Constitution Unit, July 2004, 5, https://www.ucl.ac.uk/constitution-unit/sites/constitution-unit/files/112_0.pdf, accessed March 19, 2020.
[23] "Key findings about Americans' declining trust in government and each other", https://www.pewresearch.org/fact-tank/2019/07/22/key-findings-about-americans-declining-trust-in-government-and-each-other/, accessed June 22, 2020.
[24] Pippa Norris, op. cit., 257.

Party seems to have greatly capitalised on the strong mobilisation of African American voters who supported massively Joe Biden in battleground states such as Georgia, Pennsylvania, or Michigan, confirming once more that the black vote is a key factor for any successful Democrat's presidential bid since the late twentieth century[25] (one of the key factors for any successful Democrat's presidential bid since the late twentieth century).

A large amount of literature has been published on party communication and its impact on voters' participation. Most of these studies, however, have been led by political analysts and have concentrated on a single country and on the means used. Our aim here is to offer a historical approach to the issue and, through case studies, expand the field's research agenda by taking into account less familiar mobilising strategies in Britain and the United States and paying attention to the message sent to potential participants. Two different yet complementary approaches will be used, one from the top down with political parties, the other from the bottom up with grassroots organisations, to analyse how these groups either (re)connect citizens with politics or give birth to social movements which durably occupy the political landscape of the United States and Britain.

1 Empowering Racial Minorities: Legal Measures, Grassroots Mobilisation and Political Strategies

In June 2020, along with other black athletes and entertainers, African-American basketball player Lebron James decided to launch an organisation called "More than a Vote" to encourage Blacks to mobilise politically and to raise awareness about the necessity to preserve everyone's right to vote in the United States, especially ethno-racial minorities. Set up in the context of renewed racial tensions in the U.S., this new grassroots organisation, composed of prominent public figures from civil society, offers a new significant example, in the twenty-first century, of the willingness to continue the historical journey to empower racial minorities.

---

25 Rashawn Ray, in a Brookings article published in the aftermath of the elections recalls that black voters constituted 50% of all Democratic voters in Georgia, 20% in Michigan, and 21% in Pennsylvania. Rashawn Ray, "How Black Americans Saved Biden and the American Democracy", Brookings, November 24, 2020, https://www.brookings.edu/blog/how-we-rise/2020/11/24/how-black-americans-saved-biden-and-american-democracy/, accessed January 6, 2021.

From the early days of the American Republic, the question of the economic, political and social integration of ethno-racial minorities, particularly Blacks, has been at the core of activists' preoccupations. As such, the issue of Blacks' enfranchisement came to occupy a central position in the political debate, in co-ordination with the abolitionist movement that intensified in the mid-nineteenth century under the impulse of influential leaders such as Frederick Douglass, for instance. As the Civil War guns fell silent, the abolition of slavery, with the 13th Amendment of 1865, became a springboard on which activists capitalised to secure the 14th Amendment (citizenship to all regardless of race) in 1868, and the 15th Amendment (right to vote for all men regardless of race) in 1870. From that point on, mobilising Blacks to go to the polls, to get elected to local and national offices and to express political opinions became priority to ensure racial and social justice. Despite a long period of transition in the aftermath of Reconstruction, which led historians such as Eric Foner[26] to denounce the inefficiency of the post-Civil War period, as early as the twentieth century, Black civil rights activists like W.E.B. Du Bois, for example, became increasingly vocal about the necessity to empower African Americans and to secure their right to vote. In defending such a vision of Blacks' integration, they paved the way for the Civil Rights Movement which reached its apex in 1964 and 1965 with the Civil Rights Act and the Voting Rights Act. If the role of the African-American community cannot be denied in this long historical process, all racial minorities were concerned by the central issue of enfranchisement and voters' mobilisation. As waves of immigration succeeded each other throughout the twentieth century, ethno-racial groups from European and Asian origins, but also Native Americans, strove to defend their civil rights and to organise politically to develop grassroots organisations. From a top-down perspective, political parties also came to acknowledge the importance of racial minorities in the local and national electoral process.

As Olivier Richomme explains, the mid-twentieth century was a turning point in that respect, as the Democratic Party tried to capitalise on the success of the Civil Rights Movement to gather the massive support of racial minorities when, conversely, Republicans became predominantly the party of white voters as part of its newly-emerging Southern strategy under the impulse of Barry Goldwater and other racial conservative politicians. Olivier Richomme thus draws on the consequences of the Civil Rights Act and the Voting Rights Act in the late twentieth and early twenty-first centuries, as redistricting and gerrymandering

---

26 Eric Foner, *Reconstruction, America's Unfinished Revolution, 1863–1877* (Harper Perennial Modern Classics, 2014).

tactics turned into political tools that reshaped the contours of state and federal politics. These practices have, since then, been an accurate indicator of the growing racial polarisation of American politics, leading to a clear-cut divide between the two dominant parties. On the one hand Democrats and ethno-racial minorities are now generally regarded as close electoral allies who heavily depend on each other to secure victories at all levels of the political spectrum, when Republicans almost exclusively rely on the support of the white community. This phenomenon, known as "conjoined polarization", defines the political landscape of the country up to the point that it has become virtually impossible to distinguish between race and partisanship. Yet, as Olivier Richomme demonstrates, this political reality does not necessarily facilitate the empowerment of racial minorities who seem to suffer from the intended and unintended consequences of a situation where representation becomes highly problematic. The 2020 presidential elections was another striking episode in this extremely polarised context.

If this situation persists in contemporary America and seems to intensify at a national level, it is absolutely not new, as it started in the South of the United States as early as the 1860s. As such, the chapter of John A. Kirk on the long struggle for black voting rights in Arkansas provides an illuminating case study that explores the question of African Americans' representation in the late nineteenth and early twentieth centuries, whether it be by the elite few or through grassroots mobilisation. Dr. Kirk gives some insight into a state which was in the spotlight during the Civil Rights Movement[27] and was representative of a more national movement which tried to combine top-down and bottom-up strategies to serve the interests of the African-American community. John Kirk's chapter offers a historical perspective on the case of Arkansas by identifying the different phases that saw the mobilisation of Blacks evolve from an exclusively middle-class oriented fight to a struggle which the masses embraced with enthusiasm, as the birth of organisations demonstrates and as more black politicians won local elections that rewarded the efforts of the whole community. However, as John Kirk puts forward in the last part of his chapter, the case of Arkansas remains one of vivid interest since it is the last former confederate state to have never elected a black politician statewide or nationwide, proving that voters' mobilisation sometimes fails to parlay into significant electoral victories.

If the question of race has always been central in the history of the United States, the case of the United Kingdom is also one to be analysed when it

---

[27] It is in Little Rock, Arkansas, that one of the most mediatised events of the Civil Rights Movement took place in 1957, when the Governor of the state, Orval Faubus, tried to prevent the implementation of school desegregation, forcing President Eisenhower to resort to the National Guard to ensure the safety of black students.

comes to empowering racial minorities. As Sharon Baptiste underlines, the issue of mobilising ethno-racial minorities in the United Kingdom has become closely linked with the country's decolonisation process that occurred in the aftermath of World War II and concerned voters with origins in Africa, the Caribbean, Asia, India, or Bangladesh, primarily. It is only in the 1970s that the participation of minorities in British General Elections became a priority for some organisations and independent think tanks nationwide. Researchers' interest for minorities' political participation in the UK intensified in the twenty-first century with surveys being conducted with a view to analysing and understanding the attitudes and behaviours of black voters particularly. As such, Sharon Baptiste primarily focuses on Black and Minority Ethnic (BME) voters over the period between 1996 and 2019, from the creation of Operation Black Vote (OBV) to the latest General elections of 2019. On the occasion of the December 2019 General elections, which were broadly seen as one of the most important political events in generations, OBV's central message was that if BAME communities, and young people in general, did not register to vote, others with possibly controversial views would speak on their behalf. This was illustrated, as part of a campaign created by Saatchi & Saatchi London, by some controversial statements uttered by politicians on the issue of race, religion, women, sexuality and climate change. Sharon Baptiste thus strives to determine whether it is possible to precisely evaluate the success of Operation Black Vote, in terms of voters' mobilisation, but also in the long run as far as influencing policymaking is concerned.

2 Mobilising Women: Grassroots Action and Political Discourse

The enfranchisement of women, whether in Britain or the United States, undoubtedly represents a major event in the history of suffrage extensions. Cutting through all social classes, it gave political representation to unprecedented numbers, nearly doubling the number of citizens eligible to vote: more than 26 million throughout the United States with the ratification of the 19th Amendment in 1920[28] and 8 million in Britain with the Representation of the People Act in 1918

---

[28] Only a minority of women registered to vote however. Statistics in New York and Illinois from the early 1920s indicate that between 35 and 46 per cent of eligible women actually voted, against 75 per cent of men; Margaret Smith Crocco and Della Barr Brooks, "The Nineteenth Amendment: Reform or Revolution?", *Social Education* 59, no. 5 (1995): 279–284, 279.

(to be completed by an additional 5.24 million with the Representation of the People Act 1928).[29]

From a historical perspective, the extension of women's suffrage in the U.S. is of particular interest as the country's states and territories were among the first political entities in modern times to grant women voting rights. Wyoming was the first territory to enfranchise women in 1869, as well as the first state, in 1890, followed before the end of the century by Colorado (1893), Utah and Idaho (1896). Western states and territories, possibly, it has been argued, because of the shortage of women they faced on the frontier and so as to make themselves more "attractive" to women, were more favourable to women's suffrage than eastern states. Suffrage, however, was not the only means through which women could express their claims and grievances. Farmers' Alliances, as shown by Jean-Louis Marin-Lamellet, also provided women with a means for advancement. Born in rural Texas before spreading across the cotton South, merging with other organisations and then reaching into the Kansas, California and the Rocky Mountain States, Farmers' Alliances in the 1880s and 1890s mobilised "periphery agrarians" – farmers, storekeepers, miners, railroad workers – in a progressive farmer-labour movement. The fact that these regions were the first to enfranchise women is no coincidence: Farmers' Alliances also attracted all sorts of middle class reformers and radicals who, when they entered politics in 1892 through the Populist Party, campaigned for women's rights. Populist state governments in Colorado and Idaho thus helped women win the right to vote and Farmers' Alliances in the Midwest and West supported women's suffrage at local and state level. Jean-Louis Marin-Lamellet's study therefore not only sheds new light on the history of Farmers' Alliances but also as, in his own words, "there is no clear-cut separation between the two movements" on the beginning of Populism. In addition to examining the strategies, tools and institutions that made it possible for a movement that started with a dozen farmers to eventually mobilise millions of Americans, his chapter focuses on one militant group that was particularly galvanized into action – women.

Less than three months after the ratification of the 19th Amendment, more than eight million women across the U.S. voted in elections for the first time, raising both fears and expectations among political parties as to how they would use their votes. While feminist organisations such as the National League of Women Voters rapidly realised how mobilising women could prove an effi-

---

29 An age limit requirement – 30 – was explicitly set in 1918 to ensure women did not become the majority of the electorate, which would have been the case had women been enfranchised on the same basis as men, all the more so following the loss of men in the war.

cient means of pressure to obtain reform, politicians also took great care to show interest for the new voters and emphasise issues that were believed to be of special interest to women (at the time prohibition, child health, public schools and world peace).[30] That trend continued and was reinforced from the 1980s onwards by growing talk both in the press and academic literature about the existence of a gender gap[31] and the fact that, while in all presidential elections prior to 1980 the turnout rate for women had been lower than that for men, the proportion of eligible female adults who voted now exceeded that of men. This can make a huge difference, as illustrated by the 2004 elections, when 8.8 million more women than men voted.

While the enfranchisement of more than eight million women in Britain in 1918 had also led to massive mobilisation efforts,[32] the phenomenon had already died out by the beginning of World War Two and British political parties, unlike their American counterparts, did not resume paying attention to the female electorate until the mid-1990s.[33] This lack of interest for women voters, which was reflected in the media,[34] might seem paradoxical in a country which had been led for the past 11 years by a woman Prime Minister – Margaret Thatcher – the first woman in the Western world to have been elected at the head of a major political party (the Conservative Party in 1975) and to have occupied such a position. Yet, as illustrated by Karine Rivière-de-Franco's case study of Margaret Thatcher's and Theresa May's political communication, correlation between descriptive representation and substantive representation is a complex phenomenon and shared experience does not guarantee good representation. Political and electoral sources thus not only reveal divergence in the two politicians' conception of the female electorate, but also in their means of engaging

---

30 Lorraine Gates Schuyler, *The Weight of Their Votes: Southern Women and Political Leverage in the 1920s* (The University of North Carolina Press, 2006), 17; J. Kevin Corder and Christina Wolbrecht, "Political Context and the Turnout of New Women Voters after Suffrage", *Journal of Politics* 68, no. 1 (2006): 34–49.
31 Pippa Norris, "The Gender Gap in Britain and America", *Parliamentary Affairs* 38, no. 2 (1985): 192–201; Eleanor Smeal, *How and Why Women Will Elect the Next President* (New York: Harper and Row, 1984); Carol M. Mueller (ed.), *The Politics of the Gender Gap* (Newbury Pk: Sage, 1988).
32 Véronique Molinari, "Educating and Mobilising the New Voter: Interwar Handbooks and Female Citizenship in Great-Britain, 1918–1931", *Journal of International Women's Studies* 15, no. 1 (2014).
33 Véronique Molinari, "Mobilisation des électrices", op. cit.
34 Labour MP Angela Eagle declared about the media coverage of the 1992 General elections that "It was as if a glass trap door had opened and the women disappeared"; Mary-Ann Stephenson, *The Glass Trapdoor* (London: Frawcett Society, 1998).

and communicating with women voters, be it to mobilise these voters in favour of the Conservative Party or to promote perceived "women's issues". Rivière-de-Franco's study covers two different periods of British politics: the 11 years of Thatcher in office, from 1979 to 1990, and Theresa May's brief premiership (2016–19), dominated by the consequences of the Brexit referendum. Although these only two female British Prime Ministers shared the same political partisanship (Conservatism), nearly 30 years therefore separated them during which the country underwent profound economic, social and cultural transformations. The "female vote," following on the American example, had also become an object of interest for political parties,[35] leading in turn to substantial efforts at mobilisation between 2005 and 2015 on the part of some grassroots organisations, such as Fawcett Society and the Young Women's Christian Association England and Wales.[36] On the occasion of the 2005 elections, a campaign targeting women aged 19 to 24 was even launched by Cosmopolitan UK, both within the pages of the magazine and through posters placed in a couple of cities. Mixing humour and stereotypes,[37] inspiration for the latter was acknowledged by the chief editor of the magazine to have been found in the campaign led by Rock the Vote[38] in the United States the previous year – providing yet another example of the process of Americanisation of British political campaigns.

---

35 Véronique Molinari, "Du 'vote des flappers' au 'vote à talons hauts': évolutions et constantes dans la mobilisation de l'électorat féminin par les partis politiques britanniques entre les années vingt et aujourd'hui", Recherches Féministes, revue interdisciplinaire francophone d'études féministes, GREMF, Université Laval, Québec, Canada, 20, no. 1 (2007): 167–190.
36 Véronique Molinari, "Mobilisation des électrices", op. cit.
37 Sensually parted, glossy lips and gold dangle-earrings to illustrate the slogan "Prove you've something between your earrings", a road-sign, "No parking, except for women with lots of shopping", followed by "If we all vote, who knows what we can achieve".
38 Founded in 1990 and a pioneer in the youth-vote movement, Rock the Vote's stated mission was "to engage and build the political power of young people. See Brian Cogan, *Mosh the Polls: Youth Voters, Popular Culture, and Democratic Engagement* (Plymouth: Lexington Books, 2008), 63–78; and Kathryn C. Montgomery, *Generation Digital: Politics, Commerce, and Childhood in the Age of the Internet* (The MIT Press, 2007), 180–185.

3 Digital Mobilisation: Revolutionising Politics in the Twenty-first Century?

Despite different political and electoral systems, common features have been identified between British and American campaigning strategies,[39] a trend that has intensified over the past 50 years with a phenomenon of "Americanisation" of electoral campaigns among Western countries.[40] In Britain, the 1970 election was thus identified as "the most notable for initiating the importation of commercial, marketing-based campaigning techniques developed in U.S. presidential contests"[41] and the 1987 campaign as having marked "the full migration of American political packaging techniques,"[42] offering what Mughan defined as "the most personalized contest in British political history to that point".[43] While the Conservatives were the first to take the initiative and rapidly committed to the use of political marketing expertise, Labour remained long reluctant to use the same techniques, disregarding the media and preferring to concentrate on traditional methods.[44] Even then, however, political marketing remained circumscribed by different factors as compared to the U.S.: relatively low budgets, equal time rulings concerning TV appearances, impossibility for the candidate to by-pass the party.[45]

Literature has shown that individuals or groups "contacted by parties, campaigns, or interest groups are more likely to participate in politics than those who are not" and that "a successful mobilization strategy can play a small,

---

[39] Karine Rivière de Franco, "Introduction", in Renée Dickason, David Haigron and Karine Rivière-de Franco, *Stratégies et campagnes électorales en Grande-Bretagne et aux Etats-Unis* (Paris: L'Harmattan, 2009), 13.
[40] Dennis Kavanagh, *Election campaigning, the New Marketing of Politics* (London: Blackwell, 1995).
[41] Anthony Mughan, *Media and the Presidentialization of Parliamentary Elections*, 28
[42] Nicholas Jackson O'Shaughnessy, *The Phenomenon of Political Marketing* (New York: Palgrave Macmillan, 1990), 218.
[43] Mughan, op. cit., 33.
[44] Anthony Mughan, op. cit., 31. "Some problems have arisen from the party's ethos," Kavanagh writes, "particularly the notion that it has been the party of the working class and trade unions and has an ideology. For many Labour politicians this self-image has defined the party's message and its electoral market; they claimed to know what ordinary people wanted without the help of market research", 77.
[45] Ibid., 210.

but decisive role in winning elections".[46] As a consequence, both scholars and politicians have been eager to measure the impact and effectiveness of the means/media used (television appeals versus door-to-door canvassing...).[47] These techniques have, quite naturally, gradually changed over the past century, along with developments in communication technology. From public meetings, small "at homes", posters and pamphlets used before the Second World War, the three major parties in Britain progressively adopted the radio then, from 1951, TV broadcasts and, finally, digital technologies, all this with more and more professional help. As early as 1989, J.D.H. Downing demonstrated in *Computers for Political Change*[48] the potential of new technology for grassroots political movements. In the United Kingdom, the first experiments in this sector took place in the 1990s. Initially limited to isolated initiatives, they were then gradually deployed more widely, in particular as part of strategies to counter demobilisation in a context of declining membership and increasing abstention. For while political demobilisation was taking place, the use of social media exploded, with over half of British adults now using social media platforms regularly and the population spending more time on social networks than on any other online activity.[49] For the past 10 years, campaigners have therefore increasingly used new means of communication to reach voters, including advertising services bought from digital and social media companies like Facebook, Google, YouTube, Snapchat, Twitter or Instagram.[50] The idea of marketing on Facebook is said to have been brought to the UK when incumbent Prime minister Cameron hired Jim Messina, Obama's 2012 campaign manager, as a campaign strategy adviser in 2015. While British political parties nationally spent about £1.3 million on Facebook during

---

[46] Kenneth M Goldstein and Matthew Holleque, "Getting up off the canvass: Rethinking the study of mobilization", in Jan E. Leighley, *The Oxford Handbook of American Elections and Political Behavior* (OUP, 2010), 578.
[47] John M. Bochel and David D. Denver, "Canvassing, Turnout and Party Support", *British Journal of Political Science* 1 (1971): 257–269; Ian McAllister, "Campaign Activities and Electoral Outcomes in Britain 1979 and 1983", *Public Opinion Quarterly* 49 (1985): 489–503; Paul F. Whiteley and Patrick Seyd, "Party Election Campaigning in Britain", *Party Politics* 9 (2003): 637–652.
[48] John D.H. Downing, "Computers for Political Change: PeaceNet and Public Data Access", *Journal of Communication* 39, no. 3 (1989): 154–162.
[49] Miller, op. cit., 17.
[50] While in 2011, spending by campaigners on digital advertising was 0.3 per cent of total spend, this increased to 1.7 per cent in 2014, 23.9 per cent in 2015, 32.3 per cent in 2016 and 42.8 per cent in 2017; Report: Digital campaigning – increasing transparency for voters, Electoral Commission, June 2018, https://www.electoralcommission.org.uk/who-we-are-and-what-we-do/changing-electoral-law/transparent-digital-campaigning/report-digital-campaigning-increasing-transparency-voters.

the 2015 general election campaign; the figure soared to £3.2 million on the occasion of the June 2017 elections.[51] This gradual adoption of digital technology by the major British political parties over the past two decades is the object of Géraldine Castel's study, in which the author focuses more particularly on the latter's capacity to use ICT to reach out to the public and encourage involvement with their activities at organisational level or for voters' mobilisation. The chapter provides an overview of the evolution of platforms, actors, tools, contents and objectives from the introduction of Excalibur in 1994 by Tony Blair's team to the general election of 2019 and addresses issues pertaining to the impact of such technological development on election results, parties and, more broadly, democracy.

In the recent history of U.S. politics one example came to illustrate the newly acquired importance of digital tactics and strategies in mobilising a wide range of citizens for a common cause: the rise of the Tea Party in the aftermath of Barack Obama's election in 2008. The Tea Party movement, which was born out of the defiance within conservative groups towards an alleged liberal president who came from a racial minority, appears as an interesting case study when it comes to analysing the power of the media and the various digital tools to mobilise voters and activists. Indeed, as Marion Douzou shows, the different Tea Party-affiliated organisations and activists intensively used new technologies to spread their message and educate potential voters to the principles and values of a movement generally presented as grassroots-based. The role and usage of Facebook, Twitter and YouTube serve as a good example to demonstrate that conservatives also resort to such devices to influence the political sphere even though, as Marion Douzou explains, liberal movements have recently been more active in the world of digital politics. Yet, the fact that conservatives and liberals alike are now highly dependent on new technologies attests to the undeniable impact of these devices on politics in the twenty-first century.

---

51 Dan Sabbagh, "Rise of digital politics: why UK parties spend big on Facebook", *The Guardian*, March 23, 2018, https://www.theguardian.com/technology/2018/mar/23/facebook-digital-politics-tories-labour-online-advertising-marketing.

4 When Grassroots and Party Mobilisation Interact: the Case of the Republican Party in the Twentieth Century

Interestingly enough, in some cases, bottom-up and top-down mobilisation converge and complete each other as part of a strategy that aims at getting citizens involved in the political process. Throughout history, this phenomenon has been observed in different English-speaking countries, and more particularly in Britain and in the United States. However, when grassroots and institutional mobilisation interact, this may also be the result of a context of political tension within a political organisation. This is exactly what happened in the early twentieth century for the Republican Party in the United States, after a series of defeats against the New Deal coalition supporting the Democratic president, Franklin Delano Roosevelt. The decline of Republicans precipitated the G.O.P. into a minority status throughout the 1930s and 1940s, which provoked an identity crisis and divided party members and activists with regards to the new approach to adopt to regain legitimacy with U.S. voters. In the last chapter of this work, Robert Mason explores this crucial period which saw the Republican Party gradually reorganise and reinvent itself, leading to an ideological transformation symbolised by the rise of Barry Goldwater's Southern and conservative strategy. As Robert Mason demonstrates, the intraparty tension, which also impacted party activists at the grassroots level, put in perspective the necessity for Republicans to find their policy direction while navigating between a moderate and an increasingly conservative path. Notwithstanding, whether it be at the grassroots level or among the elites of the G.O.P., the whole point of these intense, and sometimes divisive, debates consisted in getting voters' support and mobilisation to revitalise the Republican Party and mount a new challenge that would jeopardise and weaken the Democratic New Deal coalition and its heritage in the aftermath of Franklin Delano Roosevelt's passing.

Through the lens of the specific example of Republicans between 1933 and the mid-1960s, it is thus worth noticing that the question of voters' commitment remains a central issue. Grassroots and top-down mobilisation(s) often converge, sometimes conflict, but on the whole, they epitomise the need for political parties to maintain, preserve and potentially increase the support of voters to secure electoral victories, both at a local and a national level. Future elections in Britain and in the United States, in the short term, as well as the long run, will prove again that the legitimacy of elected officials will be reinforced by a robust and steady voters' mobilisation, especially in two countries where the first-past-the-post and the winner take all systems remain regularly contested.

Bibliography

Bara, Judith. Democratic politics and party competition. Routledge, 2006.

Birch, Sarah. "Our new voters: Brexit, political mobilisation and the emerging electoral cleavage." IPPR Progressive Review 23, no. 2 (2016).

Bochel, John M., and David D. Denver. "Canvassing, Turnout and Party Support". British Journal of Political Science 1 (1971): 257–269.

Brody, Richard. "The puzzle of political participation in America". In The New American political system, 287–324. Washington: American Enterprise Institute for Public Policy Research, 1978.

Bromley, Catherine, John Curtice and Ben Seyd. "Is Britain Facing a Crisis of Democracy?" The Constitution Unit, July 2004, 5. https://www.ucl.ac.uk/constitution-unit/sites/constitution-unit/files/112_0.pdf.

Budge, Ian, and Ivan Crewe. Party Identification and beyond: representations of voting and party competition. ECPR Press, 1976.

Budge, Ian, and Ivor Crew et al. The New British Politics. Longman, 2001.

Cogan, Brian. Mosh the Polls: Youth Voters, Popular Culture, and Democratic Engagement. Plymouth: Lexington Books, 2008.

Corder, J. Kevin, and Christina Wolbrecht. "Political Context and the Turnout of New Women Voters after Suffrage". Journal of Politics 68, no. 1 (2006): 34–49.

Cox, Gary. "Swing voters, core voters, and distributive politics". In Political Representation, edited by I. Shapiro, S. Stokes, E. Wood and A. Kirshner. Cambridge: Cambridge University Press, 2010.

Crewe, Ivor, B. Särlvik and J. Alt. "Partisan Dealignment in Britain 1964–1974". British Journal of Political Science 7, no. 2 (1977): 129–190.

Crocco, Margaret Smith, and Della Barr Brooks. "The Nineteenth Amendment: Reform or Revolution?" Social Education 59, no. 5 (1995): 279–284.

Downing, John D.H. "Computers for Political Change: PeaceNet and Public Data Access". Journal of Communication 39, no. 3 (1989): 154–162.

Foner, Eric. Reconstruction, America's Unfinished Revolution, 1863–1877. Harper Perennial Modern Classics, 2014.

Gates Schuyler, Lorraine. The Weight of Their Votes: Southern Women and Political Leverage in the 1920s. The University of North Carolina Press, 2006.

Goldstein, Kenneth M., and Matthew Holleque. "Getting up off the canvass: Rethinking the study of mobilization". In Jan E. Leighley, The Oxford Handbook of American Elections and Political Behavior, 578. OUP, 2010.

Karp, Jeffrey A. et al. "Getting out the Vote: Party Mobilisation in a Comparative Perspective." British Journal of Political Science 38, no. 1 (2008): 91–112.

Kavanagh, Dennis. Election campaigning, the New Marketing of Politics. London: Blackwell, 1995.

Key, V.O. Jr. "A Theory of Critical Elections". The Journal of Politics 17, no. 1 (1955): 11. https://www.jstor.org/stable/2126401. Accessed March 22, 2020.

King, Anthony, ed. Britain at the polls, 2001. Chatham House Publishers, 2002.
McAllister, Ian. "Campaign Activities and Electoral Outcomes in Britain 1979 and 1983." Public Opinion Quarterly 49 (1985): 489–503.
Miller, Car. "We are living through a radical shift in the nature of political engagement." The Rise of Digital Politics. Demos, 2016.
Molinari, Véronique. "Du 'vote des flappers' au 'vote à talons hauts': évolutions et constantes dans la mobilisation de l'électorat féminin par les partis politiques britanniques entre les années vingt et aujourd'hui". Recherches Féministes, revue interdisciplinaire francophone d'études féministes, GREMF, Université Laval, Québec, Canada, 20, no. 1 (2007): 167–190.
Molinari, Véronique. "Educating and Mobilising the New Voter: Interwar Handbooks and Female Citizenship in Great-Britain, 1918–1931". Journal of International Women's Studies 15, no. 1 (2014).
Molinari, Véronique. "Mobilisation des électrices et instrumentalisation de la différence: les campagnes électorales de 2004 et 2005 en Grande-Bretagne et aux États-Unis". In Renée Dickason, David Haigron and Karine Rivière-De Franco (dir.), Stratégies et campagnes électorales en Grande-Bretagne et aux Etats-Unis. L'Harmattan, 2009.
Montgomery, Kathryn C. Generation Digital: Politics, Commerce, and Childhood in the Age of the Internet. The MIT Press, 2007.
Mueller, Carol M., ed. The Politics of the Gender Gap. Newbury Pk: Sage, 1988.
Mughan, Anthony. Media and the Presidentialization of Parliamentary Elections. Palgrave Macmillan, 2000.
Norris, Pippa. Critical Citizens: Global Support for Democratic Government. Oxford: OUP, 1999.
Norris, Pippa. "The Gender Gap in Britain and America". Parliamentary Affairs 38, no. 2 (1985): 192–201.
O'Shaughnessy, Nicholas Jackson. The Phenomenon of Political Marketing. New York: Palgrave Macmillan, 1990.
Rivière de Franco, Karine. "Introduction." In Renée Dickason, David Haigron and Karine Rivière-de Franco, Stratégies et campagnes électorales en Grande-Bretagne et aux États-Unis. Paris: L'Harmattan, 2009.
Rivière-De Franco, Karine. La communication électorale en Grande-Bretagne de Margaret Thatcher à Tony Blair. Paris: l'Harmattan, 2008.
Rosenstone, Steven J., and John Mark Hansen. Mobilisation, Participation, and Democracy in America. Macmillan, 1993.
Ruy A. Teixeira. Why Americans don't vote: turnout decline in the United States, 1960–1984. New York: Greenwood Press, 1987.
Sabbagh, Dan. "Rise of digital politics: why UK parties spend big on Facebook." The Guardian, March 23, 2018.
Sarlvik, Bo, and Ivor Crewe. Decade of Dealignment: The Conservative Victory of 1979 and Electoral Trends in the 1970s. New York: Cambridge University Press, 1983.
Schofield, Norman, Gary Miller and Andrew Martin. "Critical Elections and Political Realignments in the USA: 1860–2000." Political Studies 51, no. 2 (2003): 217–240.
Smeal, Eleanor. How and Why Women Will Elect the Next President. New York: Harper and Row, 1984.

Stephens, Hugh W. "Party Realignment in Britain, 1900–1925: A Preliminary Analysis." Social Science History 6, no. 1 (1982): 35–66.
Stephenson, Mary-Ann. The Glass Trapdoor. London: Fawcett Society, 1998.
Whiteley, Paul F., and Patrick Seyd. "Party Election Campaigning in Britain". Party Politics 9 (2003): 637–652.
Whiteley, Paul. Political Participation in Britain. London: Palgrave Macmillan, 2012.

Part 1: **Empowering Racial Minorities: Legal Measures, Grassroots Mobilisation and Political Strategies**

Olivier Richomme

1 Empowering Minority Voters in the U.S.

The Paradoxes of Redistricting in the Age of Conjoined Polarisation

Introduction

The American political landscape has been upended since the 1960s Minority Rights Revolution and the passage of the 1965 Voting Rights Act (VRA).[1] These episodes and their consequences have changed the way Americans perceive political representation. The absence of non-White elected officials became the symbol of institutional discrimination, especially in the eye of minorities, that delegitimised the entire political system and threatened the very core of the political compromise the nation was believed to have been built upon. The challenges of the period ushered by the Civil Rights Movement was that the U.S. Congress, state legislatures and other governing bodies were only composed of older White males. As long as this was the case, the American democracy would not be representative of the entire country. A diverse population required a diverse body of representatives. Furthermore, the United States could no longer be considered a democracy without an unhindered right to vote. But the franchise was meaningless if it did not translate into the election of representatives that carried the voices of the historically marginalised minority groups. Otherwise it meant that many political communities' interests were not represented and their grievances would not be heard and addressed.

This voting rights revolution impacted many aspects of the American political system. One aspect often overlooked is the importance of redistricting that led to the emergence of minority elected officials. While the first goal of the Civil Rights Movement was access to the ballot and enforcement of the Fifteenth Amendment of the U.S. Constitution,[2] it soon became clear that enfranchisement

---

[1] John D. Skrentny, *The Minority Rights Revolution* (Cambridge, MA: Harvard University Press, 2002).

[2] The 15th Amendment states that the "right of citizens of the United States to vote shall not be denied or abridged by the United States or by any State on account of race, color, or previous condition of servitude". It also gives Congress the power to "enforce this article by appropriate legislation."

alone could not achieve political representation in a racially polarised environment and in a winner-take-all electoral system.[3] Racial polarisation, or racial bloc voting, can simply be defined as members of a community voting systematically for candidates they perceive as a member to their own racial group.[4] Using racial polarisation and residential segregation, redistricting was used to keep racial minorities out of office. After the 1960s, thanks to federal legislation and court intervention, one solution was to use redistricting to help minorities get elected to office in a majoritarian system. Instead of opting for a form of proportional representation to guarantee that minorities might have a chance to elect a candidate representing their interest, American reformers opted to keep a winner-take-all system in which some electoral districts would be composed of large numbers of ethno-racial minorities.[5] This policy raises a series of complex issues. One of them is the interaction of race and partisanship in American politics. It is in this context that voter mobilisation strategies need to be analysed.

The Minority Rights Revolution and the Republican "Southern strategy" completed a racial partisan realignment that has its roots in President Roosevelt's coalition of the 1930s.[6] The Democratic Party came to champion minority rights as its electoral base was reshaped by the integration of minority groups, starting with African Americans. Therefore, the issue of minority political representation, understood as necessarily including some sort of descriptive representation, became intertwined with partisanship.[7] Most White voters prefer to vote

---

[3] Bernard Grofman, Lisa Handley and Richard G. Niemi, *Minority Representation and the Quest for Voting Equality* (New York: Cambridge University Press, 1992).

[4] Stephen Ansolabehere, Nathaniel Persily and Charles Stewart III, "Regional Differences in Racial Polarization in the 2012 Presidential Election: Implications for the Constitutionality of Section 5 of the Voting Rights Act," *Harvard Law Review Forum* 126 (2013): 205–220.

[5] I use the expression ethno-racial to emphasise the conflation of race and ethnicity in the U.S. in the same way as David Hollinger (1995). In the case of ethno-racial groups, what is striking in the U.S. is the fairly stable nature of these statistical categories or at least the presence of a mechanism to make those statistics appear as stable over time and space. For understandable historical reasons, interest groups coalesce around ethno-racial identities, which puts great emphasis on ethno-racial statistics in the context of redistricting. It must be noted that some of these ethno-racial categories often taken for granted did not exist when the VRA was passed, such as the "Hispanic" category.

[6] Eric Shickler, *Racial Realignment: The Transformation of American Liberalism, 1932–1965* (Princeton, NJ: Princeton University Press, 2016).

[7] According to Hanna Pitkin's definition, descriptive representation is concerned with representing the identity of a voter, while substantive representation is concerned with representing the interests of a voter; Hanna Fenichel Pitkin, *The Concept of Representation* (University of California Press, 1967).

for White candidates. Most African Americans (and to some extent other ethno-racial minorities), when given the option, prefer to vote for an African American candidate. Racial polarisation rates are especially high in the U.S. South but this phenomenon is by no means limited to this region.[8] The Democratic Party has become the party of minority rights, thereby preferred by ethno-racial minorities, in particular among African Americans. As many scholars have observed, "it is often difficult to untangle racial consideration from partisan consideration".[9] After all, as Rick Hasen remarked, "Liberal and conservative scholars have long recognized that the Voting Rights Act's enforcement and interpretation can have partisan implications and motivations".[10] Since the 1980s at least, over 90 per cent of African Americans and about two-thirds of Latinos have consistently supported the Democratic Party for presidential or congressional elections. By contrast, the Democratic Party has not won the white vote in a presidential election for more than 50 years, that is since the Civil Rights Movement and the voting rights revolution reached its apex.[11] Partisan and racial polarisation are so high and intertwined that Professor Bruce Cain considered that they are now "two sides of the same coin".[12] The interconnection between race and partisanship is such that Cain and Zhang have astutely called this phenomenon "conjoined polarization":

> Racial sorting and party sorting trends have been closely intertwined. Civil rights policies gave socially conservative white Democrats reason to defect to the Republican Party. Immigration policies also enabled the non-white and non-European population to grow and eventually enter a coalition with liberal whites. At the same time, both parties became

---

[8] Ansolabehere, Persily and Stewart, "Regional Differences in Racial Polarization in the 2012 Presidential Election," 205–220.

[9] Richard H. Pildes, "Voting Rights The Next Generation", in *Race, Reform and Regulation of the electoral Process*, ed. Guy-Uriel E. Charles, Heather Gerken and Michael Kang (Cambridge University Press, 2011), 30.

[10] Richard Hasen, "Race or Party: How Courts Should Think About Republican Efforts to Make it Harder to Vote in North Carolina and Elsewhere," *Harvard Law Review Forum* 127 (2014): 58–75.

[11] "Election Polls – Vote by Groups, 1960–1964," *Gallup*, accessed September 21, 2018, http://www.gallup.com/poll/9454/election-polls-vote-groups-19601964.aspx._

[12] Alan I. Abramowitz, *The Disappearing Center: Engaged Citizens, Polarization and American Democracy* (Yale University Press, 2010); *The Great Realignment: Race, Party Transformation and the Rise of Donald Trump* (Yale University Press, 2018); James E. Campbell, *Polarized: Making Sense of a Divided America* (Princeton, NJ: Princeton University Press, 2016); James A. Thurber and Antoine Yoshinaka (eds.), *American Gridlocked: The Sources, Character, Impact of Political Polarization* (Cambridge University Press, 2016); Bruce Cain, "Moving Past Section 5: More Fingers or a New Dike," *Election Law Journal* 13, no. 2 (2013): 338–340.

more ideologically consistent, with more within-party conformity in social and economic policy. This undercut the ideological heterogeneity that in the immediate post World War II era had limited the polarization of activists, donors, and representatives in both parties. The Democratic and Republican parties became more ideologically consistent and racially distinctive.[13]

In today's United States, distinguishing between race and partisanship has become much more difficult than it used to be. As partisan and racial polarisation have increased, they have also aligned to the point that considering one without the other is, at least for the purpose of redistricting, simply untenable. Conjoined polarisation has tremendous political implications in a time of representative democracy crisis in the U.S. Parties have used every aspect of redistricting to mobilise the electorate or to counterbalance the other party's voter mobilisation efforts. And because the number of districts that are left competitive is so small they concentrate all of the resources and attention, increasing the stakes for partisan gains or minority representation.

This chapter proposes to analyse how the interaction of race and partisanship complicates minority political representation. We will study the challenges of using redistricting as the preferred solution to achieve diversity in post-civil rights American politics. However, in order to understand the contradictions of the public policies designed to help elect minorities in the U.S. today, we first need to go back to the implementation of the 1965 Voting Rights Act.

The 1965 Voting Rights Act

During the period that is sometimes called the second Reconstruction,[14] due to the fact that Southern states and local governments resisted attempts to remove obstacles that prevented African Americans from voting, Congress enacted the Voting Rights Act in 1965 to try and make the Fifteenth Amendment a reality.[15]

---

[13] Bruce E. Cain and Emily R. Zhang, "Blurred Lines: Conjoined Polarization and Voting Rights," *Ohio State Law Journal* 77, no. 4 (2016): 867–904.

[14] Morgan Kousser, *Colorblind Injustice: Minority Voting Rights and the Undoing of the Second Reconstruction*, (Chapel Hill, NC: North Carolina Press, 1999); Richard Vallely, *The Two Reconstructions: The Struggle for Black Enfranchisement* (Chicago, IL: University of Chicago Press, 2004).

[15] David Epstein, Richard Pildes, Rodolfo De La Garza and Sharyn O'Hallaran (eds.), *The Future of the Voting Rights Act* (New York: Russell Sage, 2006); Daniel McCool (ed.), *The Most Fundamental Right: Contrasting Perspectives on the Voting Rights Act* (Bloomington: Indiana Press University, 2012).

The VRA is a unique piece of legislation that contains permanent and temporary sections. Section 2 is permanent: it outlaws electoral procedures that "result in the denial or abridgement of the right of any citizen of the U.S. to vote on account of race or color." Sections 4 through 9 are temporary and need to be renewed regularly. Out of these sections, Section 5 is probably the most controversial, and also the most efficient. It created an exception to federalism and was decried, especially by Southerners, as an attack on state sovereignty. Through Section 5, the VRA specifically targeted certain state and local government jurisdictions in the South. Southern States used tests or devices, such as literacy tests, as a prerequisite for voter registration. Section 4 of the VRA created a triggering formula that measured voter registration and turnout levels in states and local governments that used the above-mentioned prerequisites. The VRA ultimately forbade the use of these tests or devices in these jurisdictions for a five-year period. Section 5 sought to prevent the implementation of any change affecting the right to vote unless federal approval was obtained from the U.S. Attorney General in an administrative proceeding or in a judicial action from the U.S. District Court for the District of Columbia. The revolutionary aspect of Section 5 is that it placed the burden of proof on the covered jurisdiction that submitted the proposed voting change. The jurisdictions covered by Section 5 had to demonstrate that the proposed voting change did not have a discriminatory effect on minority voting strength and that the change was not adopted with a discriminatory purpose. In 1965, the covered jurisdictions where those in which less than 50 per cent of persons of voting age were registered on November 1, 1964, or in which less than 50 per cent of persons of voting age voted in the presidential election of 1964.[16]

U.S. Congress then prolonged and amended the 1965 VRA several times. In order to extend the temporary provisions of the VRA, Congress modified the triggering formula found in Section 4. In 1970, Congress extended the regional ban on tests or devices to the entire nation and not only in the South. Moreover, Congress prolonged Section 5 preclearance requirement,[17] as well as the national ban on tests or devices, for another seven years. In 1975, Congress permanently banned tests or devices and extended the Section 5 preclearance requirement for an additional seven years. In addition, Congress realised that voting discrimination was not limited only to African Americans, but also applied to other ethnoracial groups, such as Latinos and Asians. Consequently, Congress expanded the definition of a test or device to include English-only elections in those jurisdic-

---

16 Voting Rights Act of 1965, 1965 § 4(c).
17 Preclearance means covered jurisdictions had to ask for authorization from federal courts or the Justice Department to implement new electoral changes.

tions where more than five per cent of the eligible voters were members of an applicable language minority group. This extended definition mainly concerned states with an important Latino population, such as Arizona and Texas, or a large Native American population, such as Alaska. The 1975 amendments also aimed to help limited-English proficiency citizens to vote. Furthermore, the newly-enacted Section 203 provided language assistance during elections in jurisdictions that met certain criteria.[18] Under the 1975 VRA amendments, a jurisdiction could simultaneously be subject to the language assistance provisions of Section 5 and Section 203.

The Voting Rights Act went under another drastic change when in 1982 Congress was faced with its prolongation. In 1980, the U.S. Supreme Court had held, in a plurality opinion on the case *City of Mobile v. Bolden*, that invalidating an at-large method of election on the basis of violation of the Fourteenth and Fifteenth Amendments or Section 2 of the VRA required proof of a discriminatory intent.[19] In response, Congress amended Section 2 to eliminate the discriminatory intent requirement. The newly-amended Section 2 required proof only of a discriminatory effect on minority voting strength. This is a good example of the back and forth between the Legislative and the Judiciary branches in the field of voting rights enforcement. The Senate Report accompanying the 1982 VRA amendments further defined the standard: Section 2 is violated when it is demonstrated that, under the "totality of circumstances", minority voters did not have an equal opportunity to participate in the political process and elect "candidates of their choice".[20] That same year Congress also extended the preclearance requirement of Section 5 for 25 years. In addition, Congress established a new mechanism to create an incentive for covered jurisdictions to comply with Section 5 of the VRA. Congress provided an expanded "bail out" mechanism that permitted Section 5-covered jurisdictions to be exempt from Section 5 preclearance upon meeting

---

18 James Thomas Tucker, *The Battle over Bilingual Ballot: Language Minorities and Political Access Under the Voting Rights Act* (Burlington, VT: Ashgate 2009).
19 *City of Mobile v. Bolden*, 446 U.S. 55, 60–62, 66–67 (1980).
20 Senate Report No. 97–417 (1982), 28. In *Thornburg v. Gingles*, 478 U.S. 30 (1986) the Supreme Court further interpreted Section 2 in a case involving a challenge to multimember and single-member legislative districts in North Carolina. The majority opinion established a three-pronged test to analyse vote dilution claims in parallel to the "totality of circumstances" test. First, the minority group must be "sufficiently large and geographically compact to constitute a majority of a single member district". Second, the minority group must be "politically cohesive". And third, the "white majority votes sufficiently as a bloc" to enable it to "usually defeat the minority's preferred candidate." *Thornburg v. Gingles*, 50–51. The precise definition of these new concepts (geographical compactness, political cohesion, candidate of choice, racial bloc voting) was not given by the Court.

certain criteria. The language assistance provisions in Section 203 were extended for a 10-year period until 1992; Congress then extended the language assistance provisions to 2007. As a result of these amendments, the triggering formula was modified.

As the VRA was up for renewal in 2007, Congress prolonged it for 25 years in 2006 and amended it significantly again as a reaction of a U.S. Supreme Court jurisprudence that appeared contrary to its initial legislative intent. In another fascinating example of the inter-branch dialogue between the Legislative and the Judiciary branches on voting rights enforcement, proponents of the VRA tried to correct three Supreme Court cases, two that dealt with Section 5 and one that dealt with expert witness fees.

The first case, *Reno v. Bossier Parish School Board*, 528 U.S. 320 (2000) (known as Bossier II) dealt with the Section 5 requirement. Before *Bossier II* the standard was that any change that had a discriminatory purpose or intent would not be approved. In *Bossier II* the U.S. Supreme Court ruled that Section 5 only outlawed "retrogressive dilution," that is voting changes that made things worse for minorities. After *Bossier II*, simply maintaining the initial situation, that is to say keeping the same number of minorities elected, passed constitutional muster. Section 5 of the VRA was amended by Congress to replace the phrase "does not have the purpose and will not have the effect" with "neither have the purpose nor will have the effect." Congress also added a subsection that forbade preclearance of any voting change "that has the purpose or will have the effect" of discrimination. The word "purpose" was defined to include "any discriminatory purpose."

The second Supreme Court case was *Georgia v. Ashcroft*, 539 U.S. 461 (2003). Before this decision the standard for Section 5 preclearance was whether an election procedure had the potential to dilute minority voting strength (*Beer v. U.S.*, 425 U.S. 130 (1976)). The 2003 Supreme Court decision lowered this standard in granting approval by simply giving minorities the capacity to influence elections even if they were not able to elect the candidate of their choice. Congress responded to this ruling by amending Section 5 to specify that the purpose of this section was to protect the ability of minority citizens to "elect their preferred candidates of choice."

The third, less famous, case was *West Virginia University Hospitals, Inc. v. Casey*, 499 U.S. 83 (1991). Private Section 2 challenges can be very complex, long and expensive. Section 14 of the VRA allowed private parties that prevailed in court to recover attorney's fees, but in 1991 the Supreme Court limited it to legal fees excluding expert witness fees. Congress added language into the act covering "reasonable expert fees."

The Act was renewed by a majority Republican Congress and signed by a Republican president but with a strong Republican opposition that appeared in a rare *post hoc* report of the Senate Judiciary committee.[21] This opposition materialised in two subsequent U.S. Supreme Court decisions. In *Northwest Austin Municipal Utility District No. 1 v. Holder*, 557 U.S. 193 (2009), known as NAMUNDNO, the conservative Supreme Court majority declined to rule on the constitutionality of Section 5 but some Justices strongly indicated that they were bothered by Section 5 as it stood. In *Shelby County v. Holder*, 570 U.S. 2 (2013) the Court ruled, by a five to four vote, that Section 4(b) was unconstitutional because the coverage formula is based on data over 40 years old, making it no longer responsive to current needs and therefore an impermissible burden on the constitutional principles of federalism and equal sovereignty of the states. The Court did not strike down Section 5, but without Section 4(b), no jurisdiction will be subject to Section 5 preclearance unless Congress enacts a new coverage formula. The 2021 round of redistricting will be the first one taking place without Section 5 protection in more than 50 years.

Impact of the 1965 Voting Rights Act

There are several ways one can measure the impact of the Voting Rights Act (VRA). Statistics depicting the increase of minority voting and political participation in the years following the passage of the law are nothing but spectacular. In the seven states covered by the VRA in 1965,[22] the average African American registration rate was 29.3 per cent before the Act and had reached 52.1 per cent by 1967. African American voting registration rate in the eleven states of the former Confederacy increased from 43.1 per cent in 1964 to 62 per cent in 1968. In Mississippi, the discrepancy between the White and African American voter registration rates went from 63.2 per cent in 1965 to 6.3 per cent in 1988.[23] African American turnout also increased tremendously as a result. For instance, in Alabama

---

[21] James Thomas Tucker, "The Politics of Persuasion: Passage of the Voting Rights Act reauthorization Act of 2006," *Journal of Legislation* 33, no. 2 (2007): 205–267; Nathaniel Persily, "The Promises and Pitfalls of the New VRA," *Yale Law Journal* 117 (2007): 174–253.

[22] The states of Alabama, Georgia, Louisiana, Mississippi, South Carolina and Virginia were covered in their entirety, along with 40 counties in North Carolina.

[23] Lisa Handley and Bernard Grofman, "The Impact of the Voting Rights Act on Minority Representation: Black Officeholders in Southern State Legislatures and Congressional Delegations," in *Quiet Revolution in the South*, ed. Chandler Davidson and Bernard Grofman (Princeton, NJ: Princeton University Press, 1994), 335–350.

and Mississippi, between the two presidential elections of 1964 and 1968, African American turnout increased by respectively 19.3 per cent and 16.8 per cent.[24]

There were only 1,469 African American office holders in the U.S. in 1970. By 2002 there were 9,430 of them.[25] According to National Association of Latino Elected Officials (NALEO) figures, there were 4,004 Latino elected officials in the U.S. in 1990.[26] By 2004, that number had reached 4,853 and by 2014 it was at 6,084.[27] The first National Asian Pacific American Political Almanac printed in 1976 listed just over 100 Asian-Americans who were elected or appointed to public office in only four states: California, Hawaii, Oregon and Washington. The 2015 issue lists more than 4,000 in the U.S. and its territories.[28] Not all of these figures are attributable to the VRA but its impact on all types of voting statistics is undeniable.

For instance, in 1965, the number of African Americans elected in the U.S. House of Representatives was six. In 1995, that number had ballooned to 41. In 2005 and 2015, it reached its peak of 44.[29] Most of these gains were due to redistricting. Most congressional minority elected officials represent majority-minority districts. By contrast, in state-wide elections ethno-racial minorities usually struggle to get elected. In 2016, no African American governor held office and by then there had only been four in American history. That same year there was a grand total of four non-White governors. The same is true in the U.S. Senate where minorities have historically been exceptions, sometimes the result of appointments. In 2017, a historic year for diversity in Congress, there were four African Americans, two Asian Americans and four Latinos in the Senate. Therefore, minorities represented a record 10 per cent of the U.S. Senate.[30]

---

[24] Grofman, Handley and Niemi, *Minority Representation and the Quest for Voting Equality* (1992), 22.
[25] "Black Elected Officials by Office, 1970 to 2002, and State, 2002," U.S. Census Bureau, Statistical Abstract of the U.S. 2011, table 413, 258, http://www2.census.gov/library/publications/2010/compendia/statab/130ed/tables/11s0413.pdf.
[26] NALEO, http://www.naleo.org/at_a_glance.
[27] Ibid.; Luis Ricardo Fraga and Sharon A. Navarro, "Latinos in Latino Politics," in *Latino Politics: Identity, Mobilization and Representation*, ed. Roldfo Espino, David L. Leal and Kenneth J. Meier (Charlottesville, VA: University Press of Virginia, 2007), 180.
[28] Don T. Nkanishi, and James Lai (eds.), *National Asian Pacific Political Almanac*, 15th Edition (UCLA Asian American Studies Center Press, 2014).
[29] Anna Brown and Sara Atske, "Blacks have made gains in U.S. political leadership, but gaps remain", *Pew Research Center*, June 28, 2016, http://www.pewresearch.org/fact-tank/2016/06/28/blacks-have-made-gains-in-u-s-political-leadership-but-gaps-remain/.
[30] Before the 2016 elections there were two African Americans, one Asian-American and three Latinos. That represents a 40 per cent jump in one election cycle.

Between its two chambers, Congress reached a new historical high for ethno-racial diversity with 19 per cent of legislators being non-White. In the House of Representatives 22 per cent of all members belonged in 2017 to an ethno-racial minority. Between the two chambers the total breakdown of minority members was: 50 African Americans, 39 Latinos, 15 Asian Americans and two Native Americans.[31] In 2001, minorities accounted for 12 per cent of all members compared to 31 per cent of the population.[32] In 1981, only six per cent of Congress members were from ethno-racial minority groups, while these groups represented 20 per cent of the American population.

These figures suggest that the VRA was a success in reforming the American political system. Yet it also raises the issue of substantive versus descriptive representation and the conundrum of proportional representation. Does the election of an African American candidate (descriptive representation) guarantee that the interests of the African American community be adequately represented (substantive representation)? Should not a skilful White candidate that accumulates seniority in the legislature and sits on powerful committees be more likely to deliver tangible results for this community? Some studies have suggested that African Americans that are elected in very safe majority-minority districts operate too far left on the political spectrum and therefore end up being marginalised in the legislative bargaining processes that usually takes place at the centre.[33] Would not a form of proportional representation solve, in part, the issues raised by majority-minority districts in a winner take all system? If minority representation is so crucial for the American society, should not the electoral system be designed to achieve such a goal?

In spite of the disclaimer included in Section 2 by Congress, and despite numerous reiterations by the U.S. Supreme Court that the Constitution does not guarantee proportional representation to minorities,[34] one can clearly see that ethno-racial minorities advocacy groups are not satisfied by levels of descriptive

---

31 These figures include California Senator Kamala Harris as both Asian and African American and Representative Adriano Espaillat (D-NY) as both Latino and African American.
32 Kristen Bialik and Jens Manuel Krogstad, "115th Congress sets new high for racial, ethnic diversity," *Pew Research Center*, January 24, 2017, http://www.pewresearch.org/fact-tank/2017/01/24/115th-congress-sets-new-high-for-racial-ethnic-diversity/.
33 David T. Canon, *Race, Redistricting, and Representation: The Unintended Consequences of Black Majority Districts* (Chicago, IL: University of Chicago Press, 1999).
34 *City of Mobile v. Bolden*, 446 U.S. 55 (1980) at 78–79 (plurality opinion of Stewart, J.) ("political groups have no constitutional claim to representation"); id. at 86 (J. Stevens, concurring) (no case "establishes a constitutional right to proportional representation for racial minorities"); *Chapman v. Meier*, 420 U.S. 1, 17 (1975); *White v. Regester*, 412 U.S. 755 (1973) at 765–766; *Whitcomb v. Chavis*, 403 U.S. 124 (1971) at 149.

representation that are lower than their proportion in the general population. The debate over voting rights in the U.S. has revolved around the determination, a process that is by nature a political bargain, of how much ethno-racial disproportionality mandates corrective action in a winner-take-all and geographical district-based electoral system.

Redistricting in the U.S.

One of the main characteristics of the American electoral system is its reliance on single member districts with a plurality vote. In the U.S., most districts use single-member plurality systems (SMD) and not some form of proportional voting (PR). This has tremendous implications since many groups try to achieve through redistricting some form of proportional representation and feel frustrated with the system when they do not reach their goal. Redistricting is therefore quite different from what happens in most other democracies. Other countries in the world also use single member districts yet "American practice has diverged more and more from those employed elsewhere."[35] A number of prominent American scholars have supported some form of proportional representation.[36] Nevertheless, one of the most striking features of the American electoral reform is the absence of proportional representation and the unwillingness to experiment with such electoral systems.[37] The irony of redistricting in the U.S. is that as the jurisprudence on racial representation has evolved toward an implicit

---

[35] David Butler and Bruce E. Cain, *Congressional Redistricting: Comparative and Theoretical Perspectives* (McMillan, 1992), 118.

[36] Lani Guinier, *The Tyranny of the Majority: Fundamental Fairness in Representative Democracy* (New York: Free Press, 1994); Douglas J. Amy, *Real Choices/New Voices: How Proportional Representation Elections Could Revitalize American Democracy*, 2nd Edition (New York: Columbia University Press, 2002); Mark Rush and Richard Engstrom, *Fair and Effective Representation: Debating Electoral Reform and Minority Rights* (Rowman and Littlefield, 2001); Shaun Bowler, Todd Donovan and David Brockington, *Electoral Reform and Minority Representation: Local Experiments with Alternative Elections* (Ohio State University Press, 2003).

[37] Some cities adopted some form of PR system with mixed results. Very few courts have used PR voting as a remedy for minority discrimination; Olivier Richomme, "'Fair' Minority Representation and the California Voting Rights Act", *National Political Science Review* 20, no. 2 (2019): 55–75. The most notable exception is the state of Maine that adopted ranked-choice voting in 2018.

norm of ethno-racial proportionality[38] as the proof of a "fair and effective representation," proportional electoral systems have not gained much traction.

Another important difference with other countries is that, in most U.S. states, redistricting is still in the hands of the legislature. In many nations, this was considered a clear conflict of interest. Many Americans seem to agree if we judge by opinion polls or the increasing number of attempts at creating independent redistricting commissions. Political parties see redistricting as a way to assert their power. Incumbents see it as an opportunity to stay in office. Minority groups see an opportunity to increase their descriptive, or substantive, representation. Reform groups worry about the fairness of this process. The fact that redistricting is done by legislatures means that every other legislative activity takes a back seat to line-drawing negotiations, while it consumes all the political oxygen. Important policy matters or impending legislation become engulfed in the process and every political dispute becomes fair game in redistricting negotiations. Redistricting can also be used to favour an incumbent or for retaliation against a member that refuses to follow his or her leadership or the party's line.

Another feature of redistricting in the U.S. is the degree to which plans are litigated in the courts. Court intervention in the 1960s quickly focused on the redistricting process. The first generation of voting rights cases broadened the electorate and made the process more open than ever before in American history. The amended Voting Rights Act has subjected line-drawers' decisions to judicial review. In the 1940s, the U.S. Supreme Court considered that the U.S. Congress, not the courts, had the authority to supervise states' political activity such as redistricting. In *Colgrove v. Green*, 328 U.S. 549 (1946), Justice Frankfurter warned the judiciary not to enter the "political thicket" by ruling on redistricting and vote dilution claims.[39] As a political endeavour it was, according to him, not justiciable. However, in the early 1960s in *Gomillon v. Lightfoot*, 364 U.S. 339 (1960), the same Justice wrote the majority opinion that struck down the new district in the city of Tuskegee, Alabama, not because of the vote dilution claim but be-

---

[38] This norm of ethno-racial proportionality can also be found in affirmative action jurisprudence and almost every time judges are asked to define what would be the proof of an absence of discrimination.

[39] In this case Illinois congressional district lines had not changed since 1901. Vote dilution is defined by Dick Engstrom as "the practice of reducing the potential effectiveness of a group's strength by limiting its ability to translate that strength into the control of (or at least influence with) elected public officials"; Richard Engstrom, "Racial Discrimination in the Electoral Process: the Voting Rights Act and the Vote Dilution Issue," in *Party Politics in the South*, ed. Robert Steed, Laurence Moreland and Ted Baker (New York: Praeger, 1980), 197.

cause the new map denied Tuskegee African American residents a vote in municipal elections. Frankfurter held that the legislature's law did violate the provision of the Fifteenth Amendment. Justice Whitaker concurred but wrote in his opinion that the law should have been struck down under the Equal Protection Clause of the Fourteenth Amendment. As it turns out, *Gomillon* was the bridge between *Colgrove* and *Baker v. Carr*, 369 U.S. 186 (1962), a Tennessee malapportionment case, with which the Court plunged into the proverbial "political thicket". *Baker* required state legislatures to redistrict based on population, in order to reflect demographic changes and enable representation of urban populations. *Baker* opened the door to more litigation such as *Gray v. Sanders*, 372 U.S. 368 (1963), which established the principle of "one person, one vote" under the Equal Protection Clause.[40] In *Wesberry v. Sanders*, 376 U.S. 1 (1964), a case involving U.S. Congressional districts in the State of Georgia, the U.S. Supreme Court required each state to draw its congressional districts so that they would be approximately equal in population. In the related case, *Reynolds v. Sims*, 377 U.S. 533 (1964), the U.S. Supreme Court held that seats in both houses of a bicameral state legislature must also represent districts as equal in population as practicably possible. At the same time that the U.S. Supreme Court started its redistricting revolution, Congress passed the 1965 Voting Rights Act.

Therefore, the passage of the VRA and courts intervention involving the Fourteenth and the Fifteenth Amendments changed everything as it created what does not exist in many other countries: minority vote dilution and racial gerrymandering.[41] Both stem from a tension inside American law between group-based harm and individual-based harm. The conflict between the two has been at the heart of the fight over the definition of the Equal Protection doctrine. The intervention of the courts has had two important consequences. Firstly, because the American judiciary is quite politicised (some judges are elected, appointed by partisan elected officials, subject to recall in some states), it is often accused of partisan bias.[42] Secondly, the willingness of the courts to review redistricting cases has led to the expectation of strict statistically measurable standards. This approach has shown its limits in partisan gerrymandering

---

[40] Stephen Ansolabehere and James M. Snyder, *The End of Inequality: One Person, One Vote and the Transformation of American Politics* (Norton, 2008).
[41] Heather Gerken, "Understanding the Right to an Undiluted Vote", *Harvard Law Review* 114, no. 6 (2001): 1663–1743.
[42] Hasen, Richard, *The Supreme Court and Election Law: Judging Equality from Baker v. Carr to Bush v. Gore* (New York University Press, 2003); Heather K. Gerken and Michael S. Kang, "The Institutional Turn in Election Law Scholarship," in *Race, Reform, and Regulation of the Electoral Process* (2011), 86–100.

cases since the U.S. Supreme Court has been incapable on agreeing on a workable standard.[43] For 30 years after *Baker v. Carr* the courts used racial vote dilution doctrine focused exclusively on group rights, that to say the ability of a racially defined community to participate in the political processes and to elect legislators of their choice, instead of addressing the rights of individual voters. As a result, voting rights were administered by Equal Protection standards that differed markedly from those applied in other areas. Then in 1993, in the new jurisprudence following the case *Shaw v. Reno*, the U.S. Supreme Court tried to "merge the analysis governing race-conscious districting back into general-purpose equal protection doctrine".[44] Trying to administer voting rights cases through its already tortuous affirmative action framework, emphasising individual rights versus competing state interest, led the Court to establish an especially meandering jurisprudence when it came to race.[45] The crux of the matter is that under current jurisprudence partisan gerrymandering is permissible while racial gerrymandering is inherently suspect and may be subjected to strict scrutiny.[46] As Cain and Zhang have observed, "Such a distinction between race and party is meaningless in the context of conjoined polarization. Nearly every decision to discriminate against racial minorities in voting has an electoral purpose. Considered in that light, all manipulations of the electoral process are partisan at heart".[47] One of the most interesting consequences of the absence of standard for partisanship and a strict standard for race is that racial gerrymandering claims or equal population deviation claims have therefore been used as a proxy for partisan vote dilution claims. Republicans can hide behind the partisan argument to justify ethno-racial discrimination and Democrats have used

---

43 In 1986, the Court held that partisan gerrymandering claims are justiciable under the Constitution, but the justices disagreed about how to identify unconstitutional partisan gerrymanders; *Davis v. Bandemer*, 478 U.S. 109 (1986). Since then, a majority of the Court has repeatedly declined to overturn *Bandemer* yet it has rejected every allegation of unconstitutional partisan gerrymandering that has come before it: *Vieth v. Jubelirer*, 541 U.S. 267 (2004); *League of United Latin American Citizens v. Perry*, 548 U.S. 399 (2006); *Gill v. Witford*, 585 US (2018).
44 Pamela S. Karlan and Daryl J. Levinson, "Why Voting is Different," *California Law Review* 84, no. 4 (1996): 1202.
45 The *Shaw* jurisprudence and its progeny, with their emphasis on individual rights versus competing state interests doctrine, was instrumental in the creation of election law as a distinct field from constitutional law.
46 On the justiciability of partisan gerrymandering since *Vieth* see for example Anthony J. McGann, Charles Anthony Smith, Michael Latner and Alex Keena, *Gerrymandering in America: The House of Representatives, the Supreme Court and the Future of Popular Sovereignty* (Cambridge University Press, 2016); Nicolas R. Seabrook, *Drawing the Lines: Constraints on Partisan Gerrymandering in U.S. Politics* (Cornell University Press, 2017).
47 Cain and Zhang, "Blurred Lines," 886.

ethno-racial dilution claims to achieve partisan goals. Thirdly, court intervention changed the nature of redistricting because legislators and governors now had to take into consideration what types of maps the judiciary might draw in case of gridlock and took the habit of hedging their bets. Or as Gary Cox and Johnathan Katz put it: "Endowing the lower courts with the power to set the reversion meant that the courts became players in all subsequent redistricting actions. The possibility always existed that a state's plan would be litigated. Thus, those devising new redistricting plans had to consider which court would hear the case and its likely view of matters".[48]

While constitutional constraints are now much greater, it seems the stakes are still as high for people involved in redistricting, be it parties, elected officials, ethno-racial minorities, political activists or "good government" groups. Malapportionment has been banned by the courts since *Baker v. Carr* so now the fight over boundaries is between equally populated districts. But redistricting can still advantage one group over the other, usually one party over the other (partisan gerrymandering) or one ethno-racial group over the other (racial gerrymandering). Both have become intertwined to the point that most of the time it is illusory to attempt to differentiate between the two. When can race be considered "a predominant factor" as the courts have asked? When is race used as a proxy for partisanship and vice-versa?[49] The U.S. Supreme Court maintains the theoretical distinction between the two because its view of racial gerrymandering is derived from its individual rights approach on race in affirmative action jurisprudence. Yet this approach, as opaque as in affirmative action cases, seems ill-equipped to deal with the questions raised by democratic representation whether one takes a group-rights approach, a structuralist approach or even an individual-rights approach.[50]

Starting in the 1990s, technological changes in turn have opened the redistricting process to a broader set of activists and to the public eye. Because American institutions are Madisonian in design, actors in the political system are not supposed to be neutral or disinterested. Americans expect different groups to lobby for their interest. Institutions expect people to be interested and therefore, in a way, encourage people to behave in a self-interested manner and not for the public welfare. Redistricting follows this norm deeply engrained in the political

---

48 Gary W. Cox, *Elbridge Gerry's Salamander: The Electoral Consequences of the Apportionment Revolution* (Cambridge University Press, 2002), 210–211.
49 Hasen, Richard, "Race or Party," 2014.
50 Gerken, "Understanding the Right to an Undiluted Vote," 2001; Guy-Uriel Charles, "Judging the Law of Politics," *Michigan Law Review* 103 (2005): 1099–1141; Joseph Fishkin, "Equal Citizenship and the Equal Right to Vote," *Indiana Law Journal* 86 (2011): 1289–1360.

culture. Redistricting is the product of various interests competing against one another. Over the years, the number of competing factions has increased. While redistricting became a more open process, a constantly growing number of interests needed to be satisfied.

The sum total of all these factors is a redistricting process under greater pressure, under greater public scrutiny and judicial oversight, and still unable to deliver the promise of five decades of Supreme Court jurisprudence about fair political representation. These unrealised expectations are now more obvious than ever and are ultimately destabilising to the redistricting process.[51] Renewed attention to alternatives and redistricting reform attempts have come to respond to this frustration.

Conclusion: the Challenges of Minority Representation through Redistricting

One of the main challenges for the future of redistricting in the U.S. is the context of conjoined polarisation because it has tremendous electoral consequences. Scholars seem to have reached a consensus on the partisan implications of majority-minority districts.[52] Creating districts that contain a majority of minority voters, as is often required by the Voting Rights Act, is obviously intended to help minority candidates get elected in those districts but it harms the Democratic Party overall by packing Democratic supporters into too few districts.[53] Besides, the Voting Rights Act, as it is enforced by the Executive branch, can be used as a partisan tool for electoral gain, independent of the party in control. Scholars suggest that when either party oversees the Department of Justice

---

[51] Samuel Issacharoff, "Supreme Court Destabilization of Single-Member Districts," *University of Chicago Legal Forum* 1 (1995): 238–239.

[52] Richard L. Engstrom, "Race and Southern Politics: The Special Case of Congressional Districting," in *Writing Southern Politics: Contemporary Interpretations and Future Directions*, ed. Robert P. Steed and Laurence W. Moreland (University of Kentucky Press, 2006), 110; Kenneth W. Shotts, "The Effect of Majority-Minority Mandates on Partisan Gerrymandering," *American Journal of Political Science* 45 (2001): 121; Adam B. Cox and Richard T. Holden, "Reconsidering Racial and Partisan Gerrymandering," *The University of Chicago Law Review* 78, no. 2 (2011): 553–604.

[53] Carol M. Swain, *Black Faces, Black Interests: The Representation of African Americans in Congress* (Cambridge, MA: Harvard University Press, 1993); David Lublin, *The Paradox of Representation: Racial Gerrymandering and Minority Interests in Congress* (Princeton, NJ: Princeton University Press, 1997); Canon, *Race, Redistricting, and Representation*.

they seem to enforce the Voting Rights Act in partisan ways.[54] Republicans openly complain about the Voting Rights Act infringement of states' electoral rights but seem to find that majority-minority districts, especially if they contain large Democratic majorities, are a source of electoral gains in other districts. Democrats, on the other hand, have pushed for the creation of those districts to help minority candidates get elected, especially African Americans, as these candidates are almost exclusively Democrats. Yet, these "sure shot" elections put them at a disadvantage in adjacent districts. Consequently, when Republicans in Congress supported the reauthorisation of the Voting Rights Act in 2006 it was perceived as a simple strategic calculation being in their partisan interest.[55] The Republican Party did not necessarily support minority groups' voting rights and interest representation but only saw majority-minority districts as a way to concentrate, and therefore weaken, Democratic voters. Any written work on redistricting is fundamentally about representation, or more precisely "fair and effective representation," and this debate shows that in the U.S. this implies a questioning of the interaction of race and politics.

The interaction of race and partisanship means the future of redistricting is very uncertain. One of the main conundrums for redistricters is that taking race into consideration is a dangerous sport. The jurisprudence on racial gerrymandering is so opaque that a legislature or a commission can be sued for taking race too much, or not enough, into consideration. Before Section 5 was rendered inoperative by the *Shelby County* Supreme Court decision in 2013, line drawers had to take race into consideration especially for jurisdictions covered by the formula contained in Section 4. Because of Section 2 of the Voting Rights Act, race still needs to be taken into consideration, but it is not clear how much leeway the courts will be willing to give to legislatures or commissions.

The second main problem faced by map makers is that some factors can be in direct contradiction of others. The post-*Shaw* jurisprudence puts the emphasis on the shape of districts. During racial gerrymandering trials, courts have routinely considered districts' shapes as circumstantial evidence. In states, or areas within a state, where minorities are not neatly clustered, redistricters have to draw irregularly shaped districts to make sure a certain percentage of a district population belongs to a minority. But more importantly, neat, squarish districts do not guarantee that minorities have not been discri-

---

[54] Katz, Ellen D. "Democrats at DOJ: Why Partisan Use of the Voting Rights Act Might Not Be So Bad After All." Stanford Law and Policy Review 23 (2012): 417.
[55] Persily, "The Promises and Pitfalls of the New VRA," 2007.

minated against or that they have the opportunity to elect the candidate of their choice. Since the courts have never established any standard for shape (and how could they), it is anybody's guess what will constitute a suspicious-looking district. The absence of Section 5 preclearance, the erratic jurisprudence of the *Shaw*-line of cases, and the deficiency of any standard for partisan gerrymandering post-*Whitford* make redistricting unpredictable, and place the burden of redistricting enforcement on Section 2. However, Section 2 and its interpretation (the *Gingles* test) are from a different era when the main goal was to identify racial division inside the Democratic Party that controlled the South at the time. Today, conjoined polarisation and the increase in diversity complicate all three parts of the *Gingles* test. And the question of minority representation is not limited to the South anymore.[56]

But unless the U.S. adopts another voting system, and this is very unlikely, redistricting will continue to be more conflictual as minority groups grow in number and demand increases of their representation, that is to say in proportion to their demographic weight. The American concept of political representation is that of a body of elected officials that mirrors the diversity of the population. As long as redistricting is perceived as the main instrument to achieve ethno-racial diversity in a racially polarised environment, it will concentrate all the tensions inherent to the political representation conundrum of the American society. Redistricting concentrates so many of the contradictions at the heart of representative democracy that redistricting reform is sometimes presented as the panacea for everything that hails American democracy: partisan polarisation, incumbent advantage, lack of competition or underrepresentation of minority groups. It is neither negligible nor the key to electoral success that many elected officials believe it to be. Nor is it the source of all the shortcomings of democracy. If it generates so much passion, it is because redistricting concentrates all the paradoxes and tensions inherent to representative democracy.

This interaction between race and partisanship also changes the dynamic inside both parties. As African Americans, Latinos and Asian Americans joined the Democratic coalition in the 1980s and 1990s, their fight was no longer about access to the polls but about pushing out White Democratic incumbents to increase their descriptive representation because that party was the only avenue open to them. Yet in most cases, in a "winner-take-all" system with a high degree of racial polarisation, minority groups found that their electoral preferences were

---

[56] Sydney Moncrief (ed.), *Reapportionment and Redistricting in the West* (Lexington, 2011); Olivier Richomme, *Race and Redistricting in California: From the 1965 Voting Rights Act to Present* (Lexington, 2019).

thwarted by racial, partisan or incumbent interests, and did not lead to a body of representatives in the image of the population. The Republican Party on the other hand, has evolved into the party capitalising on older White males' anxieties. Both parties, therefore, have now diametrically opposed strategies when it comes to voting rights that extend way beyond the scope of redistricting. One party is convinced that an expansive approach to voting rights is in its electoral interest while the other is convinced that a restrictive definition of voting rights is in its electoral, albeit short-term, interest. It's under this broader framework that voter mobilisation strategies will be elaborated in the U.S. in the foreseeable future.

Bibliography

"Black Elected Officials by Office, 1970 to 2002, and State, 2002." U.S. Census Bureau, Statistical Abstract of the U.S. 2011, table 413, 258. http://www2.census.gov/library/publications/2010/compendia/statab/130ed/tables/11s0413.pdf.

"Election Polls – Vote by Groups, 1960–1964." Gallup. Accessed September, 21 2018. http://www.gallup.com/poll/9454/election-polls-vote-groups-19601964.aspx.

Abramowitz, Alan I. *The Great Realignment: Race, Party Transformation and the Rise of Donald Trump.* Yale University Press, 2018.

Abramowitz, Alan I. *The Disappearing Center: Engaged Citizens, Polarization and American Democracy.* Yale University Press, 2010.

Amy, Douglas J. *Real Choices/New Voices: How Proportional Representation Elections Could Revitalize American Democracy*, 2nd Edition. New York: Columbia University Press, 2002.

Ansolabehere, Stephen, and James M. Snyder. *The End of Inequality: One Person, One Vote and the Transformation of American Politics.* Norton, 2008.

Ansolabehere, Stephen, Nathaniel Persily and Charles Stewart III. "Regional Differences in Racial Polarization in the 2012 Presidential Election: Implications for the Constitutionality of Section 5 of the Voting Rights Act." *Harvard Law Review Forum* 126 (2013): 205–220.

Bialik, Kristen, and Jens Manuel Krogstad. "115th Congress sets new high for racial, ethnic diversity." Pew Research Center, January 24, 2017. http://www.pewresearch.org/fact-tank/2017/01/24/115th-congress-sets-new-high-for-racial-ethnic-diversity/.

Bowler, Shaun, Todd Donovan and David Brockington. *Electoral Reform and Minority Representation: Local Experiments with Alternative Elections.* Ohio State University Press, 2003.

Brown, Anna, and Sara Atske. "Blacks have made gains in U.S. political leadership, but gaps remain." Pew Research Center, June 28, 2016. http://www.pewresearch.org/fact-tank/2016/06/28/blacks-have-made-gains-in-u-s-political-leadership-but-gaps-remain/.

Butler, David, and Bruce E. Cain. *Congressional Redistricting: Comparative and Theoretical Perspectives.* McMillan, 1992.

Cain, Bruce E., and Emily R. Zhang. "Blurred Lines: Conjoined Polarization and Voting Rights." *Ohio State Law Journal* 77, no. 4 (2016): 867–904.

Cain, Bruce. "Moving Past Section 5: More Fingers or a New Dike." *Election Law Journal* 13, no. 2 (2013): 338–340.
Campbell, James E. *Polarized: Making Sense of a Divided America*. Princeton, NJ: Princeton University Press, 2016.
Canon, David T. *Race, Redistricting, and Representation: The Unintended Consequences of Black Majority Districts*. Chicago, IL: University of Chicago Press, 1999.
Charles, Guy-Uriel. "Judging the Law of Politics." *Michigan Law Review* 103 (2005): 1099–1141.
Cox, Adam B., and Richard T. Holden. "Reconsidering Racial and Partisan Gerrymandering." *The University of Chicago Law Review* 78, no. 2 (2011): 553–604.
Cox, Gary W. *Elbridge Gerry's Salamander: The Electoral Consequences of the Apportionment Revolution*. Cambridge University Press, 2002.
Engstrom, Richard L. "Race and Southern Politics: The Special Case of Congressional Districting." In *Writing Southern Politics: Contemporary Interpretations and Future Directions*, edited by Robert P. Steed and Laurence W. Moreland. University of Kentucky Press, 2006.
Engstrom, Richard. "Racial Discrimination in the Electoral Process: the Voting Rights Act and the Vote Dilution Issue." In *Party Politics in the South*, edited by Robert Steed, Laurence Moreland and Ted Baker. New York: Praeger, 1980.
Epstein, David L., Richard H. Pildes, Rodolfo De La Garza and Sharyn O'Hallaran, eds. *The Future of the Voting Rights Act*. New York: Russell Sage, 2006.
Fishkin, Joseph. "Equal Citizenship and the Equal Right to Vote." *Indiana Law Journal* 86 (2011): 1289–1360.
Fraga Luis, Ricardo, and Sharon A. Navarro. "Latinos in Latino Politics." In *Latino Politics: Identity, Mobilization and Representation*, edited by Roldfo Espino, David L. Leal and Kenneth J. Meier. Charlottesville, VA: University Press of Virginia, 2007.
Gerken, Heather K., and Michael S. Kang. "The Institutional Turn in Election Law Scholarship." In *Race, Reform, and Regulation of the Electoral Process*, edited by Guy-Uriel E. Charles, Heather K. Gerken and Michael S. Kang, 86–100. Cambridge University Press, 2011.
Gerken, Heather. "Understanding the Right to an Undiluted Vote". *Harvard Law Review* 114, no. 6 (2001): 1663–1743.
Gerken, Heather. "Keynote Address: What Election Law has to say to Constitutional Law." *Indiana Law Review* 44 (2010): 7–22.
Grofman, Bernard, Lisa Handley and Richard G. Niemi. *Minority Representation and the Quest for Voting Equality*. New York: Cambridge University Press, 1992.
Guinier, Lani. *The Tyranny of the Majority: Fundamental Fairness in Representative Democracy*. New York: Free Press, 1994.
Handley, Lisa, and Bernard Grofman. "The Impact of the Voting Rights Act on Minority Representation: Black Officeholders in Southern State Legislatures and Congressional Delegations." In *Quiet Revolution in the South*, edited by Chandler Davidson and Bernard Grofman, 335–350. Princeton, NJ: Princeton University Press, 1994.
Hasen, Richard L. "Racial Gerrymandering's Questionable Revival." *Alabama Law Review* 67, (2016): 365.

Hasen, Richard. "Race or Party: How Courts Should Think About Republican Efforts to Make it Harder to Vote in North Carolina and Elsewhere." *Harvard Law Review Forum* 127 (2014): 58–75.

Hasen, Richard. *The Supreme Court and Election Law: Judging Equality from Baker v. Carr to Bush v. Gore.* New York University Press, 2003.

Hollinger, David. *Postethnic America: Beyond Multiculturalism.* New York: Basic Books, 1995.

Issacharoff, Samuel. "Supreme Court Destabilization of Single-Member Districts." *University of Chicago Legal Forum* 1 (1995): 238–239.

Karlan, Pamela S., and Daryl J. Levinson. "Why Voting is Different." *California Law Review* 84, no. 4 (1996): 1202.

Katz, Ellen D. "Democrats at DOJ: Why Partisan Use of the Voting Rights Act Might Not Be So Bad After All." *Stanford Law and Policy Review* 23 (2012): 417.

Kousser, Morgan. *Colorblind Injustice: Minority Voting Rights and the Undoing of the Second Reconstruction.* Chapel Hill, NC: North Carolina Press, 1999.

Lublin, David. *The Paradox of Representation: Racial Gerrymandering and Minority Interests in Congress.* Princeton, NJ: Princeton University Press, 1997.

McCool, Daniel, ed. *The Most Fundamental Right: Contrasting Perspectives on the Voting Rights Act.* Bloomington: Indiana Press University, 2012.

McGann, Anthony J., Charles Anthony Smith, Michael Latner and Alex Keena. *Gerrymandering in America: The House of Representatives, the Supreme Court and the Future of Popular Sovereignty.* Cambridge University Press, 2016.

Moncrief, Sydney, ed. *Reapportionment and Redistricting in the West.* Lexington, 2011.

NALEO, https://naleo.org/at-a-glance/

Nkanishi, Don T., and James Lai, eds. *National Asian Pacific Political Almanac*, 15th Edition. UCLA Asian American Studies Center Press, 2014.

Persily, Nathaniel. "The Promises and Pitfalls of the New VRA." *Yale Law Journal* 117 (2007): 174–253.

Pildes, Richard H. "Voting Rights The Next Generation." In *Race, Reform and Regulation of the electoral Process*, edited by Guy-Uriel E. Charles, Heather Gerken and Michael Kang, 30. Cambridge University Press, 2011.

Pitkin, Hanna Fenichel. *The Concept of Representation.* University of California Press, 1967.

Richomme, Olivier. *Race and Redistricting in California: From the 1965 Voting Rights Act to Present.* Lexington, 2019.

Richomme, Olivier. "'Fair' Minority Representation and the California Voting Rights Act." *National Political Science Review* 20, no. 2 (2019): 55–75.

Rush, Mark, and Richard Engstrom. *Fair and Effective Representation: Debating Electoral Reform and Minority Rights.* Rowman and Littlefield, 2001.

Seabrook, Nicolas R. *Drawing the Lines: Constraints on Partisan Gerrymandering in U.S. Politics.* Cornell University Press, 2017.

Shickler, Eric. *Racial Realignment: The Transformation of American Liberalism, 1932–1965.* Princeton, NJ: Princeton University Press, 2016.

Shotts, Kenneth W. "The Effect of Majority-Minority Mandates on Partisan Gerrymandering." *American Journal of Political Science* 45 (2001): 121.

Skrentny, John D. *The Minority Rights Revolution.* Cambridge, MA: Harvard University Press, 2002.

Swain, Carol M. *Black Faces, Black Interests: The Representation of African Americans in Congress.* Cambridge, MA: Harvard University Press, 1993.

Thurber, James A., and Antoine Yoshinaka, eds. *American Gridlocked: The Sources, Character, Impact of Political Polarization.* Cambridge University Press, 2016.

Tucker, James Thomas. "The Politics of Persuasion: Passage of the Voting Rights Act reauthorization Act of 2006." *Journal of Legislation* 33, no. 2 (2007): 205–267.

Tucker, James Thomas. *The Battle over Bilingual Ballot: Language Minorities and Political Access Under the Voting Rights Act.* Burlington, VT: Ashgate, 2009.

Vallely, Richard. *The Two Reconstructions: The Struggle for Black Enfranchisement.* Chicago, IL: University of Chicago Press, 2004.

John A. Kirk
2 From Representation by the Elite Few to the Mobilisation of the Masses

The Long Grassroots Struggle for Black Voting Rights in Arkansas since the 1860s

Introduction

The struggle for black political representation and participation in Arkansas since the 1860s has been defined by a gradual move away from a select few members of the black elite who claimed to speak for the interests of the race as a whole to the organisation and mobilisation of the black masses for voting rights. This occurred in four main stages.

The Four Stages of Black Political Representation, Participation and Voting Rights

Firstly, black Arkansans, as in other southern states, experienced political representation under Republican Reconstruction governments after the Civil War. In practical terms this meant a select number of black politicians, mainly drawn from the small black professional, merchant, and land-owning class, serving in the Arkansas General Assembly.[1] The collapse of Reconstruction in the South by 1877 (in Arkansas effectively by 1874) led to a retrenchment of political power by former Confederates under the banner of the Democratic Party.[2] Disenfranchisement and segregation laws passed in the early 1890s consolidated white supremacy by introducing racial cleavages that marginalised the black

---

[1] Blake J. Wintory, "African-American Legislators in the Arkansas General Assembly, 1868–1893," *Arkansas Historical Quarterly* 65 (Winter 2006): 385–434.
[2] On Reconstruction in the South see Eric Foner, *Reconstruction: America's Unfinished Revolution, 1863–1867* (New York: Harper & Row, 1988). On Reconstruction in Arkansas see Carl Moneyhon, *The Impact of the Civil War and Reconstruction on Arkansas: Persistence in the Midst of Ruin* (Baton Rouge: Louisiana State University Press, 1994).

population in politics and society. This led to black politicians being excluded from the Arkansas General Assembly for the next 80 years.³

Secondly, attempts to maintain black political representation during the age of segregation and disenfranchisement were continued by members of the black elite that looked to exercise their limited influence with whites.⁴ These efforts coalesced around attempts to provide a black voice and presence in Arkansas's main political parties. Black attorney Scipio Africanus Jones emerged as the leading black politician in the Republican Party of Arkansas (RPA), while black physician Dr. John Marshall Robinson battled with the Democratic Party of Arkansas (DPA), which excluded blacks entirely, to permit them a say in its party affairs. Both men met with victories and setbacks in their efforts.

Thirdly, during the 1930s and 1940s, the Great Depression, the New Deal and the United States' entry into World War II all profoundly reshaped the struggle for black voting rights. In the 1940s, young black Arkansas attorney William Harold Flowers articulated a more expansive agenda for what black political power might achieve. Rather than seeking to solely provide a representative voice for the black population as others in the black elite had previously done, Flowers advocated the mass organisation and mobilisation of the black population through an independent black political organisation called the Committee on Negro Organizations (CNO). Flowers and the CNO successfully grew the number of black voters in the state. This, in turn, provided leverage for further voting rights and civil rights demands. Eventually, this forced the DPA to open its doors to black membership in 1950, paving the way for greater black access to state politics.

Fourthly, since the 1950s black Arkansans have had greater opportunities for representation and participation in mainstream state politics. National developments such as the abolition of the poll tax in federal elections and the passage of voting and civil rights legislation in the 1960s made an impact in Arkansas, as did grassroots activism within the state. In 1972, the first black legislators were elected to the Arkansas General Assembly in the twentieth century. Soon after, black voter registration levels in the state reached a record high. Nevertheless,

---

3 The best overview about the onset of the age of disenfranchisement and segregation in Arkansas is John William Graves, *Town and Country: Race Relations in an Urban/Rural Context, Arkansas, 1865–1905* (Fayetteville: University of Arkansas Press, 1990). For a regional perspective on developments, see R. Volney Riser, *Defying Disfranchisement: Black Voting Rights Activism in the Jim Crow South, 1890–1908* (Baton Rouge: Louisiana State University Press, 2010).
4 On Little Rock's black elite, and the black elite in other southern cities, see Willard B. Gatewood, *Aristocrats of Color: The Black Elite, 1880–1920* (Bloomington: Indiana University Press, 1990).

the struggle for black representation and participation in state politics continued. A landmark court case in *Jeffers v. Clinton* (1989) successfully won the creation of more black majority districts, increasing the numbers of black politicians in the Arkansas General Assembly. However, Arkansas remains the only former Confederate state to have never elected a black person to a statewide or federal office. As in other states, more recently new barriers to black political representation and participation in Arkansas have emerged, such as the state's 2018 voter I.D. law. The struggle for black voting rights in Arkansas is by no means over yet.[5]

Historiographical Context

For many years historians have endeavoured to chart the larger and longer struggle for voting rights and civil rights at local, county, state, regional, national and even international levels.[6] Historian Jaquelyn Dowd Hall has outlined the idea of a "long" civil rights movement.[7] This concept seeks to extend the chronology of the civil rights movement beyond what black activist Bayard Rustin termed its "classic" phase in the 1950s and 1960s. This phase was composed of what have become familiar and recognisable events beginning with the U.S. Supreme Court's 1954 *Brown v. Board of Education* school desegregation decision, the 1955 murder of Emmett Till and the 1955–1956 Montgomery bus boycott in the mid-1950s, and ending with Martin Luther King, Jr.'s assassination in Memphis in 1968.[8] By stretching the chronology of the civil rights movement back before the 1950s, and forward after the 1960s, we can view the classic phase of the civil rights movement that unfolded in those decades as forming part of a much longer black struggle for freedom and equality.

This essay adds another piece to that ever-growing mosaic of scholarship by examining black efforts to win political representation and participation in Ar-

---

[5] For a more expansive overview of the long civil rights movement in Arkansas see John A. Kirk, *Redefining the Color Line: Black Activism in Little Rock, Arkansas, 1940–1970* (Gainesville: University Press of Florida, 2002).

[6] For a useful overview of and commentary on these developments, see John A. Kirk, "The Long and the Short of It: New Perspectives in Civil Rights Studies," *Journal of Contemporary History* 46, no. 2 (April 2011): 425–436.

[7] Jacquelyn Dowd Hall, "The Long Civil Rights Movement and the Political Uses of the Past," *Journal of American History* 91, no. 4 (March 2005): 1233–1263.

[8] Bayard Rustin, "From Protest to Politics: The Future of the Civil Rights Movement," *Commentary* 39 (February 1965): 25–31.

kansas. The state is best known for its place in civil rights history because of the 1957 Little Rock school crisis, when President Dwight D. Eisenhower sent federal soldiers to Central High School in Arkansas's capital city to ensure the safe entry of nine black students following the U.S. Supreme Court's landmark *Brown* decision.[9] These events, like so many others in the "classic" decades of the civil rights movement in the 1950s and 1960s, were profoundly shaped by the tireless groundwork laid by black activists over many years as they chiseled away at the edifice of white supremacy, including the political struggles outlined here.[10]

In line with many other histories of local black activism in the long, grassroots struggle for freedom and equality, there are elements of this history in Arkansas that were shaped by the specific local, county and state political cultures they emerged from. There are also elements of this history that connect those struggles to others which unfolded in other localities, and at regional and national levels.[11] Therefore, the campaigns for black political representation, participation and voting rights in Arkansas help illuminate the specific contours of how black activism developed in that state while also providing a window on broader developments that shaped similar campaigns elsewhere.

Black Politics in the Late Nineteenth Century: Representation of the Many by the Elite Few

Black political representation in Arkansas began even before the passage of the Fifteenth Amendment to the U.S. Constitution in 1870 that guaranteed all black men the right to vote without "account of race, color, or previous condition of servitude."[12] Just three years after the abolition of slavery, in 1868 six black men served in the Arkansas General Assembly under the state's Republican Reconstruction government. Between 1868 and 1893, a total of 84 blacks were elected: six in the senate, 74 in the house, and four in both chambers. These politicians were drawn mainly from the ranks of the small black elite in the state that was composed of professionals, businessmen and landowners. Most came from the heavily black populated areas of the Arkansas delta, where the state's

---

9 See, for example, Tony A. Freyer, *Little Rock on Trial: Cooper v Aaron and School Desegregation* (University Press of Kansas, 2007); Elizabeth Jacoway, *Turn Away Thy Son: Little Rock, the Crisis that Shocked a Nation* (New York: Free Press, 2007); and Karen Anderson, *Little Rock: Race and Resistance at Central High School* (Princeton: Princeton University Press, 2010).
10 For Rustin's use of this term, see Rustin, "From Protest to Politics."
11 See Hall, "The Long Civil Rights Movement."
12 U.S. Const. amend. XV.

cotton production and enslaved labour had been concentrated.¹³ Collectively, these black politicians gave voice to black aspirations after the Civil War, although they were far from representative of the black population as a whole, many of whom were left as landless farmers under the emerging exploitative systems of sharecropping and tenant farming.¹⁴

Twenty-five continuous years of black political representation in Arkansas politics came to a screeching halt in 1893. After the last black legislator left the Arkansas General Assembly that year, it was another 80 years before the next arrived. The emergence of disenfranchisement measures and segregation laws sidelined blacks from mainstream politics and society. Arkansas's election law of 1891 began the process of disenfranchisement in the state. Although passed with the stated intention of combating electoral fraud, its measures proved disastrous for black political participation. The law centralised the electoral system and put it under the control of the avowedly white supremacist and resurgent DPA. A secret ballot and a standardised ballot paper required by the act appeared innocuous enough on the face of it, but it essentially introduced a form of literacy test. Over a quarter of the population in the state could not read or write, including 93,090 whites and 116,665 blacks.¹⁵

In 1892, the first election governed by the new rules, voters also passed a poll tax amendment. By requiring the purchase of a poll tax receipt to vote, many poorer Arkansans, black and white, were excluded from the electoral process. Because of these combined measures, the vote in the 1894 elections was a third lower than in the 1890 elections, a drop of around 65,000 people. Such disenfranchisement measures allowed white Democrats to seize political control in the state and to place further limits on black citizenship by passing segregation laws that provided for the separation of the races in virtually every sphere of life.¹⁶

Despite the emergence of this much more hostile environment for voting rights and civil rights, the struggle for black political representation continued. This initially followed the same pattern as Reconstruction politics in focusing on maintaining representation in the RPA led by members of the black elite. Black political representation did notably differ during this period in shifting

---

13 Wintory, "African-American Legislators in the Arkansas General Assembly."
14 On the emergence of sharecropping and tenant farming see Edward Royce, *The Origins of Southern Sharecropping* (Philadelphia, PA: Temple University Press, 2010).
15 John William Graves, "Negro Disfranchisement in Arkansas," *Arkansas Historical Quarterly* 26 (1967): 199–225; and Chris M. Branam, "Another Look at Disfranchisement in Arkansas, 1888–1894," *Arkansas Historical Quarterly* 69 (2010): 245–256.
16 See Graves, *Town and Country*.

its focus to the state capital of Little Rock rather than the Arkansas delta. A more urban environment, Little Rock offered greater protections in terms of collective security for blacks in the state, and it was generally less susceptible to the violence and intimidation that stood in the way of black political representation and participation in rural areas.[17]

Blacks and Political Parties in the Early Twentieth Century: Republican Scipio Africanus Jones and Democrat Dr. John Marshall Robinson

Scipio Africanus Jones and Black Republicans

Scipio Africanus Jones was at the forefront of the struggle for black political representation in the early twentieth century. Born a slave in Tulip, southwest Arkansas, Jones worked as a field hand after emancipation, moving to Little Rock in 1881. After gaining an education at the historically black institutions Philander Smith College and then Shorter College, he became a self-taught lawyer, opening a practice in 1889. Jones was a talented attorney and became counsel to many of the black fraternal and Masonic groups in Little Rock, as well as an early advocate for civil rights in the courtroom.[18] Jones' most celebrated cases came after the 1919 Elaine Massacre, when whites killed what some estimates put at hundreds of black men, women and children after they attempted to organise a sharecroppers' union in the Arkansas delta.[19] Employed by the National Association for the Advancement of Colored People (NAACP), Jones won custodial rather than death sentences for the 12 black prisoners convicted for their alleged role in events. He then successfully negotiated with white politicians for their release from prison.[20]

---

[17] For a discussion of race relations in Little Rock in a statewide context see the introduction to Kirk, *Refining the Color Line*.
[18] Tom Dillard, "Scipio A. Jones," *Arkansas Historical Quarterly* 31 (Autumn 1972): 201–219.
[19] On the Elaine Massacre see Grif Stockley, *Blood in Their Eyes: The Elaine Race Massacres of 1919* (Fayetteville: University of Arkansas Press, 2001); and Robert Whitaker, *On the Laps of Gods: The Red Summer of 1919 and the Struggle for Justice that Remade a Nation* (New York: Crown, 2008).
[20] On the trials of the Elaine Twelve see Richard C. Cortner, *A Mob Intent on Death: The NAACP and the Arkansas Riot Cases* (Middletown: University of Connecticut Press, 1988). See also Dillard, "Scipio Jones," 201–219; and Tom Dillard, "Perseverance: Black History in Pulaski County, Arkansas—An Excerpt," *Pulaski County Historical Review* 31 (1983): 62–73.

These exploits undoubtedly helped Jones in his political career that centred upon taking on the so-called "lily-whites" in the Republican ranks who tried to prevent black participation in the party after the collapse of Reconstruction. Jones and his followers won the long, bitter and hard-fought battle against this political faction in 1928. That year, Jones gained election as a delegate to the Republican National Convention, forcing the RPA to acknowledge and accept the legitimacy of black participation in the state organisation.[21] By the time that Jones had successfully asserted an ongoing black voice in the RPA, however, the almost complete dominance of the DPA in state politics meant that the struggle of black Republicans counted for relatively little.[22]

Dr. John Marshall Robinson and the Arkansas Negro Democratic Association

The decisive shift in political power from the Republican Party to the Democratic Party in Arkansas meant a parallel shift in the focus of efforts for black political representation. Little Rock black physician Dr. John Marshall Robinson spearheaded attempts to establish a black voice in the DPA by founding the Arkansas Negro Democratic Association (ANDA) in 1928.[23] Marshall, born in Pickens, Mississippi, in 1879, attended Rust College in his home state before graduating from Meharry Medical College in Nashville, Tennessee, in 1904. He opened a medical practice at Seventh and Main Streets in downtown Little Rock in 1906, and he was a founder member of the Little Rock NAACP branch, the first NAACP branch established in the state, in 1918. Robinson did not share the mainly Republican loyalties of the established black elite and his attempts to promote black participation in the DPA offered a new direction in black political leadership.[24]

ANDA's first action was to sue white Democrats for the right to vote in the party's primary elections. Since the DPA dominated virtually every political office

---

[21] Dillard, "Scipio Jones," 201–219; Tom Dillard, "To the Back of the Elephant: Racial Conflict in the Arkansas Republican Party," *Arkansas Historical Quarterly* 33 (1974): 3–15.
[22] V.O. Key, Jr., *Southern Politics in State and Nation* (New York: Alfred A. Knopf, 1949), 183.
[23] Text of speech delivered by Dr. J.M. Robinson to the Jefferson County Democratic Association, Pine Bluff, Arkansas, July 18, 1952, Dr. John Marshall Robinson Papers (privately held in possession of Terry Pierson, Little Rock, Arkansas).
[24] For more details on Robinson and ANDA, see John A. Kirk, "Dr. J. M. Robinson, the Arkansas Negro Democratic Association and Black Politics in Little Rock, Arkansas, 1928–1952," *Pulaski County Historical Review* 41 (1993): 2–16 (part one); *Pulaski County Historical Review* 41 (1993): 39–47 (part two); and Dale Lya Pierson, "John M. Robinson, M.D., 1879–1970," *Pulaski County Historical Review* 41 (1993): 91–93.

in Arkansas at the time, its primary elections were the true source of political power in the state. General elections provided for little more than the ratification of a Democratic nominee. DPA regulations forbade black participation in the party's primary elections, thereby denying blacks any meaningful say in state politics—yet another disenfranchisement measure to accompany literacy tests and the poll tax.[25]

ANDA's attack on the white primary system built upon regional developments in political activism initiated by black Democrats in Texas who, aided by the NAACP, won an important ruling before the U.S. Supreme Court in *Nixon v. Herndon* (1927). In the *Nixon* case, the Court ruled that state laws preventing black suffrage in Democratic Party primaries were unconstitutional. This victory proved only a partial triumph, since the Court did not rule on the constitutional rights of black voters *per se*, but rather on the use of state laws to prevent blacks from voting. This left the way open for state Democratic parties to claim that they were private organisations and therefore constitutionally allowed to introduce rules preventing black suffrage in their party primaries since voting rights and civil rights laws only extended to state action. Since the white primary system in Arkansas was identical to that used in Texas, ANDA sought to clarify and extend the *Nixon* ruling. What ANDA specifically wanted was a court decision that would rule out the use of exclusively white party primaries.[26]

On November 27, 1928, Judge Richard M. Mann of the Second Division Circuit Court, sitting in the absence of Chancellor Frank H. Dodge in the Pulaski County Chancery Court (Pulaski County was home to the state capital of Little Rock), upheld an application by Dr. Robinson and other ANDA members for an injunction against the DPA to prevent it from barring black voters from their party primaries. Meanwhile, he ordered the separation of black and white ballots in primary elections pending an appeal.[27] On August 30, 1929, Chancellor Dodge, having returned to court, again revoked the voting rights of black Democrats. ANDA's ap-

---

25 Key, *Southern Politics*, 183.
26 Dr. J.M. Robinson to J.F. McClerkin, August 6, 1928, Robinson Papers; John A. Hibbler to William T. Andrews, September 27, 1929, group I, series D, container 44, folder "Cases Supported—Arkansas Primary Case 1928–1929," National Association for the Advancement of Colored People Papers, Manuscript Division, Library of Congress, Washington, D.C.; Darlene Clark Hine, *Black Victory: The Rise and Fall of the White Primary in Texas* (Millwood, NY: KTO Press, 1979), 72–85.
27 *Arkansas Gazette* (Little Rock), November 27, 1928, clipping in Pulaski County Democratic Committee (PCDC) Scrapbooks, Arkansas History Commission, Little Rock.

peals to the Arkansas and U.S. Supreme Court both failed to overturn the decision.[28]

The Emergence of Mass Black Political Organisation and Mobilisation in the 1940s: William Harold Flowers and the Committee on Negro Organisations

The Impact of the Great Depression, the New Deal and World War II

During the 1930s and 1940s, a significant shift took place in the struggle for voting rights and civil rights in Arkansas. Many in the black elite found their position and status undermined as the Great Depression destroyed a number of black businesses and enterprises in the state. At the same time, a new agenda for black advancement was emerging that went beyond the capacity of existing black leaders to handle. The majority of blacks in the state suffered far more at the hands of the Depression than the black elite. Increasingly, they looked to the federal government for help. In return, the national Democratic Party under President Franklin D. Roosevelt offered a set of New Deal programs and policies that brought with them the potential to challenge racial discrimination, which in turn raised hopes throughout the state's black population.[29]

While the limited impact of the New Deal on black lives was ultimately ambiguous, and its positive aspects very often undermined by segregation and unchecked racial discrimination, it did provide some hope for blacks that the federal government could make a difference in their daily lives. In the 1936

---

28 William T. Andrews to John A. Hibbler, July 19, 1930, group I, series D, container 44, folder "Cases Supported—Arkansas Primary Case 1928–1929," NAACP Papers (Washington, D.C.); Hine, *Black Victory*, 115.
29 For the national and regional impact of the New Deal on blacks see, for example, Ralph J. Bunche, *The Political Status of the Negro in the Age of FDR* (Chicago, IL: University of Chicago Press, 1973); Harvard Sitkoff, *A New Deal for Blacks: The Emergence of Civil Rights as a National Issue: Volume 1: The Depression Decade* (New York: Oxford University Press, 1978); John B. Kirby, *Black Americans in the Roosevelt Era: Liberalism and Race* (Knoxville: Tennessee University Press, 1980); Nancy J. Weiss, *Farewell to the Party of Lincoln: Black Politics in the Age of FDR* (Princeton, NJ: Princeton University Press, 1983); and Patricia Sullivan, *Days of Hope: Race and Democracy in the New Deal Era* (Chapel Hill: University of North Carolina Press, 1996).

elections, blacks left their traditional political home in the Republican Party, which they had previously viewed a natural ally as the party of President Abraham Lincoln and Emancipation, and began to move *en masse* to the Democratic Party as it became, at least at the national level, perceived as the pro-civil rights party. In the South, meanwhile, state and local Democrats remained the stoutest defenders of white supremacy. Demographic shifts helped to consolidate black political aspirations and with it the potential to exercise collective political power as the movement of blacks from rural areas to villages, towns and cities created a growing base for political mobilisation.[30]

World War II acted as a further catalyst for change. Wartime army bases that located in the South helped its ailing economy, which President Roosevelt recognised as the nation's "number one economic problem," with 12 billion dollars of investment. Encroaching industrialisation went hand in hand with further black urbanisation. Blacks pushed hard to win their share of wartime prosperity not only in the South but nationwide. The threat of a mass march on Washington by black labour leader A. Philip Randolph in 1941 led to the formation of the Fair Employment Practice Committee (FEPC) by Roosevelt to monitor racial discrimination in federal employment.[31] Even with its shortcomings, the FEPC contributed to a tripling in the federal employment of blacks.[32] Hundreds of thousands of blacks enlisted to help fight in the war for democracy. They did so with the firm intention of winning support for what the black press termed the "double V"—victory at home for democracy and equality, as well as abroad.[33]

---

30 John B. Mitchell, "An Analysis of Arkansas's Population by Race and Nativity, and Residence," *Arkansas Historical Quarterly* 8 (1949): 115–132.

31 See Herbert Garfinkle, *When Negroes March: The March on Washington Movement in the Organizational Politics for the FEPC* (Glencoe, IL: Free Press, 1959); Cornelius L. Bynum, *A. Philip Randolph and the Struggle for Civil Rights* (Urbana: University of Illinois Press, 2010); and David Lucander, *Winning the War for Democracy: The March on Washington Movement, 1941–1946* (Urbana and Chicago: University of Illinois Press, 2014).

32 On the FEPC see Merle E. Reed, *Seedtime for the Modern Civil Rights Movement: The President's Committee on Fair Employment Practice, 1941–1946* (Baton Rouge: Louisiana State University Press, 1991).

33 On blacks and World War II see, for example, Neil R. McMillen (ed.), *Remaking Dixie: The Impact of World War II on the American South* (Jackson: University Press of Mississippi, 1997); Daniel Kryder, *Divided Arsenal: Race and the American State during World War II* (New York: Cambridge University Press, 2000); Charles D. Chamberlin, *Victory at Home: Manpower and Race in the American South during World War II* (Athens: University of Georgia Press, 2003); Kevin M. Kruse and Stephen Tuck (eds.), *Fog of War: The Second World War and the Civil Rights Movement* (New York: Oxford University Press, 2012); Kimberley L. Phillips, *War! What Is It Good For? Black Freedom Struggles and the U.S. Military from World War II to Iraq* (Chapel Hill: University of North Carolina Press, 2012); Paul Alkebulan, *The African American Press in World*

NAACP membership grew tenfold, and much of this growth came from newly established and burgeoning local southern branches.³⁴

William Harold Flowers

Looking to build upon the promise of change that the New Deal had brought and which the United States' entry into World War II held the potential to fulfill, there was an ever-growing constituency for mass black political engagement in Arkansas. It was precisely this constituency that young attorney William Harold Flowers sought to address. Flowers, born in Stamps, southwest Arkansas, in 1911, was the son of an insurance salesman and a schoolteacher. The Flowers family belonged to a small black elite in Stamps and lived in an integrated neighbourhood. Yet rather than sharing the narrow vision of merely being a representative voice of the black masses that others in the black elite did, Flowers' early experiences gave him a more expansive and democratic outlook. Enamoured by childhood trips to the courthouse with his father, Flowers finally determined to pursue a legal career after a harrowing and graphic introduction to another side of southern justice. At the age of 16, on a visit to Little Rock, he witnessed the burning of lynching victim John Carter on West Ninth Street, the city's main black business downtown thoroughfare. It was at this sight, Flowers recalled in later years, that he was "truly converted to be a lawyer."³⁵

Flowers attended Lincoln High School in East St. Louis, Illinois, for two years before completing his education at Philander Smith College. He then worked his way through law school, taking part-time classes at the Robert H. Terrell School of Law in Washington, D.C., a night school founded by black lawyer George A. Parker in 1931. After graduation from law school, Flowers returned to Arkansas and set up a legal practice in Pine Bluff in 1938. Some 40 miles south of Little Rock, Pine Bluff was a thriving hub for black enterprises, organisations and institutions, and it was home to Arkansas's black land grant campus Arkan-

---

War II: Toward Victory at Home and Abroad (Lanham, MD: Lexington Books, 2014); and Christine Knauer, *Let Us Fight as Free Men: Black Soldiers and Civil Rights* (Philadelphia: University of Pennsylvania Press, 2014).
34 Adam Fairclough, *Better Day Coming: Blacks and Equality, 1890–2000* (New York: Viking Penguin, 2001), 182.
35 Maya Angelou, *I Know Why the Caged Bird Sings* (New York: Random House, 1969), 47; *Arkansas Gazette*, July 31, 1988.

sas Agricultural, Mechanical & Normal College.[36] Young, eager, and idealistic, with first-hand experiences of southern injustice, from his first days in Pine Bluff Flowers set about trying to use his legal talents in the pursuit of voting rights and civil rights. Initially, Flowers looked to the NAACP to help in this ambitious task. In October 1938, Flowers wrote to NAACP executive secretary Walter White informing him that Arkansas badly needed organisation and leadership and that he wanted to try to provide it. But, Flowers explained, he needed financial assistance to do so. As a novice lawyer just starting to build up his business he could not afford to take time away from his livelihood without recompense.[37]

Despite these pleadings, no help from the NAACP's national office in New York was forthcoming. Letters arrived from special counsel to the NAACP, Charles Houston, and his aspiring protégé, assistant special counsel to the NAACP, Thurgood Marshall, both offering sympathy but little practical help.[38] Although Houston and Marshall initially stalled, Flowers' call for black lawyers to take a more active role in the struggle for voting rights and civil rights was very much in line with developments taking place in the NAACP's national office in the late 1930s. Under pressure from the Internal Revenue Service (IRS), which denied the NAACP tax-exempt status because of its lobbying activities, in 1939 the NAACP created the NAACP Legal Defense and Educational Fund, Inc., known later as the LDF or "Inc. Fund." The LDF dealt with legal and educational matters only, thus ensuring its tax-exempt status. Although the NAACP and the LDF remained closely intertwined, with overlapping board membership, the creation of the LDF signaled the beginning of an increasing emphasis on litigation by black activists in the NAACP's national office during the 1940s. In particular, it provided Thurgood Marshall, who became director-counsel of the LDF and special counsel to the NAACP, and other talented black lawyers, with a platform to pursue voting rights and civil rights through the courts.[39]

---

36 For a portrait of black Pine Bluff in the age of segregation see George Lipsitz, *Ivory Perry and the Culture of Opposition* (Philadelphia: Temple University Press, 1988), 15–38.
37 W.H. Flowers to Walter White, October 31, 1938, William Harold Flowers Papers (privately held in possession of Stephanie Flowers, Pine Bluff, Arkansas).
38 Charles Houston to W.H. Flowers, November 22, 1938; Thurgood Marshall to W.H. Flowers, April 14, 1939, both in Flowers Papers.
39 Mark Tushnet, *The NAACP's Legal Strategy Against Segregated Education, 1925–1950* (Chapel Hill: University of North Carolina Press, 1987), 100; Jack Greenberg, *Crusaders in the Courts: How a Dedicated Band of Lawyers Fought for the Civil Rights Revolution* (New York: Basic Books, 1994), 19–21; and Mark Tushnet, *Making Civil Rights Law: Thurgood Marshall and the Supreme Court, 1936–1961* (New York: Oxford University Press, 1994), 27.

The Committee on Negro Organizations (CNO)

By the time that the NAACP had rebuffed his requests for assistance, Flowers decided that he could wait no longer for them to act. On March 10, 1940, at a meeting in his hometown of Stamps, Flowers officially launched a Committee on Negro Organizations (CNO) to take on the task of politically mobilising the state's black population.[40] Flowers was determined to create a "single organization sufficient to serve the social, civic, political and economic needs of the people." Such an organisation would stand up for the rights of blacks to have a say in government, fight, "un-American activities... enslaving the Negro people," and devise a "system of protest" to remove them.[41]

The cornerstone of the CNO's program was to encourage black participation in the political process. This was by no means a new idea as the efforts of Scipio Africanus Jones and black Republicans and Dr. John Marshall Robinson and black Democrats testified. Flowers and the CNO were part of an already established long tradition of black political activity in Arkansas. However, in direct contrast to all previous attempts to secure black political participation, Flowers had a much broader vision of what the vote could achieve. Black political leaders such as Jones and Robinson had viewed politics as a platform for the black elite to represent their own interests, and to a lesser extent those of the black masses. Flowers viewed black political participation as a vehicle for advancing the black community as a whole.[42]

Flowers, although a staunch Republican, insisted that efforts to mobilise the black population in Arkansas should be non-partisan. Moving beyond the confines of white-dominated party politics, Flowers proposed the creation of an independent black political organisation that could represent the interests of all blacks in the state and tackle the common problems that they collectively encountered. The first step toward the kind of mass black political participation that Flowers and the CNO envisaged was payment of the state poll tax. They were convinced that if blacks began to purchase poll tax receipts and cast their vote at elections, it would prove a vital first step in raising black political consciousness to challenge the all-white DPA primaries.[43]

The goal of mass political mobilisation called for coordination and organisation. The CNO's first objective was to "seek the endorsement of Negro church,

---

40 Press Release, n.d., Flowers Papers.
41 *The CNO Spectator* (Pine Bluff), July 1, 1940, Flowers Papers.
42 Ibid.
43 Ibid.

civic, fraternal and social organizations."[44] Only by bringing about unity, direction of purpose, and exerting power through an expansive statewide representative body could the task of raising black political consciousness be effectively carried out. Flowers believed that he was well suited to such a task. His father was not only a businessman but also a leading Mason. His mother was a schoolteacher. He was a lawyer. The Flowers family, which was well respected and well known in black Arkansas, had strong links to the church. Flowers possessed first-hand knowledge of these different organisational power structures within Arkansas's black community and had direct contact with its various strands. Flowers therefore understood exactly which channels he needed to work thorough in order for the campaign to be effective.[45]

After the initial meeting at Stamps that launched the CNO, Flowers set off on a speaking tour to secure support from grassroots organisations across the state.[46] The series of meetings culminated in the "First Conference on Negro Organization" on September 27, 1940, held at Lakeview Junior High School. In his opening address, Flowers told the crowd that they had been brought together to "devise a program of action," to combat discrimination against blacks, "merely because of the color of their skin." He claimed that, "For six months we have obtained the endorsement of twenty-one organizations, with a numerical strength of approximately ten thousand Negro citizens." Further, Flowers outlined the achievements of the CNO to date. There had been 35 investigations over charges of color discrimination in public works employment. This had led to the lifting of a ban that had previously prevented blacks from participating in opportunities provided by the New Deal's National Youth Administration (NYA). The state had employed its first black census enumerator. Sixteen mass meetings had taken place with a total attendance of over 4,000 people. Blacks were beginning to show their disdain of disenfranchisement and segregation in significant numbers and the white power structure in the state, albeit on a small scale, was responding by acquiescing to some black demands.[47]

The next step, of converting organisational strength and enthusiasm into direct political gains, came with poll tax drives in September 1941. Under the direction of the CNO, a physician from the town of Hope, Dr. Roscoe C. Lewis, ran a

---

44 Ibid.
45 *Arkansas Gazette*, July 31, 1988.
46 *The CNO Spectator*, July 1, 1940, Flowers Papers.
47 "Partial Text of Keynote Address of W. Harold Flowers, delivered Friday Evening, September 27, 1940 at the opening of the 'First Conference on Negro Organization' held at Lakeview, Arkansas," September 27, 1940; CNO Press release, October 12, 1940; Flowers to William H. Nunn, October 5, 1940, all in Flowers Papers.

poll tax purchasing campaign in southern Arkansas, while an undertaker from Morrilton, W. L. Jarrett, supervised in the North. "Drive to Increase Race Votes Is Successful" headlined the *Arkansas State Press*, the Little Rock-based black newspaper owned by husband and wife team L.C. and Daisy Bates, at the end of the CNO's campaign. The newspaper anticipated a record turnout of black voters.[48] The following year, the newspaper printed Flowers' photograph with a caption acknowledging that "He Founded A Movement."[49] In 1940, black voter registration in Arkansas had stood at only 1.5 per cent. By 1947, that number had increased to 17.3 per cent. Through poll tax drives, voter education rallies and the general raising of political awareness and activity, Flowers and the CNO made sure that black political organisation pre-dated, and could therefore take full advantage of, subsequent national rulings.[50] Having established this foundation, Flowers chose to focus his efforts on building the NAACP's organisational structure in the state by founding an Arkansas NAACP state conference of branches in 1945. The NAACP national office proved far more responsive to his overtures for help following his success with the CNO. As an attorney, Flowers went on to blaze a trail for civil rights in the Arkansas courts by winning numerous landmark cases.[51]

The Impact of William Harold Flowers and the CNO

Flowers and the CNO effectively provided the inspiration for other local political groups who worked alongside the NAACP in unfolding voting rights and civil rights struggles. These groups dedicated themselves to mobilising the black vote and using it as a tool to elicit concessions from the white power structure. In Little Rock, black soldiers returning from World War II formed the Veterans' Good Government Association (VGGA) under the leadership of Charles Bussey who, like Flowers, hailed from Stamps. In 1947, Bussey successfully ran for the position of "bronze mayor," an annual election that was usually a formality of ratifying an unofficial mayor for blacks handpicked by whites. Bussey and the

---

48 *Arkansas State Press*, September 19, 1941.
49 Ibid., March 6, 1942.
50 Steven F. Lawson, *Running for Freedom: Civil Rights and Black Politics Since 1941* (New York: McGraw-Hill, 1991), 85.
51 On Flowers' civil rights activism, see John A. Kirk, "'He Founded a Movement': W. H. Flowers, the Committee on Negro Organizations and Black Activism in Arkansas, 1940–1957," in *The Making of Martin Luther King and the Civil Rights Movement in America*, ed. Brian Ward and Tony Badger (London: Macmillan, 1996), 29–44.

VGGA upset the usual smooth running of the election by persuading blacks to vote for him instead of the white-supported candidate, a result that clearly upset whites since they canceled the usual celebration banquet after his victory.[52] Bussey also had a hand in helping to form the East End Civic League (EECL) that represented a depressed black area in Little Rock. The EECL, run by Jeffrey Hawkins, helped to put pressure on white politicians for the improvement of street lighting, roads and pavements in the community. These groups became part of the wider struggle to translate a raised black political consciousness throughout the state into various forms of political activism, assisting blacks in securing material improvements in their everyday lives.[53]

The campaigns run by Flowers and the CNO in the early to mid-1940s also reinvigorated existing black leaders and organisations. After its defeat in the 1928 lawsuit, ANDA lay dormant for over a decade. Yet in the wake of a new push for voting rights, in December 1940 Dr. John Marshall Robinson petitioned the Democratic State Committee (DSC) to modify its rules to allow blacks to vote in the DPA primaries. Robinson, while seeking the right to vote, still assured whites that ANDA did not seek mass voting by blacks. DSC chair Robert Knox referred the matter to a subcommittee that decided to shelve the matter indefinitely. Without the strength of numbers to back up its demands, ANDA could do little to protest the decision. Whereas Flowers and the CNO could draw upon a grassroots statewide network of members and organisations for support, the limited scope of action, aims and backing for ANDA precluded such bold measures.[54]

The Struggle to End the Democratic Party's All-white Primary Elections

It took another two years for Robinson and ANDA to take further action on voting rights. This was prompted by developments at a national level, when the *United States v. Classic* (1941) case came before the U.S. Supreme Court. The lawsuit, which concerned fraud in Louisiana primary elections, did not deal directly

---

[52] Charles Bussey interview with John A. Kirk, Little Rock, Arkansas, December 4, 1992, John Kirk Civil Rights Movement in Arkansas Materials, Special Collections Division, University of Arkansas Libraries, Fayetteville.
[53] Jeffery Hawkins interview with John A. Kirk, Little Rock, Arkansas, September 30, 1992, John Kirk Civil Rights Movement in Arkansas Materials.
[54] *Arkansas Gazette*, December 8, 1940, clipping in PCDC Scrapbooks.

with race, but rather involved the constitutional status of primary elections. The Court ruled that discriminatory practices in primary elections, "may... operate to deprive the voter of his constitutional right of choice." The Court therefore concluded, "We think the authority of Congress... includes the authority to regulate primary elections."[55] The *Classic* decision undermined claims by state and local Democrats across the South that their own private rules should govern primary elections. Certainly, Thurgood Marshall regarded the decision as "striking and far reaching" in terms of future possible attacks on the white primary system.[56] A letter from ANDA to U.S. Attorney General Francis Biddle asked for his support in allowing black Arkansans to vote in DPA primaries. Robinson informed Biddle that the DPA had ignored a petition to secure such rights.[57] Meanwhile, white Democrats in Arkansas insisted that they would still bar blacks from voting in primary elections.[58]

Robinson's reply from the U.S. Attorney General's office insisted that "the denial of the right to Negro voters to participate in the primary elections has been the subject of a series of conferences within this department." Encouraged by the news, Robinson informed ANDA supporters that he expected no trouble at the polls from whites in the forthcoming primary elections. ANDA secretary John Hamilton McConico declared that ANDA was "not asking pity or any special favors, we are simply seeking to exercise those rights and privileges guaranteed to free men in a free country."[59] The decisive test for the *Classic* ruling came at the Little Rock DPA primaries. Election officials turned away the first black voter, a Baptist minister, from the polling booth. They even refused the minister's request to see a blank ballot. Similar events occurred throughout the city, with an estimated 75 to 100 blacks denied the right to vote.[60]

After the election, Dr. Robinson filed a report of events to Thurgood Marshall. In a mood of resignation, Robinson wrote, "They [white Democrats] made their decisions and made it stick. We'll just have to let things cool off for a while until everybody gets level-headed again." Indicative of the influence that support from outside organisations could have on sustaining local black protest, discussions with the NAACP's national office brought a more emboldened statement from ANDA. Robinson declared that if Democrats did not allow blacks to vote in the following Tuesday's second primary they would ap-

---

55 Hine, *Black Victory*, 202–207.
56 Ibid.
57 *Arkansas Gazette*, April 12, 1942, clipping in PCDC Scrapbooks.
58 Ibid., July 22, 1942.
59 Ibid., July 24, 25, 27, 1942.
60 Ibid., July 29, 1942.

peal to the federal courts for relief. At the same time, Robinson sought to maintain good relations with the DPA. In a letter to DPA state secretary Harry Combs, Robinson noted, "We hope you understand that this will be a friendly suit, with no financial or penal objectives." Combs bluntly replied, "The same rule that applies to the first primary applies to the second primary."[61]

As the position of stalemate continued at the local level, it took another U.S. Supreme Court ruling three years later to again stimulate further action from ANDA. Soon after the *Classic* ruling, Thurgood Marshall launched a test case in Texas in an attempt to get the courts to apply the new precedent in party primaries to black voting rights. The *Smith v. Allwright* (1944) case, similar to litigation existing in several other states, finally declared the all-white Democratic Party primaries unconstitutional.[62] Secretary of the Pulaski County Democratic Committee (PCDC) June Wooten conceded that the *Smith v. Allwright* ruling meant that blacks would be able to vote in federal elections. But Wooten did not completely admit defeat. He still believed that white Democrats could deny blacks the vote in state elections. Even in federal elections, at which blacks were now able to vote, Wooten believed that some semblance of segregation could continue by providing separate ballot boxes for black and white voters.[63]

U.S. Assistant Attorney General Cleveland Holland provided some encouragement for Dr. Robinson and ANDA when he advanced a more liberal interpretation of the Court's ruling. Holland emphasised the "state and national" clause of the written judgement which meant that blacks "may be able to vote for state and local offices," as well as in federal elections.[64] With the backing of the federal government behind them, ANDA held another meeting, at Little Rock's Dunbar High School, to discuss plans for voting in the DPA primaries that summer. In his letter of invitation to the meeting, Robinson expressed confidence that ANDA finally had "a definite understanding with the majority group."[65] Such optimism was borne out by the announcement on May 17, 1944 that the DSC would meet in

---

[61] Text of speech delivered by Dr. J.M. Robinson to the National Voters League, Birmingham, Alabama, April 4, 1945, Robinson Papers; *Arkansas Gazette*, August 4, 1942, clipping in PCDC Scrapbooks.
[62] Text of speech delivered by Dr. J.M. Robinson to the National Voters League, Birmingham, Alabama, April 4, 1945; Hine, *Black Victory*, 212–229.
[63] *Arkansas Gazette*, April 4, 1944, clipping in PCDC Scrapbooks.
[64] Ibid., April 11, 1944.
[65] Ibid., April 22, 1944.

the morning at Little Rock's Hotel Marion to amend party rules, allowing full participation by blacks in DPA primaries.[66]

Yet in a letter to the meeting, Gov. Homer Adkins informed the DSC that the proposal to remove black voting restrictions "does not coincide with my views in any respect." Moreover, Adkins urged the DSC not to act, "as it is entirely a matter for the convention and legislature to settle."[67] In the meantime, Adkins pressed for further steps to prevent blacks from voting. Seeking to circumvent the *Smith v. Allwright* decision, in June 1944, just before the summer primaries, Adkins advocated barring black voters on another basis than "that of race or color." What he had in mind, he revealed, was a loyalty clause refusing blacks the vote because they had been loyal to, and participated in, the Republican Party. DSC chair Joe C. Barrett suggested the introduction of further membership qualifications along with procedural mechanisms to prevent blacks from voting.[68]

The DPA state convention ratified new measures to prevent the casting of black ballots the following month.[69] Shortly afterwards, when Dr. Robinson announced ANDA's support of Gov. Adkins for the forthcoming election, Adkins replied curtly that the endorsement was "neither wished or solicited by me." Adkins went on to declare that "the Democratic Party in Arkansas is the white man's party and will be kept so... If I cannot be nominated by the white voters of Arkansas I do not want the office."[70] While the DPA waited for the state to sanction their new party rules, they allowed blacks to vote in the Little Rock city primaries. This right was short-lived. In January 1945, the Arkansas General Assembly passed the Trussell Bill, which ratified changes to DPA membership rules, and the Moore Bill, which initiated a complex segregated "double primary" system to disfranchise black voters. The double primary system provided for city and statewide primaries to exclude blacks, and federal primaries at which blacks could vote, but only at segregated ballot boxes.[71]

---

[66] Text of speech delivered by Dr. J.M. Robinson to the National Voters League, Birmingham, Alabama, April 4, 1945; *Arkansas Gazette*, May 17, 1944, clipping in PCDC Scrapbooks.
[67] *Arkansas Gazette*, May 18, 1944, clipping in PCDC Scrapbooks.
[68] Dr. J.M. Robinson to Sam Rorex, July 18, 1944, group II, series B, container 210, folder "Voting, Arkansas, 1943–47," NAACP Papers (Washington, D.C.); *Arkansas Gazette*, June 4, 1944, clipping in PCDC Scrapbooks.
[69] Text of speech delivered by Dr. J.M. Robinson to the National Voters League, Birmingham, Alabama, April 4, 1945; C. Calvin Smith, "The Politics of Evasion: Arkansas's Reaction to *Smith v. Allwright*, 1944," *Journal of Negro History* 67 (1982): 47.
[70] *Arkansas Gazette*, July 20, 1944, clipping in PCDC Scrapbooks.
[71] Text of speech delivered by Dr. J.M. Robinson to the National Voters League, Birmingham, Alabama, April 4, 1945; J.R. Booker to Thurgood Marshall, March 21, 1945; Thurgood Marshall to J.R. Booker, March 27, 1945; Thurgood Marshall to Dr. E.A. Dennard, April 23, 1945, all in

Shortly after the public renouncement of Robinson's support, white Democrats contrived a direct personal smear against him to discredit black Democrats. In September 1944, Arkansas Secretary of State Claris G. Hall claimed that Robinson was not eligible to vote because of a conviction for manslaughter in 1911. The conviction came after Robinson's affair with a married woman that led to him shooting and fatally wounding the woman's husband. Robinson served two years in the penitentiary for the crime before receiving parole without pardon. Hall asserted that Robinson's lack of a pardon meant that he could not qualify as a registered voter.[72] The blatant attempt to intimidate Robinson worked. In exchange for his citizenship rights restored, Robinson offered not only to resign as the president of ANDA, but to "permanently cease and terminate all my activities, political or otherwise," linked to the organisation.[73] Adkins issued a pardon only after the elections had passed and he had been re-elected as governor. The DPA's harassment of the ANDA leader was successful in ensuring that no more attempts to assert black voting rights were forthcoming from Robinson.[74]

The Demise of the All-white Primary Elections and Black Membership of the DPA

White Democrats' attempts to intimidate Robinson into silence may have worked, but they did not prevent others from taking the cause forward. Blacks were particularly encouraged by the election of a new governor, Sidney Sanders McMath, in 1948. McMath was part of a regionwide movement in the postwar South that pressed for reforms based on a platform that pledged better public health, education and welfare. This so-called "G. I. Revolt"—McMath was formerly a U.S. Marine and many of the other new southern politicians were also ex-servicemen—promoted economic growth and industrialisation as a cure for southern financial and social ills. The G.I. politicians also recognised that to make a start on tackling poverty and social backwardness in the South also meant including blacks in their program of reform. Blacks took heart from

---

group II, series B, container 210, folder "Voting, Arkansas, 1943–1947," NAACP Papers (Washington, D.C.); *Arkansas Gazette*, July 26, 1944, clipping in PCDC Scrapbooks; Henry M. Alexander, "The Double Primary," *Arkansas Historical Quarterly* 3 (1944): 217–268; Smith, "The Politics of Evasion," 48–49.

72 *Arkansas Gazette*, September 17, 1944, clipping in PCDC Scrapbooks.
73 Ibid., September 23, 1944.
74 *Arkansas State Press*, November 17, 1944.

this, with the *Arkansas State Press* declaring that in the 1948 elections, "FOR THE FIRST TIME IN OUR LIVES we felt we were voting for SOMETHING."[75]

In May 1950, seeking to test the DPA's resolve to be more forward-looking under McMath's leadership, black Little Rock minister Rev. J. H. Gatlin announced his intention to stand as a candidate for election as a city alderman. To win nomination for the post meant running in the local DPA primaries. The initial reaction from PCDC secretary June Wooten was that he saw "no way under the rules of the State Committee that a Negro would qualify for a place on the state ballot."[76] To run for office, Gatlin had to pay a filing fee to Wooten. An attempt to do so on June 3 resulted in the return of Gatlin's money. Wooten maintained that Gatlin could not run for office since he was ineligible for membership of the DPA.[77] The final deadline for filing in the city race was June 24. On June 7, Gatlin sent a letter prepared by the legal redress committee of the Little Rock NAACP, headed by *Arkansas State Press* co-owner and editor L.C. Bates, to DSC members. In his letter, Gatlin requested a rule change that would allow his name to go on to the DPA primary election form. DPA chair Willis R. Smith subsequently called a meeting of the DSC for the following Tuesday.[78]

At the meeting on June 13, committee members decided that only the DPA state convention had the right to vote upon changes to the DPA constitution. Wooten urged members of the committee to think seriously about their actions since in the light of recent court decisions he believed that Gatlin's case stood every chance of winning. The meeting adjourned with the decision to put the matter to the DPA state convention later in the year after the party primaries had taken place.[79] In response, L.C. Bates indicated that Gatlin was ready to go to court.[80] On June 17, Little Rock attorney Joseph R. Booker and NAACP Legal Defense Fund southwest regional attorney Ulysses Simpson Tate filed Gatlin's case with the U.S. District Court. The attorneys also requested an injunction preventing the exclusion of Gatlin, "or any other person qualified... on account

---

75 *Arkansas State Press*, November 5, 1948; Sidney S. McMath interview with John A. Kirk, Little Rock, Arkansas, December 8, 1992, John Kirk Civil Rights Movement in Arkansas Materials; Jim Lester, *A Man for Arkansas: Sid McMath and the Southern Reform Tradition* (Little Rock, Arkansas: Rose Publishing Co., 1976).
76 *Arkansas State Press*, June 4, 1950.
77 Ibid.
78 Ibid., June 7, 1950; *Arkansas Gazette*, June 8, 1950.
79 *Arkansas Democrat* (Little Rock), June 13, 1950.
80 Ibid., June 15, 1950.

of race, color, religion, national origin or any other unconstitutional restriction," from the Little Rock DPA city primaries.[81]

On July 5, 1950, federal district judge Thomas C. Trimble upheld the argument of the NAACP attorneys. Trimble based his decision on precedents set in recent court rulings and finally clarified the status of the primary election. The primary was, Trimble declared, "an integral part of the state election system... tantamount to election at the general election." Furthermore, the judge continued, "it is not sufficient that a citizen have a token exercise of his right and privilege [to vote]."[82] Gatlin became the first black Arkansan to stand as DPA candidate, although he met with defeat at the election. The court victory prompted other black candidates to file for office in other elections, most notably ANDA's Rev. Fred T. Guy, who unsuccessfully made a bid for a position on the Little Rock school board.[83] The DPA state convention changed party rules to allow full black membership of the DPA later that year. Gov. McMath, in his closing speech, declared that he was "proud, and I know you are proud... [that the convention]... has said the Negro citizen is entitled to the rights and privileges of Party membership."[84]

Mass Black Political Participation in Arkansas Politics Since the 1950s—and its Limits
The 1950s and 1960s

During the 1950s, blacks became ever more integrated into the DPA and thereby exercised a greater say in state politics. This paved the way for developments in the 1960s when, in parallel with events elsewhere, black Arkansans were finally able to fully participate in the body politic.

At a national level, in 1964 Amendment Twenty-Four to the U.S. Constitution abolished the use of poll taxes in federal elections.[85] The same year, Arkansas

---

81 Ibid., June 16, 1950.
82 Ibid., July 6, 1950.
83 *Arkansas State Press*, September 1, 1950.
84 Ibid., September 23, 1950; text of speech delivered by Dr. J.M. Robinson, Chicago, Illinois, October 29, 1950, Robinson Papers. On Guthridge's later career, see Neil R. McMillen, "The White Citizens Council and Resistance to School Desegregation in Arkansas," *Arkansas Historical Quarterly* 30 (Summer 1971): 95–122.
85 U.S. Const. amend. XXIV.

abolished the poll tax in city and state elections, and it adopted a free permanent personal voter registration system that removed the last major obstacle to blacks exercising the franchise in general elections.[86] The Voting Rights Act of 1965 made less of an impact since its coverage formula excluded the state from its provisions.[87]

At a regional level, black Arkansans benefited from a number of voting rights and civil rights initiatives. A regionwide Voter Education Project (VEP), run by the interracial civil rights organisation the Southern Regional Council (SRC) in Atlanta, was directed by native Arkansan Wiley Branton, a fellow Pine Bluff attorney and protégé of William Harold Flowers.[88]

At a state and local level, the Student Nonviolent Coordinating Committee (SNCC) ran a number of community-based projects in Arkansas between 1962 and 1967, including voter registration campaigns that followed in the footsteps of Flowers and the CNO two decades earlier.[89] In 1966, Winthrop Rockefeller, a grandson of Standard Oil founder John D. Rockefeller, became the first Republican governor of Arkansas in 94 years. Rockefeller courted the black vote to break the DPA's stranglehold on state politics and appointed blacks to more state offices and jobs than ever before.[90]

The 1970s

The impact of these changes became fully apparent in the 1970s. In 1972, for the first time in the twentieth century, black legislators were elected to the Arkansas General Assembly, making it the last southern state to elect black legislators in modern times. The four black legislators were dentist Dr. Jerry Jewell in the Arkansas Senate, who was a former NAACP state president and thereby a direct

---

86 Calvin R. Ledbetter, Jr., "Arkansas Amendment for Voter Registration without Poll Tax Payment," *Arkansas Historical Quarterly* 54 (Summer 1995): 134–162.
87 See footnote 2.
88 On the Voter Education Project, see Evan Faulkenbury, *Poll Power: The Voter Education Project and the Movement for the Ballot in the American South* (Chapel Hill: University of North Carolina Press, 2019).
89 On SNCC in Arkansas, see Jennifer Jensen Wallach and John A. Kirk (eds.), *Arsnick: The Student Nonviolent Coordinating Committee in Arkansas* (Fayetteville: University of Arkansas Press, 2011).
90 On Rockefeller's election victory, see John A. Kirk, "A Southern Road Less Travelled: The 1966 Arkansas Gubernatorial Election and (Winthrop) Rockefeller Republicanism in Dixie," in *Painting Dixie Red: When, Where, Why, and How the South Became Republican*, ed. Glenn Feldman (Gainesville: University Press of Florida, 2011), 172–197.

beneficiary of William Harold Flowers' earlier creation of an Arkansas NAACP state conference of branches, optometrist Dr. William H. Townsend, attorney Richard L. Mays and university professor Henry Wilkins III in the Arkansas House of Representatives. All four were black Democrats who formed part of the long struggle to win black representation and participation in the DPA, and all four of them defeated black Republican candidates who carried forward the long struggle to win black representation and participation in the RPA. In all that year, Arkansas boasted 99 black elected officials, the second highest number of any southern state. Blacks won offices as aldermen, mayors, justices of the peace, school board members, city councilors, city recorders and city clerks. These gains further stimulated black voter registration.[91] By 1976, 94 per cent of Arkansas's voting age blacks were registered, the highest proportion of any southern state.[92]

The 1980s

The return of the first black legislators to the Arkansas General Assembly in 80 years, and the expansion of black voters and officeholders, were all significant developments although they by no means signaled the end of the struggle for voting rights in Arkansas. A defining court battle came in *Jeffers v. Clinton* (1989) when a group of black citizens sued the state on the grounds that a 1981 redistricting had diluted black voting strength. The federal court subsequently ordered the creation of two new majority-black senate districts and seven new majority-black house districts. In 1991, the number of blacks in the Arkansas General Assembly reached nine, with three senators and six representatives. The court also placed Arkansas under the preclearance requirements of the Voting Rights Act, meaning that any further changes in voting requirements would have to be approved by the U.S. Justice Department. This earned Arkansas the dubious distinction of being one of only two states, along with New Mexico, to have ever been "bailed-in" to the Voting Rights Act.[93]

---

91 *Arkansas Gazette*, February 4, 1973.
92 Lawson, *Running for Freedom*, 85.
93 Janine A. Parry and William H. Miller, "'The Great Negro State of the Country?': Black Legislators in Arkansas, 1973–2000," *Journal of Black Studies* 36 (July 2006): 837–838; Ben F. Johnson III, *Arkansas in Modern America* (Fayetteville: University of Arkansas Press, second edition 2019), 241–242.

Black Political Representation, Participation and Voting Rights Since the 1980s

The number of blacks in the Arkansas General Assembly today stands at 16, with three senators and 13 representatives out of a total of 35 senators and 100 representatives. One of the black senators is Stephanie Flowers, the daughter of William Harold Flowers, and one of the black representatives is Vivian Flowers, the grandniece of William Harold Flowers.[94] Blacks represent 15.7 per cent of the state's current population.[95]

Blacks have fared worse in higher elected offices. Arkansas remains to this day the only former Confederate state to have never elected a black person to a statewide or federal office.[96] Opportunities have been few and far between. In 1993, as president pro tempore of the senate, Dr. Jerry Jewell became governor of Arkansas for all of four days in the absence of Bill Clinton, the former Democrat governor, who was being sworn in as president of the United States. Clinton's successor, Jim Guy Tucker, the former lieutenant governor, was also in Washington, D.C. attending the ceremony.[97] In 2010, Joyce Elliott, a Democrat, became the first black politician chosen by a major party to run for the U.S. House of Representatives in Arkansas. Republican Tim Griffin defeated her in the general election.[98] Elliott is slated to run for a second time in 2020.[99] In 2012, Democrat Darrin Williams was poised to become the first black speaker of the house, only for the Republicans to win the chamber.[100]

---

94 For Arkansas House of Representatives members see https://www.arkansashouse.org/representatives/members, and for Arkansas Senate members see https://www.arkansas.gov/senate/senators.html, both accessed online January 29, 2020.
95 U.S. Census Bureau, "Quick Facts", https://www.census.gov/quickfacts/fact/table/AR/RHI225218, accessed online February 3, 2020.
96 Johnson, *Arkansas in Modern America*, 241.
97 Parry and Miller, "The Great Negro State of the Country?", 840.
98 Michael R. Wickline, "Griffin Prevails in 2nd District," *Arkansas Democrat-Gazette*, November 3, 2010 https://www.arkansasonline.com/news/2010/nov/03/griffin-prevails-2nd-district-20101103/, accessed online January 29, 2020.
99 John Moritz, "State Sen. Joyce Elliott files to challenge U.S. Rep. French Hill in Arkansas's 2nd District," Arkansas Democrat-Gazette, November 12, 2019, https://www.arkansasonline.com/news/2019/nov/12/state-sen-joyce-elliott-files-run-us-congress/, accessed online January 29, 2020.
100 Max Brantley, "Republican Davy Carter elected Arkansas House Speaker," *Arkansas Times*, November 15, 2012, https://arktimes.com/arkansas-blog/2012/11/15/republican-davy-carter-elected-arkansas-house-speaker, accessed online January 29, 2020.

Challenges facing black political representation still abound. A steadily declining black population in the state since 1940 has hindered electoral progress. The courts and congress are in retreat from ordering measures to advance black political fortunes. Meanwhile, new measures are being introduced, such as voter I.D. laws, that threaten black political participation, along with that of poor whites, which are reminiscent of the disenfranchising tactics used in the late nineteenth century. Arkansas adopted a voter I.D. law in 2018.[101] The recent conservative Republican ascendency in Arkansas does not augur well, since overwhelmingly after the nineteenth century most advances in black politics have taken place within and aided by the Democratic Party.[102]

Conclusion

The struggle for black political representation, participation and voting rights in Arkansas has been defined by a gradual transition from a select few members of the black elite representing the race as a whole to the political organisation and mobilisation of the black masses. Black political leaders like Scipio Africanus Jones, Dr. John Marshall Robinson, William Harold Flowers and others formed an essential continuity of black political activism through the age of disenfranchisement and segregation that made sure traditions of black political engagement never died, even in the most difficult of times and under the most trying of circumstances. Albeit deploying different strategies and approaches to the task, by steadfastly insisting on black political representation and participation their demands repeatedly forced white Democrats and Republicans to reckon with and to justify the very apparent injustices that white supremacy perpetrated. The work of such black political activists is often overshadowed by the more publicised events, and more dramatic and speedier transformations that took place in voting rights and civil rights in the 1950s and 1960s. But the foundations that earlier black activism laid remains a vital part of the history of the long voting rights and civil rights movements in Arkansas and in the United States. Without the groundwork of black political activists in the first half of the twentieth century, it would have been far more difficult, if not impossible, to achieve the advances that were made in the second half of the twentieth century and beyond.

---

101 Max Brantley, "Voter I.D.: It's the law, be prepared," *Arkansas Times*, October 11, 2018, https://arktimes.com/arkansas-blog/2018/10/11/voter-id-its-the-law-be-prepared, accessed online January 29, 2020.
102 Johnson, *Arkansas in Modern America*, 303–305.

Bibliography

Alkebulan, Paul. *The African American Press in World War II: Toward Victory at Home and Abroad*. Lanham, MD: Lexington Books, 2014.
Anderson, Karen. *Little Rock: Race and Resistance at Central High School*. Princeton: Princeton University Press, 2010.
Angelou, Maya. *I Know Why the Caged Bird Sings*. New York: Random House, 1969.
Arkansas Democrat newspaper. Little Rock, Arkansas.
Arkansas Gazette newspaper. Little Rock, Arkansas.
Arkansas State Press newspaper. Little Rock, Arkansas.
Berman, Ari. *Give Us the Ballot: The Modern Struggle for Voting Rights*. New York: Farrar, Straus and Giroux, 2015.
Branam, Chris M. "Another Look at Disfranchisement in Arkansas, 1888–1894." *Arkansas Historical Quarterly* 69 (2010): 245–256.
Bullock, Charles S. III, Ronald Keith Gaddie and Justin J. Wert. *The Rise and Fall of the Voting Rights Act*. Norman: University of Oklahoma Press, 2016.
Bunche, Ralph J. *The Political Status of the Negro in the Age of FDR*. Chicago, IL: University of Chicago Press, 1973.
Bussey, Charles, interview with John A. Kirk. Little Rock, Arkansas, December 4, 1992, John Kirk Civil Rights Movement in Arkansas Materials, Special Collections Division, University of Arkansas Libraries, Fayetteville.
Bynum, Cornelius L. *A. Philip Randolph and the Struggle for Civil Rights*. Urbana: University of Illinois Press, 2010.
Cagin, Seth, and Philip Dray. *We Are Not Afraid: The Story of Goodman, Schwerner and Chaney and the Civil Rights Campaign for Mississippi*. New York: Macmillan, 1988.
Chamberlin, Charles D. *Victory at Home: Manpower and Race in the American South during World War II*. Athens: University of Georgia Press, 2003.
Cortner, Richard C. *A Mob Intent on Death: The NAACP and the Arkansas Riot Cases*. Middletown: University of Connecticut Press, 1988.
Davidson, Chandler, and Bernard Grofman, eds. *Quiet Revolution in the South: The Impact of the Voting Right Act, 1965–1990*. Princeton: Princeton University Press, 1994.
Dillard, Tom. "Perseverance: Black History in Pulaski County, Arkansas—An Excerpt." *Pulaski County Historical Review* 31 (1983): 62–73.
Dillard, Tom. "Scipio A. Jones." *Arkansas Historical Quarterly* 31 (1972): 201–219.
Dillard, Tom. "To the Back of the Elephant: Racial Conflict in the Arkansas Republican Party." *Arkansas Historical Quarterly* 33 (1974): 3–15.
Dittmer, John. *Local People: The Struggle for Civil Rights in Mississippi*. Urbana: University of Illinois Press, 1994.
Dr. John Marshall Robinson Papers. Privately held in possession of Terry Pierson, Little Rock, Arkansas.
Fairclough, Adam. *Better Day Coming: Blacks and Equality, 1890–2000*. New York: Viking Penguin, 2001.
Faulkenbury, Evan. *Poll Power: The Voter Education Project and the Movement for the Ballot in the American South*. Chapel Hill: University of North Carolina Press, 2019.
Foner, Eric. *Reconstruction: America's Unfinished Revolution, 1863–1867*. New York: Harper & Row, 1988.

Freyer, Tony A. *Little Rock on Trial: Cooper v Aaron and School Desegregation.* University Press of Kansas, 2007.

Garfinkle, Herbert. *When Negroes March: The March on Washington Movement in the Organizational Politics for the FEPC.* Glencoe, IL: Free Press, 1959.

Garrow, David J. *Protest at Selma: Martin Luther King, Jr., and the Voting Rights Act of 1965.* New Haven, CT: Yale University Press, 1978.

Gatewood, Willard B. *Aristocrats of Color: The Black Elite, 1880–1920.* Bloomington: Indiana University Press, 1990.

Graves, John William. "Negro Disfranchisement in Arkansas." *Arkansas Historical Quarterly* 26 (1967): 199–225.

Graves, John William. *Town and Country: Race Relations in an Urban/Rural Context, Arkansas, 1865–1905.* Fayetteville: University of Arkansas Press, 1990.

Greenberg, Jack. *Crusaders in the Courts: How a Dedicated Band of Lawyers Fought for the Civil Rights Revolution.* New York: Basic Books, 1994.

Hall, Jaquelyn Dowd. "The Long Civil Rights Movement and the Political Uses of the Past." *Journal of American History* 91, no. 4 (2005): 1233–1263.

Hawkins, Jeffery, interview with John A. Kirk. Little Rock, Arkansas, September 30, 1992, John Kirk Civil Rights Movement in Arkansas Materials, Special Collections Division, University of Arkansas Libraries, Fayetteville.

Hine, Darlene Clark. *Black Victory: The Rise and Fall of the White Primary in Texas.* Millwood, NY: KTO Press, 1979.

Jacoway, Elizabeth. *Turn Away Thy Son: Little Rock, the Crisis that Shocked a Nation.* New York: Free Press, 2007.

Key, V.O. Jr. *Southern Politics in State and Nation.* New York: Alfred A. Knopf, 1949.

Kirby, John B. *Black Americans in the Roosevelt Era: Liberalism and Race.* Knoxville: Tennessee University Press, 1980.

Kirk, John A. "Dr. J. M. Robinson, the Arkansas Negro Democratic Association and Black Politics in Little Rock, Arkansas, 1928–1952." *Pulaski County Historical Review* 41 (Spring and Summer 1993): 2–16, 39–47.

Kirk, John A. "'He Founded a Movement': W. H. Flowers, the Committee on Negro Organizations and Black Activism in Arkansas, 1940–1957." In *The Making of Martin Luther King and the Civil Rights Movement in America,* edited by Brian Ward and Tony Badger, 29–44. London: Macmillan, 1996.

Kirk, John A. *Redefining the Color Line: Black Activism in Little Rock, Arkansas, 1940–1970.* Gainesville: University Press of Florida, 2002.

Kirk, John A. "A Southern Road Less Travelled: The 1966 Arkansas Gubernatorial Election and (Winthrop) Rockefeller Republicanism in Dixie." In *Painting Dixie Red: When, Where, Why, and How the South Became Republican,* edited by Glenn Feldman, 172–197. Gainesville: University Press of Florida, 2011.

Kirk, John A. "The Long and the Short of It: New Perspectives in Civil Rights Studies." *Journal of Contemporary History* 46, no. 2 (2011): 425–436.

Knauer, Christine. *Let Us Fight as Free Men: Black Soldiers and Civil Rights.* Philadelphia: University of Pennsylvania Press, 2014.

Kruse, Kevin M., and Stephen Tuck, eds. *Fog of War: The Second World War and the Civil Rights Movement.* New York: Oxford University Press, 2012.

Kryder, Daniel. *Divided Arsenal: Race and the American State during World War II*. New York: Cambridge University Press, 2000.

Landsberg, Brian K. *Free at Last to Vote: The Alabama Origins of the 1965 Voting Rights Act*. Lawrence: University Press of Kansas, 2007.

Lawson, Steven F. *Black Ballots: Voting Rights in the South, 1944–1969*. New York: Columbia University Press, 1976.

Lawson, Steven F. *Running for Freedom: Civil Rights and Black Politics Since 1941*. New York: McGraw-Hill, 1991.

Ledbetter, Calvin R., Jr. "Arkansas Amendment for Voter Registration without Poll Tax Payment." *Arkansas Historical Quarterly* 54 (1995): 134–162.

Lester, Jim. *A Man for Arkansas: Sid McMath and the Southern Reform Tradition*. Little Rock, AR: Rose Publishing Co., 1976.

Lipsitz, George. *Ivory Perry and the Culture of Opposition*. Philadelphia: Temple University Press, 1988.

Lucander, David. *Winning the War for Democracy: The March on Washington Movement, 1941–1946*. Urbana and Chicago: University of Illinois Press, 2014.

May, Gary. *Bending toward Justice: The Voting Rights Act and the Transformation of American Democracy*. New York: Basic Books, 2013.

McMath, Sidney S., interview with John A. Kirk. Little Rock, Arkansas, December 8, 1992, John Kirk Civil Rights Movement in Arkansas Materials, Special Collections Division, University of Arkansas Libraries, Fayetteville.

McMillen, Neil R. "The White Citizens' Council and Resistance to School Desegregation in Arkansas." *Arkansas Historical Quarterly* 30 (1971): 95–122.

McMillen, Neil R., ed. *Remaking Dixie: The Impact of World War II on the American South*. Jackson: University Press of Mississippi, 1997.

Mitchell, John B. "An Analysis of Arkansas's Population by Race and Nativity, and Residence." *Arkansas Historical Quarterly* 8 (1949): 115–132.

Moneyhon, Carl. *The Impact of the Civil War and Reconstruction on Arkansas: Persistence in the Midst of Ruin*. Baton Rouge: Louisiana State University Press, 1994.

National Association for the Advancement of Colored People Papers, Manuscript Division, Library of Congress, Washington, D.C.

Payne, Charles. *I've Got the Light of Freedom: The Organizing Tradition and the Mississippi Freedom Struggle*. Berkeley: University of California Press, 1995.

Phillips, Kimberley L. *War! What Is It Good For? Black Freedom Struggles and the U.S. Military from World War II to Iraq*. Chapel Hill: University of North Carolina Press, 2012.

Pierson, Dale Lya. "John M. Robinson, M.D., 1879–1970." *Pulaski County Historical Review* 41 (1993): 91–93.

Pulaski County Democratic Committee (PCDC) Scrapbooks, Arkansas History Commission, Little Rock.

Reed, Merle E. *Seedtime for the Modern Civil Rights Movement: The President's Committee on Fair Employment Practice, 1941–1946*. Baton Rouge: Louisiana State University Press, 1991.

Riser, R. Volney. *Defying Disfranchisement: Black Voting Rights Activism in the Jim Crow South, 1890–1908*. Baton Rouge: Louisiana State University Press, 2010.

Royce, Edward. *The Origins of Southern Sharecropping*. Philadelphia: Temple University Press, 2010.

Rustin, Bayard. "From Protest to Politics: The Future of the Civil Rights Movement." *Commentary* 39 (1965): 25–31.

Sitkoff, Harvard. *A New Deal for Blacks: The Emergence of Civil Rights as a National Issue: Volume 1: The Depression Decade*. New York: Oxford University Press, 1978.

Smith, C. Calvin. "The Politics of Evasion: Arkansas's Reaction to *Smith v. Allwright*, 1944." *Journal of Negro History* 67 (1982).

Stockley, Grif. *Blood in Their Eyes: The Elaine Race Massacres of 1919*. Fayetteville: University of Arkansas Press, 2001.

Sullivan, Patricia. *Days of Hope: Race and Democracy in the New Deal Era*. Chapel Hill: University of North Carolina Press, 1996.

The CNO Spectator newspaper (Pine Bluff, Arkansas).

Thornton, J. Mills. *Dividing Lines: Municipal Politics and the Struggle for Civil Rights in Montgomery, Birmingham, and Selma*. Tuscaloosa: University of Alabama Press, 2002.

Tushnet, Mark. *The NAACP's Legal Strategy Against Segregated Education, 1925–1950*. Chapel Hill: University of North Carolina Press, 1987.

Tushnet, Mark. *Making Civil Rights Law: Thurgood Marshall and the Supreme Court, 1936–1961*. New York: Oxford University Press, 1994.

United States Constitution.

Wallach, Jennifer Jensen, and John A. Kirk, eds. *Arsnick: The Student Nonviolent Coordinating Committee in Arkansas*. Fayetteville: University of Arkansas Press, 2011.

Weiss, Nancy J. *Farewell to the Party of Lincoln: Black Politics in the Age of FDR*. Princeton, NJ: Princeton University Press, 1983.

Whitaker, Robert. *On the Laps of Gods: The Red Summer of 1919 and the Struggle for Justice that Remade a Nation*. New York: Crown, 2008.

William Harold Flowers Papers. Privately held in possession of Stephanie Flowers, Pine Bluff, Arkansas.

Wintory, Blake J. "African-American Legislators in the Arkansas General Assembly, 1868–1893." *Arkansas Historical Quarterly* 65 (2006): 385–434.

Sharon Baptiste
3 Mobilising Black and Minority Ethnic (BME) Voters in the United Kingdom

The Political Strategies of Operation Black Vote (1996 – 2019)

Introduction

The political representation and participation of the black and minority ethnic population in the United Kingdom has been the subject of numerous research projects, surveys and studies for the last 50 years. This period corresponds to the post-war arrival and settlement in the country of tens of thousands of British colonial or British Commonwealth-born people from Africa, the Caribbean, India, Pakistan and Bangladesh. The 1974, 1979 and 1983 Community for Racial Equality (CRE) reports are among the first publications to deal with the specific topic of the participation of ethnic minorities in UK General Elections.[1] Muhammad Anwar, Harry Goulbourne and Shamit Saggar are three examples of academic researchers who have been publishing articles and monographs about black and minority ethnic attitudes, behaviour and participation in the UK political system since the 1980s and 1990s.[2] In addition to researchers, independent bodies such as the think tank Runnymede Trust and the Electoral Commission[3] have also undertaken studies and published reports in these fields.

---

[1] CRC, *Participation of Ethnic Minorities in the General Election of October 1974* (London: The Community Relations Commission, 1975); CRE, *Votes and Policies: Ethnic Minorities and the General Election 1979* (London: Commission for Racial Equality, 1980); CRE, *Ethnic Minorities and the 1983 General Election: A Research Report* (London: Commission for Racial Equality, 1984). In 1976, the Community Relations Commission (CRC) was replaced by the Committee for Racial Equality (CRE).
[2] Shamit Saggar is Emeritus Professor of Political Science and Public Policy at the Institute for Social and Economic Research (ISER) at the University of Essex. In the 1990s, he published several monographs analysing ethnic minority political participation and representation in UK General Elections, including *Race and Politics in Britain* (London: Harvester Wheatsheaf, 1992) and *Race and British Electoral Politics* (London: UCL Press, 1998). Harry Goulbourne is Professor Emeritus of Sociology at London South Bank University.
[3] The Electoral Commission is an independent body that was created in 2001. It regulates party and election finance and sets standards for how elections should be run.

https://doi.org/10.1515/9783110710403-004

In 1997, the British Election Survey (BES)[4] carried out its first small-scale stand-alone study of ethnic minorities' political attitudes and behaviour in the UK. However, it was not until the Ethnic Minority British Election Survey (EMBES) was set up for the 2010 General Election that researchers were able to access and exploit samples large enough to enable detailed analysis and reliable findings. Funded by the Economic and Social Research Council (ESRC) and involving a team of researchers from the Universities of Oxford, Manchester and Essex,[5] the Ethnic Minority British Election Survey is the largest and most authoritative study of ethnic minority voting behaviour during a General Election in the UK to date.[6] Since the 2010s, new research focus and debates have emerged. The political integration and representation of ethnic minorities in Britain since the historic General Election of 1987,[7] the impact of descriptive and substantive representation in the UK parliament on ethnic minority voter mobilisation and religious political mobilisation are some examples of these.[8]

Parallel to research studies and government surveys on BME political integration and mobilisation in the United Kingdom, a plethora of small, local, "on the ground" BME groups and associations have also sought to increase the awareness and involvement of their members in the British political system over the last 50 years.

The present chapter will present and analyse the political strategies adopted by a BME-led organisation, Operation Black Vote[9] (OBV), in order to mobilise

---

[4] The British Election Survey has examined every General Election since 1964.
[5] The research team was composed of Anthony F. Heath (University of Oxford and Institute for Social Change [ISC] at University of Manchester), Stephen Fisher (University of Oxford), Gemma Rosenblatt (Electoral Commission), David Sanders (University of Essex and director of main British Election Study [BES] in 2010) and Maria Sobolewska (University of Manchester).
[6] Anthony Heath and Omar Khan, *Ethnic Minority British Election Study – Key Findings* (London: Runneymede Trust, 2012), 1–2.
[7] In the 1987 General Election, Diane Abbot, Paul Boateng, Bernie Grant and Keith Vaz became the first post-war BME MPs elected to the UK parliament.
[8] Examples of recent fields of research are Rebecca McKee, "The Substantive Representation of Ethnic Minorities in the UK Parliament," (PhD diss., University of Manchester, 2017); Nicole S. Martin, "Do Ethnic Minority Candidates Mobilise Ethnic Minority Voters? Evidence from the 2010 General Election," *Parliamentary Affairs* 69 (2016): 159–180; and Maria Sobolewska, "Religious Political Mobilisation of British Ethnic Minorities," in *Race and Elections*, ed. Omar Khan (London: Runneymede, 2015), 18–20. A major study on the political integration and representation of ethnic minorities, called Racism30YearsOn, is also being conducted by Maria Sobolewska at the University of Manchester's Centre on Dynamics of Ethnicity (CoDE).
[9] The term "black" is used by Operation Black Vote as a political term in keeping with the rest of the British anti-racist movement of the 1970s–1990s. It refers to all people of African, Caribbean and Asian descent. Likewise, in this chapter, the term is used to designate all ethnic categories

Black and Minority Ethnic (BME) voters in the United Kingdom.[10] The analysis will cover the 23-year period between the inception of Operation Black Vote in 1996 and the snap UK General Election of December 12, 2019. The overall purpose is to provide an in-depth case study of the first cross-ethnic BME-led organisation to address and attempt to redress ethnic deficiencies in the UK's electoral and political systems. The study will thus be a useful addition to recent quantitative and qualitative analyses on the topic.

After briefly describing the historical context within which Operation Black Vote emerged as a central actor in the attempt to raise awareness and boost the electoral mobilisation of BME communities in the UK, the first part of the chapter will present the political strategies favoured by Operation Black Vote nationally and locally. Although Operation Black Vote systematically intensifies its activities in the run-up to national and local elections, many of its schemes, programmes and events are also organised outside of these periods. The second part of the chapter will attempt to evaluate the impact of Operation Black Vote's voter mobilisation strategies. Can success be quantified? And if so, what are the measurable outcomes? Criticism aimed at Operation Black Vote's intention to foster the BME vote in order to influence policymaking will also be discussed in this part.[11]

Operation Black Vote: a Brief History of the Beginnings of a Grassroots Political Organisation

Operation Black Vote (OBV) is a non-partisan, non-profit organisation that was set up in London, England, on July 16, 1996. It was formed from the amalgama-

---

with the exception of the "white" category, as outlined in the 2011 Census for England and Wales. The BME categories classified in the 2011 Census are: (1) Gypsy/Traveller/Irish Traveller; (2) Mixed/Multiple Ethnic Group; (3) Asian/Asian British: Indian; (4) Asian/Asian British: Pakistani; (5) Asian/Asian British: Bangladeshi; (6) Asian/Asian British: Chinese; (7) Asian/Asian British: Other Asian; (8) Black/African/Caribbean/Black British; (9) Other Ethnic Group. http://www.nomisweb.co.uk/census/2011/ks201uk.pdf, accessed November 6, 2019.

10 Operation Black Vote's schemes and programmes are organised exclusively in England and Wales.

11 Kehinde Andrews, "There is no such thing as the black vote – this election proves it," *The Guardian*, May 26, 2015, https://www.theguardian.com/commentisfree/2015/may/26/black-vote-election-ethnic-minority-non-white, accessed November 4, 2019.

tion of two previously existing political grassroots organisations: Charter 88,[12] a pressure group advocating constitutional and electoral reform in Britain, and the 1990 Trust,[13] the first UK national black organisation to protect and pioneer the interest of Britain's black communities by engaging in policy development and articulating the needs of black communities.[14]

It is important to remember that Operation Black Vote was set up at a time when relations between the police and London's black community, especially young black men of African-Caribbean heritage, had already been severely damaged for over a decade, and had reached tipping point. Racial tension in Britain had been growing steadily since the arrival of post-war non-white Commonwealth migrants from the Caribbean and South Asia in the 1950s and 1960s. The so-called "race" riots of 1980, 1981 and 1985[15] saw these tensions shift from the post-war migrants themselves to their children, who represented the first generation of black British youth born and/or raised in the UK. It was the suspicious death of a young man of African-Caribbean heritage, 26-year-old Wayne Douglas, in a police station in Brixton, London, in December 1995 that led not only to new "race" riots in the troubled neighbourhood, but also to the birth of Operation Black Vote.

In the 1980s and 1990s the police regularly targeted black youth who lived in areas with large concentrations of non-white Commonwealth-heritage populations[16] during coordinated "operations", which, like the military operations from which they took their name, always had code names.[17] The co-founders

---

[12] In 1996 Simon Woolley, co-founder and present director of Operation Black Vote, was a volunteer activist at Charter 88. British sociologist and cultural theorist Stuart Hall is among the 348 British intellectuals and activists who were the first of approximately 5,000 people to sign the Charter when it was set up in 1988.

[13] Lee Jasper, another OBV co-founder, was a key figure at the 1990 Trust at the time.

[14] https://www.obv.org.uk/about-us/history, accessed November 6, 2019.

[15] The first "race" riots opposing mainly black and minority ethnic young men on the one hand, and the police on the other hand, began in the St. Paul's neighbourhood of Bristol in April 1980. They were followed by street battles between BME youth and police in Brixton, London, in April 1981 and Toxteth, Liverpool, in July of the same year. Finally, unrest between police and BME youth flared up once again in Brixton, London, in September 1985, in Handsworth, Birmingham, in September 1985 and on the Broadwater Farm Estate in Tottenham, London, in October 1985.

[16] For example, in cities such as London, Birmingham, Manchester, Leeds, Liverpool and Bristol.

[17] *Operation Swamp 81*, which heightened tensions between the police and African-Caribbean youth, led to the Brixton riots in April 1981. The "Operation" consisted in the London Metropolitan Police's deployment of plain clothes officers, uniformed patrols and the Special Patrol Group to stop and search over 1,000 people in six days using the controversial "sus law", in

of Operation Black Vote[18] deliberately reclaimed this military reference, giving it a positive connotation by combining it with "Black Vote" which is what they aimed to promote. Operation Black Vote, therefore, is a well thought-out, strategic "operation" to mobilise BME individuals into exercising their democratic right to vote in UK elections. Operation Black Vote's co-founders believed that two paths needed to be embarked upon to put an end to what they considered to be the social, economic and racial injustices suffered by BME communities throughout the country. The first path was that of civic society; the second that of political engagement.[19] They agreed that real change for BME communities could only be achieved via the ballot box and long-term political strategies and not by rioting.[20] Although unapologetic of the violent methods that had been used by BME youth in the 1980s, a group to which they themselves belonged, in 1996 the organisation's co-founders felt that their response to police violence had to evolve if it were to bring about societal change and reduce social and racial inequality. In the same way that they and their counterparts of 15 years earlier had matured, so should their response to continuing police brutality towards BME communities.

Operation Black Vote's Political Strategy during the 1997 General Election

Operation Black Vote was officially set up 10 months prior to the date of the May 1, 1997 UK General Election, leaving the organisation sufficient time to convince BME communities of the potential power of their vote at the impending election. This promised to be a crucial period in the history of British politics. Labour Party leader Tony Blair was determined to replace John Major's Conservative government with a Labour one and thus end 18 years of successive Conservative governments at the head of the country. For Operation Black Vote, too, this was a potential watershed moment. Six months before the official July 16,

---

a bid to cut street crime in Brixton, London. *Operation Eagle Eye*, launched in August 1995 by the London Metropolitan Police, was announced as a new police crackdown campaign to combat the rising number of muggings in London.

18 The six co-founders of Operation Black Vote are Simon Woolley, Lee Jasper, Rita Patel, Ashok Viswanathan, Dave Weaver and Derek Hinds.

19 Simon Woolley, "Happy birthday Operation Black Vote," *The Guardian*, July 20, 2007, https://www.theguardian.com/commentisfree/2007/jul/20/happybirthdayoperationblackvote, accessed October 29, 2019.

20 *OBV News*, issue no. 6, Summer 2011, 4.

1997 launch of its campaign, the organisation had commissioned a research report from Professor Muhammad Anwar of the Centre of Ethnic Relations at Warwick University to analyse the extent of the importance of the BME vote in the UK.[21] The pioneering research revealed that in over 100 seats countrywide, the BME vote could play a decisive role in the outcome of the General Election. Indeed, the high percentage of BME communities in many urban areas, such as the parliamentary constituencies of Wolverhampton South West, Birmingham Edgbaston and Bristol West,[22] gave them considerable potential political clout.[23] For Operation Black Vote this was the perfect time to ensure that the three major parties publicly announce their positions and policy suggestions pertaining to the social issues faced by many BME communities, among which were disproportionately high rates of unemployment (particularly among young men), poor housing conditions and racism.

This first Operation Black Vote campaign consisted in distributing hundreds of thousands of voter registration cards and holding public information meetings at schools, colleges and community centres. As coverage of their initiative grew in the national and international press and in radio and television broadcasts throughout the country, the mainstream parties began to react. The positive attention to BME community problems by British political parties was unprecedented.

It was then that Operation Black Vote put in place the first of its political strategies. It organised a lobbying campaign, obliging incumbent MPs and candidates to host "Question Time"[24] meetings at constitutional level. During these meetings the BME electorate was able to interact directly with party political rep-

---

[21] Muhammad Anwar, *Ethnic Minorities and the British Electoral System: A Research Report* (Coventry: University of Coventry/Centre for Research in Ethnic Studies, 1998).

[22] The Labour Party candidate obtained the highest number of votes in these three constituencies during the 1997 General Election. All three constituencies had been Conservative strongholds for many decades. Both the Birmingham Edgbaston and the Bristol West seats had previously been held without interruption by the Conservative Party since 1931. The Wolverhampton South West constituency had been a stronghold for the Conservative Party since the constituency was first formed in 1950; "United Kingdom Election Results," http://www.election.demon.co.uk/, accessed May 19, 2020.

[23] https://operationblackvote.wordpress.com/2009/07/17/obv-the-birth-of-a-political-institution/, accessed March 16, 2020.

[24] Question Time is the BBC's flagship political debate programme. Question Time panels are typically composed of five public figures, generally including a representative of the UK government and the Official Opposition. The panel also sometimes features representatives of other political parties, taking as a guide the level of electoral support at national level which each party enjoys; https://twitter.com/bbcquestiontime?lang=fr, accessed April 8, 2020.

resentatives and demand answers to their questions. Operation Black Vote hoped these initiatives would set off a ripple. If the organisation succeeded in creating opportunities for dialogue between BME community members and politicians, the latter might seize the chance to woo potential new voters by making pre-election pledges. BME individuals, keen to hold the politicians to their word, would thus be more likely to register to vote and then actually cast their vote on election day. In the event of success by the politicians in question, Operation Black Vote would make sure that they honoured their pre-election pledge.

Operation Black Vote's political strategy was a great success. During a press conference called by the organisation, the then Labour MP and Shadow Home Secretary Jack Straw announced the Labour Party's intention, if elected to power, to open a public inquiry into the 1993 racially-motivated murder of 18-year-old Stephen Lawrence, a brutal killing that had moved the entire nation.[25] The Conservative government had controversially refused to open an inquiry at the time of the killing. For the Conservative Party, Prime Minister John Major made a speech acknowledging that the prospects of a young black man from Brixton[26] were not as good as that of a young white man from the Home Counties, and then sent a copy of the speech to Operation Black Vote, no doubt expecting the organisation to reproduce it in media that the BME population would be likely to read. Paddy Ashdown, then leader of the Liberal Democrat party, pledged to make the House of Commons more ethnically representative if he were voted into power. Finally, Tony Blair, leader of the Labour Party, declared that his lifetime commitment was to fight against racism.[27]

The Labour Party won the May 1 1997 elections and Tony Blair became the first Labour Prime Minister after almost 20 years of Conservative Party rule, succeeding Margaret Thatcher (1979–1990) and John Major (1990–1997). A few months later the new Home Secretary, Jack Straw, honoured his pre-election pledge and opened a public inquiry into Stephen Lawrence's death.

---

25 Stephen Lawrence was stabbed to death in an unprovoked attack by a gang of white youths while he was waiting at a bus stop with a friend in Eltham, South-East London, on April 22, 1993. Police arrested five suspects a few months later. Two of them were charged with murder but later released. In April 1996 – just three months before Operation Black Vote was officially established – three of the five original suspects were brought to trial for murder at the Old Bailey. The case collapsed when the judge ruled that identification evidence provided by Stephen Lawrence's friend who was present on the night of the murder was not admissible in court. All three suspects were acquitted.
26 https://www.obv.org.uk/about-us/history, accessed January 10, 2019.
27 Ibid.

BME voters as a whole, irrespective of their ethnic groups, have traditionally voted massively in favour of the Labour Party candidate in UK General Elections.[28] In the 1960s and 1970s, the new post-war electorate from Africa, South Asia and the Caribbean supported the Labour Party for at least three reasons. The first reason was the Party's sympathetic position towards decolonisation – an important factor for many new settlers whose country of birth still belonged to the British Empire. The second reason was that the Labour Party was largely seen as an "ethnic minority-friendly" party,[29] in spite of its somewhat chequered history concerning immigration legislation.[30] Finally, the new settlers were working-class voters and the Labour Party was considered to be the party of the working class. As for the Conservative Party, it has historically largely failed to attract ethnic minority voters, principally because of a lack of trust towards the Conservative Party's traditional hard line on immigration. The 1959–1964 Conservative administration, for example, introduced the 1962 Commonwealth Immigrants Act, Britain's first piece of post-war anti-immigrant legislation. By introducing a system of employment vouchers, the Act drastically reduced the number of Commonwealth citizens authorised to reside in Britain after July 1, 1962. Since the late 1990s, however, the growing wealth among parts of the Asian community, especially in the British Indian community and the appeal of Conservative middle-class values, have seen about a quarter of Asians voting for the Conservative Party.[31] BME electoral support for the Conservative Party in general has also risen but not to the same degree (see Table 1).

---

[28] For example, at least 80 per cent of BME voters in the 1983 General Election supported the Labour Party. In the 1987 General Election, although the statistics were similar for the Caribbean ethnic group, they had dropped to below 70 per cent amongst the Asian ethnic groups. In spite of this, BME voters were still largely in favour of the Labour Party candidate; Brian Spittles, *Britain since 1960: An Introduction* (Basingstoke: Palgrave Macmillan Press Ltd., 1995), 100.

[29] The term is borrowed from Shamit Saggar's article, "Race Relations", in *Britain Since 1945*, ed. Jonathan Hollowell (Oxford: Blackwell Publishers Ltd., 2003), 323.

[30] Although the 1965, 1968 and 1976 Race Relations Acts were all introduced under Labour governments, the 1966–1970 Labour government was also responsible for the 1968 Commonwealth Immigrants Act which withdrew the right of entry into Britain of Kenyan Asian refugees with British passports, following the introduction by President Jomo Kenyatta of "Africanisation" policies in Kenya.

[31] Matt Cole and Helen Deighan, *Political Parties in Britain* (Edinburgh: Edinburgh University Press, 2012), 104.

Table 1: Party support by ethnic minorities at the 1974, 1979, 1983, 1987, 1992 and 1997 UK General Elections (%).

	1974[a]	1979	1983[b]	1987	1992[b]	1997
Labour	81	86	83	72	81	85
Conservative	9	8	7	18	10	11
Other Party	10	6	10	10	9	4

[a] October 1974 General Election.
[b] Recalculated average of Asian and Afro-Caribbean support levels.
Source: Shamit Saggar, "Race Relations" (2003), 323.[32]

Reasons behind Operation Black Vote's BME Drive for Voter Mobilisation

In the mid-1990s, many BME individuals, in particular young people, were disappointed and disillusioned with mainstream politics. They had little confidence in British institutions, including the political system, which they felt had sidestepped core race and minority issues. Their response to politicians ignoring their ethnic-specific needs was to turn their back on British politics. A parliament that neither looked representative nor sounded inclusive gave little incentive to register to vote.[33]

Operation Black Vote was aware that it was crucial to mobilise and empower these individuals if they were to be successful in challenging and overcoming race inequality in Britain. That is why, in 1997, Operation Black Vote began to develop three main political strategies, which it continues to upgrade and enhance today.

Into the Millennium: Strategies to Boost BME Voter Mobilisation in the Twenty-First Century

"Into the Millennium" was the title of an Operation Black Vote document published on the organisation's website in 1997. The document was both an assess-

---

[32] Shamit Saggar, "Race Relations," in *Britain Since 1945*, ed. Jonathan Hollowell (Oxford: Blackwell Publishers Ltd, 2003), 323.
[33] http://blogs.telegraph.co.uk/news/timwigmore/100263554/why-dont-more-ethnic-minorities-vote/, accessed April 28, 2019.

ment of Operation Black Vote's achievements in its first 12 months of existence and a platform for the measures to be adopted in the run-up to the 2001 General Election. Presented in the "What we do" section of the organisation's website, these actions were organised around three distinct strategies: political education, political participation and political representation.

Political Education

This strategy aimed to raise awareness and understanding of democratic and civic society through "citizenship projects". The "Citizenship in the Community" programme, conceptualised in 1997, targeted young people and adults but schoolchildren were also encouraged to get involved, notably through the "Young Citizenship in the Community" programme. The political education programmes for young people and schoolchildren were accomplished with the collaboration of schools, colleges, universities, the National Union of Students (NUS) and other relevant youth bodies.

The political education strategy was devised to provide BME individuals with an accessible and informal introduction to the workings of the UK's national and local political systems. One of many fitting examples of this is *Understanding Power*, the civic and political education programme Operation Black Vote introduced in 2004, especially for schoolchildren. This programme, launched by the then Minister of Education and Skills, the Rt. Hon. Charles Clarke, was seen as a long-term investment, the return on which would be reaped when the schoolchildren reached the age of 18, the minimum legal voting age for General Elections in England and Wales.

Understanding Power: A Citizen Education Programme for Schoolchildren

Schoolchildren are the electorate of the future and are perhaps an easier group than young adults to inspire as they generally have very little prior knowledge of the world of politics. They have no fixed opinions and their minds are open unlike their parents' and grandparents' who may harbour negative memories of the main political parties' attitudes towards the settlement of non-white Commonwealth migrants in Britain during the second half of the twentieth century.

Aware of the importance of acquainting children with the democratic process at an early age, Operation Black Vote came up with a programme called *Un-*

derstanding Power, to capture the interest of schoolchildren in the context of the classroom. The education programme, which still exists today, was designed to be attractive and fun for schoolchildren aged 11–16. The project enables children from all ethnic backgrounds to explore the dynamics of power that influence their day-to-day lives. Operation Black Vote staff visit participating schools for a day to present the programme to both teachers and schoolchildren. The teachers then continue the programme thanks to free teaching material provided by Operation Black Vote. This education pack contains a citizenship book for the students and a detailed teachers' pack with lesson plans for each section of the booklet.

During discussion with the schoolchildren on topics with which they are familiar and will voluntarily talk about such as music, fashion, sport, news media and film, OBV staff help the schoolchildren to understand how power relations function within these topics and this then enables the schoolchildren to make the link more readily between power and civil society, in domains such as government, the law and human rights.[34] Film excerpts, interactive computer-based activities and guest speakers from the world of politics and acting are also introduced to enliven the discussion.[35] The ultimate aim is to encourage schoolchildren to play a proactive role in engaging with political and civic society that they will hopefully take with them into adulthood.[36]

Over the years, the *Understanding Power* education pack has been distributed to over 10,000 schools and colleges across England and Wales and Operation Black Vote has hosted workshops and roadshows for thousands of schoolchildren in areas with large BME communities, providing them with groundbreaking tools to become politically literate.

A second pedagogical initiative by Operation Black Vote worthy of mention is *Who runs my City?*, a project which was organised from 2006 to 2011.

Who runs my City?

In 2006, Birmingham, the second largest city in the United Kingdom, had an even more ethnically diverse population than London, the country's capital

---

[34] https://www.obv.org.uk/news-blogs/happy-birthday-operation-black-vote, accessed April 11, 2020.
[35] *OBV News*, Issue 1, Spring 2007, 6.
[36] Ibid.

city.[37] This no doubt explains why Birmingham was chosen to host the first *Who runs my city?* project. The aim was to help BME individuals of all ages to pinpoint the geographical location of key social and political institutions in their city and learn about the role of each of them. A pack comprising a fold-out poster of Birmingham and a booklet listing all of its key institutions complete with their addresses was distributed to participating schools, colleges, community and faith groups. The pack informed people of exactly where decisions concerning their city were made and who made them.[38] The project proved to be so successful in Birmingham, with over 5,000 booklets and maps distributed, that Operation Black Vote decided to reproduce the project in London. The London edition was inaugurated by both the Mayor of London and the Minister for London at City Hall, on April 25, 2007.

Between December 2010 and March 2011, the *Who runs my City?* project was offered to BME communities in six local authorities throughout Greater London,[39] providing them with the knowledge to take greater control of the governance of their daily lives. As well as online and print resources that mapped out the key public decision-making bodies and civic practitioners in their local area, a series of talks and workshops was organised. These were attended by MPs, councillors, mayoral candidates, governors and magistrates willing to dialogue with members of the public about local power and democracy. In January 2011, in partnership with London Civic Forum and the London Empowerment Partnership's Targeted Support programme,[40] Operation Black Vote took the project a step further and produced six booklets each one specific to the London authority in which the *Who runs my City?* project was run. Essentially an in-

---

[37] The 2001 Census confirmed that while 70.4% of Birmingham's population was white, 19.5% were Asian, 6.1% were Black, 0.5% were Chinese, 2.5% were of mixed ethnicity and 0.6% were of another ethnic group; World Population Review, Birmingham Population 2020, https://worldpopulationreview.com/world-cities/birmingham-population/, accessed May 15 2020; the 2001 Census percentages for the different ethnic groups in London are as follows: White: 71.1%; Asian: 13.2%, Black: 10.9%; Chinese: 1.1%; Mixed ethnicity: 3.1%; Other ethnic group: 1.58%. Percentages calculated from figures available on the following website: https://www.nomisweb.co.uk/query/asv2htm.aspx, accessed May 15, 2020.
[38] *OBV News*, Issue 1, Spring 2007, 6.
[39] The six Greater London local authorities were: Barking and Dagenham; Barnet; Tower Hamlets; Croydon; Kensington and Chelsea; and Redbridge.
[40] London Civic Forum was established in 2000. It has a cross-sector membership of over 1,300 organisations and individuals. Its aim is to develop civic participation in London. It hosts the London Empowerment Partnership which has brought together a range of statutory agencies, civil society organisations and networks in order to improve the quality, coordination and evidence of community empowerment in London; House of Commons, 2011, 176.

formation booklet, it contained a directory of local MPs' and Councillors' names and contact details as well as interesting facts and figures relating to the relevant area. The *Who Runs my City?* project ended in March 2011 after a final rally in Central London with leaders from across the political spectrum, high profile civic leaders, national charities, the BME third sector and the media.[41]

The new Conservative-Liberal Democrat government elected in May 2010,[42] announced massive central government cuts for local government.[43] These public sector budget cuts impacted on many projects funded or subsidised by local governments, including Operation Black Vote's projects. This explains not only why the *Who Runs my City?* project ended in March 2011 and was not renewed, but also why the project's activities were concentrated in the Greater London area, where the budget had been voted prior to the announcement of the government cuts.[44]

Operation Black Vote considered the "Citizen in the Community" political educational strategy to be the cornerstone on which its two other initiatives could be built. After developing political literacy thanks to its various pedagogical programmes, the organisation put the onus on political action – political participation being one way in which political action can be expressed.

Political Participation

This strategy aimed to improve engagement with civic society through local and national registration and other civic participation campaigns. Under-registration has been a longstanding issue among the BME electorate in the UK. The reasons for this are complex and due in part to the demographic profile of the British BME electorate. BME voters are more likely to be found in groups of voters who generally tend to be under-represented; groups such as the under-25s, people who live in private rented accommodation and those who do not re-register

---

[41] https://www.obv.org.uk/news-blogs/obv-rally-who-runs-london, accessed March 14, 2020.
[42] David Cameron (Conservative Party) became Prime Minister of the new coalition government, while Nick Clegg (Liberal Democrat) was appointed Deputy Prime Minister.
[43] Central government funding for local authorities in England fell by 49 per cent between 2010/2011 and 2017/2018; "Triple Whammy: The Impact of Local Government Cuts on Women," Women's Budget Group, March 2019, 1, https://wbg.org.uk/wp-content/uploads/2019/03/Triple-Whammy-the-impact-of-local-government-cuts-on-women-March-19.pdf, accessed May 22, 2020.
[44] Operation Black Vote's MP Shadowing Scheme was also affected by these cuts. The Scheme was suspended after the 2011/2012 scheme until 2017, when it was reactivated. Another casualty of the cuts was the organisation's online magazine, *OBV News*, last published in Summer 2011.

when they move to new accommodation.⁴⁵ The replacement, in 2014, of household registration with individual electoral registration, is another, more recent factor in low BME voter registration numbers.⁴⁶

In 1997, Operation Black Vote acknowledged that increasing voter registration numbers among the BME electorate was a pivotal component of its political participation strategy. At the time, 24 per cent of the BME community were not registered to vote compared to six percent of the UK white community.⁴⁷ Figures had barely changed more than a decade later. According to a study carried out in 2015 by the Runnymede Trust, as many as 20 per cent of BME voters were not registered to vote compared to seven per cent of white voters.⁴⁸ These figures are more a reflection of the quintessential complexity involved in sustaining BME electoral mobilisation, as previously outlined, rather than an indication of failure on the part of Operation Black Vote to improve BME voter registration.

In order to inspire increased BME participation at the 2010 and 2015 General Elections,⁴⁹ Operation Black Vote took a proactive stance and sent staff and volunteers into the heart of BME communities across the country in a specially designed registration bus. Christened the eXpress campaign bus, the bus toured the country, stopping in towns and cities with a substantial BME population.⁵⁰ Data analysed after the 2010 General Election showed that BME voters were just as likely to vote as white British voters if their names were on the electoral roll. The difference in electoral participation between BME and white British, therefore, was not due to voter turnout on election day but rather to the rates of registration.⁵¹ It was consequently essential to mobilise as many people as possible to register to vote before the registration deadline of April 20 for the 2015 General Election. The bright orange eXpress campaign bus enabled registrations to take

---

45 Sunder Katwala and Steve Ballinger, *Mind the Gap: How the Ethnic Minority Cost Theresa May her Majority* (London: British Future 2017), 23.
46 Individual Electoral Registration replaced Household Registration (where the head of a household was responsible for registering everyone who lived at the same address) through the UK Electoral Registration and Administration Act 2013. The Act came into effect between June 2014 (for England and Wales) and September 2014 (for Scotland).
47 https://www.obv.org.uk/about/millennium, accessed October 6, 2019.
48 Omar Khan, "Registration and Race: Achieving Equal Political Participation", in *Race and Elections*, ed. Omar Khan (London: Runneymede, 2015), 24.
49 Theresa May's announcement of a snap General Election in June 2017 meant that Operation Black Vote did not have sufficient time to organise a registration bus tour that year.
50 London, Manchester, Birmingham, Bradford, Bristol, Leicester, Loughborough and Luton were some of the locations visited by the OBV registration bus in 2010 and 2015.
51 Nicole S. Martin and Omar Khan, *Ethnic Minorities at the 2017 British General Election* (London: Runnymede, 2019), 1.

place on the spot, thanks to its Information Technology suite with 12 computer terminals connected to the online government registration form. For those people who were willing to register but not aware of the content of the major political parties' manifestoes, an educational unit at the back of the bus was available with relevant reading material. At the end of the registration drive, Operation Black Vote reported having encouraged nearly one million people – BME and white – to register to vote. No details were given as to how the organisation had arrived at this figure.[52]

Community Empowerment Roadshows: BME Engagement with Civic Society

The Community Empowerment Roadshows was a programme run jointly by Operation Black Vote and the British Association of Settlements and Social Action Centres (BASSAC) to increase BME awareness and engagement in the local democratic process.[53]

In contrast to its eXpress campaign bus, Operation Black Vote's Community Empowerment Roadshows operated on a smaller scale. They took place outside of election periods, demonstrating that political participation is to be exercised at all times, and not merely once every four years. As their name indicates, these roadshows aimed to give BME people the means to participate actively in the democratic process at the local, community level.

The first Community Empowerment Roadshows were held throughout the winter of 2010/2011 in Birmingham, Manchester and London. These travelling free public seminars and meetings facilitated discussion between the BME public and local decision-makers including local councillors and businesspeople. At the one-day sessions participants explored the functions of their local representatives, discovered their roles and responsibilities and had the opportunity to meet their local councillors. A question and answer session encouraged local residents to take an interest in local politics and interact with guest speakers such as community activists, justices of the peace and representatives of civil society organisations. During a role-play simulation, participants gained hands-on knowledge and experience as to how decisions to allocate resources were made by their local council. The role-plays highlighted the need for compromise, for

---

[52] Esmée Fairbairn Foundation Annual Report and Accounts 2015, 41.
[53] https://www.obv.org.uk/what-we-do/schemes-programmes-and-projects/magistrate-magistrates-shadowing-scheme/community-empowe-0, accessed March 20, 2020.

forming alliances and also for creative problem-solving. In the final part of the roadshow session a local councillor explained how participants could be more actively involved in local issues by becoming a housing association board member, a community organiser or a tenant inspector, for instance. The councillor also gave insight into how to engage with councillors on everyday local problems such as school admissions, fly-tipping and anti-social behaviour. Although sharing many characteristics with the *Who runs my city?* project, the community empowerment roadshows provided more than political awareness education. As well as informing participants as to how important decisions are made, they offered concrete opportunities for individuals to work alongside the local council in order to improve the daily lives of all the local residents.

Political Representation

The political representation strategy developed by Operation Black Vote took political action to its ultimate conclusion, that of BME individuals applying for membership and/or taking up positions on public bodies nationally, regionally and locally. Its "MP Parliamentary Shadowing Scheme", regularly organised since it first began in 1999, aimed to boost BME voter mobilisation based on the principle that the BME electorate would be more likely to vote for candidates who are members of an ethnic minority like themselves. The underlying assumption is that a BME MP would consistently defend ethnic minority interests in parliament. However, Operation Black Vote appears to have blurred the lines between descriptive and substantive representation. For even if the number of BME MPs increases, thus providing visual representation in the UK legislature of people from shared marginal groups, this does not signify that BME MPs will necessarily act for the BME electorate. Firstly, because considerable social and political incompatibilities may exist beween BME MPs and the BME electorate, and secondly, because the large number of BME groups and sub-groups renders comprehensive representation impossible.[54]

---

54 Rebecca McKee, "The Substantive Representation of Ethnic Minorities in the UK Parliament" (PhD diss., University of Manchester, 2017), 40–41.

MP Parliamentary Shadowing Scheme

The MP Parliamentary Shadowing Scheme is a mentoring scheme that pairs BME individuals with a member of the House of Commons or the House of Lords for a period of four to six months. During this period, the BME individuals, named "shadows", follow and closely observe their mentor carrying out their political duties at Westminster or in their constituency. The aim is for the "shadows" to discover the realities of a national political figure to see if they themselves would like to embrace a career in politics.

The "shadows" spend a minimum of two days a month with their mentor, experiencing first-hand the duties and obligations of an MP or a Lord. Six separate days are spent in Westminster observing how Parliament works and six others in the constituency of the MP, Lord or Baroness, thus providing invaluable insight into the questions that their mentor has to deal with on a daily basis. Finally, a further six days of training is provided by Operation Black Vote during which "shadows" receive instruction about policy, public speaking, media community activism and lobbying, amongst other, relevant topics.[55] The idea behind the scheme is that on completing the programme former participants will act as diplomats to either encourage BME individuals to vote for the parties whose ideas they represent as "shadows", or to vote for the former "shadow" in the event that s/he becomes an electoral candidate. Indeed, the outline that is given to candidates for the "MP Shadowing Scheme" clearly states that once they have completed the scheme, former "shadows" are expected to become community ambassadors, informing and inspiring BME communities and others to positively engage in civic and public society. During their internship, "shadows" are expected to speak at Operation Black Vote community empowerment events, both to encourage and inspire the audience to become more politically involved in their community, and also to gain experience in public speaking and to improve their oratory skills. Operation Black Vote also provides "shadows" with other opportunities to lead community activism initiatives and build on their political, civil and business knowledge, as these are all fundamental skills they will need to make the transition from voter and political mobilisation to political action.

The selection procedure for potential "shadows" is comparable to that of candidates applying for a much sought-after professional appointment. The number of applicants per Shadowing session often exceeds 500 for between 20 and 30 places available. Each applicant is required to complete an application

---

55 Steve Beebee, "Me and My Shadow," *Young People Now*, Issue 131, March 2000, 31.

form which, in addition to sections usually found on a curriculum vitae, such as Education and Qualifications, Employment History and References, contains sections with in-depth questions that are generally asked at the interview stage of a selection procedure.[56] Candidates must, for example, explain in 400 words why they want to be a participant on the scheme and how their experience, achievements and understanding of the concerns of minority communities and social inclusion would make them an ideal candidate to shadow an MP or represent a political party as a parliamentarian.[57] In accordance with its non-partisan position, Operation Black Votes allocates a roughly equal number of successful candidates to MPs and Lords/Baronesses from the three main political parties, and, where applicable, mentors are also found amongst MPs from the Scottish National Party (SNP) and Plaid Cymru, the political party of Wales.[58]

The "MP Shadowing Scheme" has been largely successful over the years, if only in terms of grooming MPs from BME communities. A number of alumni have become prominent in British politics today, including Marvin Rees, Labour Party Mayor of Bristol since May 2016; Helen Grant, Conservative MP for Maidstone and the Weald since 2010; and Sayeeda Warsi, raised to the peerage in 2007 as Baroness Warsi and a former Chairman of the Conservative Party (2010–2012).

Although the number of BME MPs elected to Parliament rose steadily over a 23-year period (see Table 2a), there is no firm evidence to suggest that Operation Black Vote's "MP Shadowing Scheme" directly contributed to this increase.

Table 2a: Black and Minority Ethnic MPs elected in UK General Elections between 1997 and 2019.

Year	No. of BME MPs	Representation (per cent)
1997	9	1%
2001	12	2%
2005	15	2%
2010	27	4%
2015	41	6%

---

[56] Candidates whose application forms are shortlisted are then invited for interview at Operation Black Vote's offices in London.

[57] The Operation Black Vote Parliamentary Shadowing Scheme Application Form is downloadable directly from the organisation's website, https://www.obv.org.uk/what-we-do/schemes-programmes-and-campaigns/mp-shadowing-scheme-2019/mp-shadowing-scheme-2019, accessed October 6, 2019.

[58] Candidates state their political party preference on their application forms.

Table 2a: Black and Minority Ethnic MPs elected in UK General Elections between 1997 and 2019. *(Continued)*

Year	No. of BME MPs	Representation (per cent)
2017	52	8%
2019	65	10%

Source: adapted from Table 8, House of Commons Briefing Paper CBP 7529, 2020, 29.[59]

Table 2b: Number of Black and Minority Ethnic MPs by political party elected in General Elections between 1997 and 2019.

Year	Total BME MPs	Labour BME MPs	Conservative BME MPs	Liberal Democrat BME MPs	Scottish National Party BME MPs
1997	9	9	-	-	-
2001	12	12	-	-	-
2005	15	12	3	-	-
2010	27	16	11	-	-
2015	41	23	17	-	1
2017	52	32	19	1	-
2019	65	41	22	2	-

Source: adapted from Table 5, House of Commons Briefing Paper CBP 7483, 2020, 9.[60]

Following the consistently high number of applications received for its "MP Shadowing Schemes" in England, the organisation launched a "Welsh Assembly Shadowing Scheme" in 2008, thus giving BME individuals living in Wales the chance to be mentored by an Assembly member and be elected to the Welsh Assembly. Operation Black Vote has also initiated similar schemes in the domain of civic leadership, including a Magistrates Shadowing Scheme, begun in 2001, a Councillor Scheme, launched in 2007 and a BME Women Councillor Scheme, which started in 2009.

Operation Black Vote claims that its different strategies and campaigns have awakened the political consciousness of many BME individuals and empowered them to register and turn out to vote. In 2009, Lee Jasper, one of the organisation's co-founders, maintained, contrary to data from sources such as the Runnymede Trust (details above. See "Political Participation"), that thanks to Oper-

---

[59] Lukas Audickas, Richard Cracknell and Philip Loft, *UK Election Statistics: 1918–2019: A Century of Elections* (London: House of Commons Library, February 2020), 29.
[60] Lukas Audickas and Richard Cracknell, *Social Background of MPs 1979–2019* (London: House of Commons Library, March 2020), 9.

ation Black Vote, the number of BME individuals who had not registered to vote had gone down from 28 per cent–30 per cent in 1996 to 18–20 per cent in 2009.[61] The source of the figures advanced by Operation Black Vote, however, is not disclosed. This leads us to question the extent to which the impact of Operation Black Vote can be quantified.

Assessing the Impact of Operation Black Vote

As far as voter registration and turnout is concerned, there is no way of knowing the exact role played by Operation Black Vote. As Sarah Pickard notes, general elections rely on secret ballots and there are consequently no official or precise demographic data published on turnout. The available data are necessarily approximate as they are collected via a number of surveys and polls each using distinct methodologies and varying sample sizes.[62] Pickard nevertheless provides useful information on the evolution of estimated BME turnout figures for the 2010, 2015 and 2017 General Elections[63] (see Table 3).

Table 3: BME and White Voter Turnout in the 2010, 2015 and 2017 UK General Elections.

	Turnout 2010 (%)	Turnout 2015 (%)	Turnout 2017 (%)
BME group	51	56	64
White ethnic group	67	68	69

Source: adapted from Table 8.3, Pickard 2019, 241.[64]

Table 3 indicates that BME turnout for all age groups rose by five per cent between 2010 and 2015 and by eight per cent between 2015 and 2017. This compares with a rise of only one per cent between 2010 and 2015 and one per cent again between 2015 and 2017 among whites of all ages.[65] The turnout percentage increase between the 2015 and 2017 elections was particularly high among BME

---

[61] https://operationblackvote.wordpress.com/2009/07/17/obv-the-birth-of-a-political-institution/, accessed March 16, 2020.
[62] Sarah Pickard, *Protest & Young People: Political Participation and Dissent in 21st Century Britain* (London: Palgrave Macmillan, 2019), 330.
[63] Data concerning BME communities appear not to have been collected by national opinion pollsters and surveys before 2010. Figures for the 2019 snap General Election were not available at the time of writing.
[64] Pickard, op. cit., 241.
[65] Ibid., 331.

members aged 18–24, rising from 38 per cent in 2015 to 54 per cent in 2017, according to an Ipsos Mori poll.⁶⁶

After the 2015 General Election, Operation Black Vote released turnout results based on its own undisclosed methodology that lend credence to the trend between 2010 and 2015. Indeed, in its blog, the organisation stated that turnout had risen considerably in the cities, towns and districts visited by its eXpress campaign bus prior to the 2015 General Election. According to the blog, BME turnout in Liverpool Riverside increased from 52 per cent in 2010 to 62.4 per cent in 2015. A seven per cent BME turnout increase was also observed in Manchester Gorton.⁶⁷ However, the extent to which the "Citizenship in the Community" programme contributed to any of these increases cannot be objectively quantified.

A study of the 2010 UK General Election revealed interesting findings in relation to BME turnout and voting behaviour and BME candidates. This investigation, by Nicole Martin, focused particularly observing on whether ethnic minority individuals were more likely to vote if they had the opportunity to vote for a candidate from the same ethnic background.⁶⁸ The results show that there is no co-ethnic or co-religion effect on voter turnout for most ethnic minorities in the UK General Elections, at least not as far as the 2010 General Election is concerned. However, a positive association was observed between the presence of a Pakistani candidate from the Labour party and the likelihood of turnout among Pakistani voters.⁶⁹ A negative association between the probability of voting among Sikhs and the Labour party candidate if the candidate was Pakistani, and the reciprocal (although considerably smaller) relationship between Sikh Labour candidates and the low probability of voting among Muslims was also observed.⁷⁰

Another study based on the same 2010 General Election results had comparable aims and yielded similar results.⁷¹ Entitled "Candidate Ethnicity and Vote Choice in Britain", this study considered whether ethnic minority voters in the UK were more inclined to vote for non-white candidates and particularly those from the same ethnic group as themselves.⁷² The study found that although

---

66 Ibid., 332.
67 https://www.obv.org.uk/news-blogs/increased-voter-turnout-bme-brits, accessed October 19, 2019.
68 Nicole S. Martin, *Parliamentary Affairs* (2016), 69, 159–180.
69 Ibid., 169.
70 Ibid., 173.
71 Stephen D. Fisher et al., "Candidate Ethnicity and Vote Choice in Britain," *British Journal of Political Science* 45, no. 4 (2015): 883.
72 Ibid., 883.

there was a strong co-ethnic voting tendency for Pakistanis, there was no candidate ethnicity effect of any kind for Indians, black Caribbeans or black Africans. White British voters, in general, proved less willing to vote for ethnic minority candidates, especially Muslim candidates.[73]

Operation Black Vote's various programmes and schemes have been offered to members of all black and minority ethnic groups. What the existing studies suggest is that more detailed data are required to establish the impact of the organisation's various initiatives. The information that the organisation regularly publishes in relation to its different campaigns, events, schemes and roadshows do not consider the different ethnic voting behaviours that exist. For example, none of Operation Black Vote's figures on BME voter mobilisation attempt to measure the impact of *biraderi* or community clan or kinship networks on Pakistani voting behaviour. Neither do they take into account other likely mediating factors, such as: (a) the *de*-mobilising effects of a non co-ethnic minority candidate on turnout; (b) religion rather than ethnicity being a factor for mobilisation or *de*-mobilisation and turnout; (c) the *de*-mobilising effects of a co-ethnic or minority candidate's political party.[74]

Testing the Power of the Black Vote Hypothesis

In its "Power of the Black Vote in 2015" report published in August 2013, Operation Black Vote claimed that the BME electorate had the power to decide the outcome of the 2015 General Election. Comparing the 2011 population census data with the results of the 2010 General Election, it calculated that 241 constituencies in England and Wales, i.e. 42 per cent of the total number of constituencies, had BME electorates larger than the 2010 majorities of the sitting MP when measured against the 2011 census and counting only what it calls "the voting electorate".[75] According to the organisation, one hundred and sixty-eight of these constituencies were in marginal seats that could probably decide which party would constitute the next government. These 168 seats were the equivalent of 29 per cent of all constituencies in England and Wales. From this data Operation Black Vote concluded that almost one third of MPs could be voted in or out

---

73 Ibid., 899, 900.
74 Nicole S. Martin, *Parliamentary Affairs* (2016), 69, 64, 166.
75 "Power of the Black Vote in 2015: The Changing Face of England and Wales", Operation Black Vote report, August 2013, 4.

of office depending on the extent to which they and their party appealed to BME voters.[76]

In the same report, Operation Black Vote also claimed that any political party that ignored the changing demographic profile of Britain's BME populations would do so at their peril. The BME percentage of the total population in England and Wales had been growing steadily since records on ethnic groups were first published in the 1991 census. From less than five per cent nationally (approximately three million people) in 1991, the BME population rose to 13 per cent (approximately eight million people) in 2011.[77] For Simon Woolley, director of Operation Black Vote, putting race equality back on the political agenda was no longer an option, but rather a question of political survival for the major parties.[78] With the combined effect of a growing BME population and increased BME voter registration numbers and turnout figures, he believed politicians would be forced to listen to BME demands and address social issues concerning BME populations that they had thus far successfully managed to sidestep or simply ignore.

In an article published in the *Guardian* after the 2015 General Election entitled, "There is no such thing as the black vote – this election proves it", Kehinde Andrews of Birmingham City University dismisses Operation Black Vote's hypotheses as a fallacy. In a scathing critique Andrews denounced any attempt to predict the election result in purely quantitative terms.[79] In his view, the BME electorate could not and should not be considered to represent a homogenous block of voters that have a potentially unified impact on election results. To support his affirmation, he cited a study commissioned by the think tank, British Future, published after the 2015 General Election results were announced.[80] The study highlights the differences in voting trends between and within different ethnic groups. Taken as a single group, British Asians were, for example, almost twice as likely to vote for the Conservative Party as Black African and Caribbean groups. However, voting patterns were very different when specific Asian sub-

---

[76] Ibid., 3.
[77] Omar Khan, "Introduction: Race and Elections in 2015 and Beyond" in *Race and Elections*, ed. Omar Khan (London: Runnymede, 2015), 4.
[78] "Power of the Black Vote in 2015: The Changing Face of England and Wales", Operation Black Vote report, August 2013, 3.
[79] Kehinde Andrews, "There's no such thing as the black vote – this election proves it," May 26, 2015, https://www.theguardian.com/commentisfree/2015/may/26/black-vote-election-ethnic-minority-non-white, accessed November 4, 2019.
[80] The survey was conducted by Survation for British Future after the election among 2,000 respondents across Britain between May 8 and 14, 2015.

groups were examined; while Muslims had voted massively for the Labour Party (64 per cent), more Sikhs and Hindus had voted Conservative than Labour.[81] It was consequently impossible for any single political party to benefit from the totality of the BME vote, Andrews argued.

Professor Andrews was equally critical of Operation Black Vote's claim that changing BME demographics could create the political leverage to decide the result of the 2015 elections. Although some BME individuals had moved out of the major industrial towns where their communities had settled on arrival in the country, to towns and more rural locations where people vote largely for the Conservative Party, their numbers were so negligible that the BME vote would carry little weight in such constituencies. Given that the vast majority of BME voters were still concentrated in cities like London, Birmingham, Manchester and Bristol and that they still traditionally voted massively for the Labour party in "safe" seats, it was logical that the growing BME population would have no homogenous effect on General Election results.

In his critique, Andrews regarded voting as a mostly passive way to engage in politics today, finding political mobilisation at the grassroots level much more empowering for all marginalised communities. In his opinion, this was the only way that the voices from these marginal communities could be heard. The overall implication in the article was that Operation Black Vote had lost its power to mobilise BME voters and was becoming increasingly obsolescent as a representative of BME communities and their political demands.

Conclusion

Operation Black Vote was the first non-partisan, non-governmental organisation to champion BME voter mobilisation in the UK. Although it is impossible to quantify the organisation's impact on the increased BME voter registration and turnout figures that were observed during the 2010, 2015 and 2017 General Elections, its innovative outreach programmes have undoubtedly increased awareness of voter registration as an important issue in UK politics.

Contrary to BME voter mobilisation, it is possible to quantify the various Operation Black Vote schemes to increase BME political participation and representation. At the end of 2019, two elected Mayors, one council leader, two elected

---

[81] Kehinde Andrews, "There's no such thing as the black vote – this election proves it," May 26, 2015, https://www.theguardian.com/commentisfree/2015/may/26/black-vote-election-ethnic-minority-non-white, accessed November 4, 2019.

Lord Mayors and over 100 magistrates in England and Wales were alumni of Operation Black Vote training programmes. At national level, 10 per cent of the UK's BME Members of Parliament were former participants of the organisation's "MP Shadowing Scheme".[82] In the light of this data, the positive effect of Operation Black Vote's strategies to encourage BME citizens in the UK to reconnect with politics and the UK political system is indisputable.

Beyond the realm of political representation, Operation Black Vote has now broadened its initial focus on boosting BME voter mobilisation to lobbying the British government for stronger racial equality policies. Within weeks of becoming Prime Minister in July 2016, Theresa May had agreed to set up a Race Disparity Unit in order to carry out a full race audit.[83] Eighteen months later, in January 2018, May appointed Simon Woolley – Operation Black Vote's director – Chair of the Race Disparity Unit's Advisory Group at Downing Street. As Chair, Woolley worked with ministers, senior civil servants, business and community leaders towards collectively closing the race equality gaps revealed by the Race Disparity Unit's groundbreaking audit of public services which had been published in October 2017.[84]

Operation Black Vote's trajectory is remarkable. Within a timespan of 23 years, it has developed from a grassroots organisation with a fairly limited agenda into a forceful pressure group, whose wider vision of a more racially equal society has influenced some of the most powerful politicians and decision-makers in the United Kingdom, even if its priority remains the promotion of BME voter mobilisation. Indeed, the organisation's efforts to this end were officially recognised in April 2020, when it received the "Best Digital Campaign or Campaigner of the Year Award" by the UK Parliament for its online voter registration campaign in the run-up to the December 2019 snap General Election. Despite a period of just over four weeks between the official announcement on October 29 and polling day on December 12, 2019, Operation Black Vote had managed to launch an electoral campaign on Twitter, create an election website in collabo-

---

82 https://www.obv.org.uk/news-blogs/looking-back-look-ahead-part-1, accessed April 13, 2020.
83 https://www.obv.org.uk/news-blogs/obvs-role-race-equality-audit, accessed April 9, 2020. In July 2020, seven months after winning the snap December 2019 UK General Election, Conservative Prime Minister, Boris Johnson, announced the disbanding of the Race Disparity Unit's Advisory Group. It was replaced by the Commission on Race and Ethnic Disparities. Dr Tony Sewell was appointed Chair of the Commission.
84 https://www.obv.org.uk/news-blogs/simon-woolley-chair-downing-st-race-disparity-advisory-group, accessed April 9, 2020; https://www.obv.org.uk/number-10-statement-race-disparity-unit, accessed April 9, 2020. The Race Disparity Unit is a cross-government initiative designed to highlight differences in treatment or outcome affecting people of different ethnicities. The Unit collects and publishes relevant government data in many areas of UK national life.

ration with the Coalition of Racial Equality Organisations (CORE),[85] produce a voter registration film and poster campaign and carry out a national voter turnout tour.

Finally, taking a broader view of voter mobilisation, Operation Black Vote's pioneering schemes, programmes and campaigns have inspired other minority groups to set up similar bodies to boost voter mobilisation among their ranks. Operation Traveller Vote, for example, was launched in the UK in 2014 while Operation Disabled Vote was set up in May 2015. The Operation Black Vote's unique approach has also been copied in Canada; Operation Black Vote Canada has been established since 2004.

Bibliography

Books

Bute, E.L., and H.J.P. Harmer. *The Black Handbook: The People, History and Politics of Africa and the African Diaspora*. London, New York: Bloomsbury Academic, 2016.

Cole, Matt, and Helen Deighan. *Political Parties in Britain*. Edinburgh: Edinburgh University Press, 2012.

Hinds, Donald. *Journey to an Illusion: The West Indian in Britain*. London: Bogle-L'Ouverture Publications Limited, 2001.

Hollowell, Jonathan, ed. *Britain Since 1945*. Oxford: Blackwell Publishers Ltd., 2003.

Philips, Mike, and Trevor Philips. *Windrush: The Irresistible Rise of Multi-Racial Britain*. London: HarperCollins, 1998.

Pickard, Sarah. *Politics, Protest & Young People: Political Participation and Dissent in 21st Century Britain*. London: Palgrave Macmillan, 2019.

Spittles, Brian. *Britain since 1960: An Introduction*. Basingstoke: Palgrave Macmillan Press Ltd., the same punctuation as above (See Hollowell, Jonathan), 1995.

Book Chapters

Saggar, Shamit. "Race Relations?" In *Britain Since 1945*, edited by Jonathan Hollowell, 313–331. Oxford: Blackwell Publishers Ltd., punctuation as above (see Spittles, Brian and Hollowell, Jonathan), 2003.

---

85 https://raceequality2019.com/, accessed December 17, 2019.

Articles in Print Journals

Beebee, Steve. "Operation Black Vote." *Young People Now*, issue 160 (2002): 18–19.
Beebee, Steve. "Me and My Shadow." *Young People Now*, issue 131 (2000): 30–31.
Fieldhouse, Edward, and Maria Sobolewska. "Introduction: Are British Ethnic Minorities Politically Under-represented?" *Parliamentary Affairs* (2012): 1–11.
Fisher, Stephen D., Anthony F. Heath, David Sanders and Maria Sobolewska. "Candidate Ethnicity and Vote Choice in Britain." *British Journal of Political Science* 45, no. 4 (2015): 883–905.
Martin, Nicole S. "Do Ethnic Minority Candidates Mobilise Ethnic Minority Voters? Evidence from the 2010 UK General Election." *Parliamentary Affairs* 69 (2016): 159–180.
Miles, Robert. "Class Relations and Racism in Britain in the 1980s". *Revue européenne des migrations internationales* 3, no. 1–2, 1er-3e trimestre (1987): 223–238.

Reports

Anwar, Muhammad. *Ethnic Minorities and the British Electoral System: A Research Report.* Commissioned by Operation Black Vote. Coventry: University of Warwick/Centre for Research in Ethnic Relations, 1998.
CRC. *Participation of Ethnic Minorities in the General Election of October 1974.* London: Community Relations Commission, 1975.
CRE. *Votes and Policies: Ethnic Minorities and the General Election 1979.* London: Commission for Racial Equality, 1980.
CRE. *Ethnic Minorities and the 1983 General Election: A Research Report.* London: Commission for Racial Equality, 1984.
Esmée Fairbairn Foundation. *Annual Report and Accounts 2015.*

Thesis

McKee, Rebecca. "The Substantive Representation of Ethnic Minorities in the UK Parliament." PhD diss., University of Manchester, 2017.

Webliography

Online Newspaper Articles

Andrews, Kehinde. "There is no such thing as the black vote – this election proves it." *The Guardian*, May 26, 2015. Accessed November 4, 2019. https://www.theguardian.com/commentisfree/2015/may/26/black-vote-election-ethnic-minority-non-white.
Templeton, Tom. "The ethnic minority vote." *The Guardian*, April 24, 2005. Accessed March 18, 2020. https://www.theguardian.com/politics/2005/apr/24/uk.election20054.

Wigmore, Tim. "Why don't more ethnic minorities vote." *Telegraph*, March 24, 2014. Accessed April 28, 2019. http://blogs.telegraph.co.uk/news/timwigmore/100263554/why-dont-more-ethnic-minorities-vote/.

Woolley, Simon. "Happy birthday Operation Black Vote." *The Guardian*, July 20, 2007. Accessed October 29, 2019. https://www.theguardian.com/commentisfree/2007/jul/20/happybirthdayoperationblackvote.

Online Magazines

OBV Special Anniversary Issue, issue 6, Summer 2011. https://www.obv.org.uk/what-we-do/obv-news-magazine/issue-6.

OBV News, issue 3, Summer 2008. https://www.obv.org.uk/what-we-do/obv-news-magazine/issue-3.

OBV News, issue 2, Autumn 2007. https://www.obv.org.uk/what-we-do/obv-news-magazine/issue-2.

OBV News, issue 1, Spring 2007. https://www.obv.org.uk/what-we-do/magazine/issue-1.

Other Downloadable Documents

Audickas, Lukas, and Richard Cracknell. *Social Background of MPs 1979–2019*. House of Commons Briefing Paper number CBP 7483. London: House of Commons Library, March 27, 2020. https://commonslibrary.parliament.uk/research-briefings/cbp-7483/.

Audickas, Lukas, Richard Cracknell and Philip Loft. *UK Election Statistics: 1918–2019: A Century of Elections*. House of Commons Briefing Paper number CPB 7529, February 27, 2020. https://commonslibrary.parliament.uk/research-briefings/cbp-7529/.

Heath, Anthony, and Khan Omar. *Ethnic Minority British Election Study – Key Findings*. London: Runneymede Trust, 2012. https://www.runnymedetrust.org/uploads/EMBES briefingFINALx.pdf.

House of Commons. *Localism: Third Report of Session 2010–2012, Volume 1 Report*. HC 547. London: The Stationery Office Limited, June 7, 2011. https://publications.parliament.uk/pa/cm201012/cmselect/cmcomloc/547/547.pdf.

Katwala, Sunder, and Steve Ballinger. *Mind the Gap: How the Ethnic Minority cost Theresa May her Majority*. London: British Future, September 2017. http://www.britishfuture.org/publication/mind-gap-ethnic-minority-vote-cost-theresa-may-majority/.

Khan, Omar, and Sveinsson Kjartan, eds. *Race and Elections*. London: Runnymede, 2015. https://www.runnymedetrust.org/uploads/RaceandElectionsFINAL_interactive.pdf.

Khan, Omar. "Registration and Race: Achieving Equal Political Participation." In *Race and Elections*, edited by Omar Khan and Kjartan Sveinsson. London: Runnymede, 2015. https://www.runnymedetrust.org/uploads/RaceandElectionsFINAL_interactive.pdf.

Khan, Omar. "Introduction: Race and Elections in 2015 and Beyond." In *Race and Elections*, edited by Omar Khan and Kjartan Sveinsson. London: Runnymede, 2015. https://www.runnymedetrust.org/uploads/RaceandElectionsFINAL_interactive.pdf.

Martin, Nicole, and Omar Khan. *Ethnic Minorities at the 2017 British General Election.* London: Runnymede, February 2019. https://www.runnymedetrust.org/uploads/2017%20Election%20Briefing.pdf.
Operation Black Vote. *Power of the Black Vote in 2017.* May 2017. https://smgbristol.files.wordpress.com/2017/06/751a5-poweroftheblackvotein2017.pdf.
Operation Black Vote. *Power of the Black Vote in 2015: The Changing Face of England and Wales.* August 2013. https://www.obv.org.uk/sites/default/files/images/downloads/Powerofthe%20BlackVotev3.pdf.
The Price of Race Inequality: The Black Manifesto 2010. n.d. https://www.diversecymru.org.uk/wp-content/uploads/The-Black-Manifesto-2010.pdf.

Websites and web pages

https://www.parliament.uk/site-information/glossary/early-day-motions/.
https://www.parliament.uk/about/how/business/edms/.
https://edm.parliament.uk/early-day-motion/13805.
https://www.electoralcommission.org.uk/i-am-a/voter/register-vote-and-update-your-details#commonwealth.
https://www.obv.org.uk.
https://www.obv.org.uk/news-blogs/obv-rally-who-runs-london.
https://www.obv.org.uk/about/millennium.
https://www.obv.org.uk/what-we-do/schemes/understanding-power/introduction.
https://www.obv.org.uk/about-us/history.
http://www.nomisweb.co.uk/census/2011/ks201uk.
https://operationblackvote.wordpress.com/2009/07/17/obv-the-birth-of-a-political-institution/.
https://www.obv.org.uk/what-we-do/schemes-programmes-and-projects/magistrate-magistrates-shadowing-scheme/community-empowe-0.
https://www.obv.org.uk/what-we-do.
https://www.obv.org.uk/news-blogs/increased-voter-turnout-bme-brits.
https://www.obv.org.uk/news-blogs/looking-back-look-ahead-part-1.
https://www.obv.org.uk/number-10-statement-race-disparity-unit.
https://www.obv.org.uk/news-blogs/obvs-role-race-equality-audit.
https://www.obv.org.uk/news-blogs/happy-birthday-operation-black-vote.
https://twitter.com/bbcquestiontime?lang=fr.

Part 2: **Mobilising Women: Grassroots Action and Political Discourse**

Jean-Louis Marin-Lamellet
4 Mobilising Agrarian Men and Women in the Late Nineteenth Century

The Case of Farmers' Alliances and the Populist Movement

Introduction

In the 1880s and 1890s, Farmers' Alliances in the American South and Midwest mobilised "periphery agrarians" – farmers, storekeepers, miners, railroad workers and nonconformist intellectuals – in a progressive farmer-labour movement advocating an antimonopoly and democratisation agenda. They were determined to give voice to all those economically and socially marginalised by Gilded Age finance capitalism: farmers at the mercy of monopolistic railroads in the Midwest, black and white sharecroppers ensnared by crop-lien system in the South but also workers exploited by corporate greed.[1] The Farmers' Alliances set up in rural Texas in the 1870s organised into a network of alliances. After Charles Macune became President of the Texas Alliance in 1886, it grew expo-

---

1 As political scientist Elizabeth Sanders argues, the term "agrarian" refers to "those agricultural regions, largely coincident with the designated southern-plains-western 'periphery,' that were devoted to one or two cash crops produced for national and international (as opposed to local) markets." Sanders distinguishes between different farmers and different city functions: agrarian peripheries were characterised by an ecosystem where cities were dependent on rural areas around them, for instance Minneapolis, Kansas City, or Chicago. Farmers' livelihoods and economic development often hinged on one railroad line, which is why they cast railroad companies as predatory and exploitative and pushed for antimonopoly legislation. "Agrarians" were also not limited to farmers: they included employees, storekeepers, craftsmen, miners and railroad workers. These groups were not only united by a producer ethos, but they actually overlapped: "farmers were often part-time coal miners, and coal miners often farmed to supplement their diet and income," as Postel explains. In "core" industrial regions, however, notably the northeast, farming did not drive cities' economic growth: diversified farmers supplied local urban markets with perishables and truck produce and depended upon metropolises. As a consequence, the abstract "urban-rural distinction *per se* has limited explanatory power in American politics" (Sanders) – another type of spatial politics, the core/ periphery divide, offers more insights into the agrarian revolt of the 1890s. Elizabeth Sanders, *Roots of Reform: Farmers, Workers, and the American State, 1877–1917* (Chicago, London: University of Chicago Press, 1999), 1–8, 16, 28; Charles Postel, *The Populist Vision* (Oxford, New York: Oxford University Press, 2007), 19.

nentially from 38,000 to 225,000 members in 1889. The Southern Alliance spread rapidly across the cotton South, merged with other organisations and then reached into the Wheat Belt, especially Kansas, and in California and the Rocky Mountain States. By 1890, the National Farmers' Alliance and Industrial Union (NFAIU) claimed 1.2 million members in 27 states, the "largest democratic mass movement in American history" according to historian Lawrence Goodwyn. Besides the NFAIU, several other organisations had similar objectives: the Chicago-based Northern Famers' Alliance and in Illinois the Farmers' Mutual Benefit Association. In the South, African Americans organised the Colored Farmers' Alliance.[2]

All these alliances mobilised agrarians who were left behind in the march of progress, overpowered by corporations and financial institutions and geographically and historically marginalised by prospering urban centres in the northeast. The different alliances pushed for radical reforms (progressive income tax and government ownership of transport and communications to name but a few) in an attempt to curb the threat wealth concentration posed for economic and political freedom. The movement also attracted all sorts of middle-class reformers and radicals. At the beginning of the 1890s, Farmers' Alliances entered politics and created the People's Party, also known as the Populist Party. This study focuses on Farmers' Alliances. However, since there is no clear-cut separation between the two movements, it also deals with the beginning of Populism.[3] As the movement was in full swing in the 1890s, the 14 founders of the original

---

[2] Lawrence Goodwyn, *The Populist Moment: A Short History of the Agrarian Revolt in America* (Oxford, New York: Oxford University Press, 1978), vii; Postel, *The Populist Vision*, 25–37; *Equality: An American Dilemma, 1866–1896* (New York: Farrar, Straus and Giroux, 2019), 302–303.

[3] For the first historians of Populism, Hicks and Parrington, the agrarian revolt of the 1890s prefigured the Progressive movement of the 1900–1910 period. Hofstadter, Wiebe and Ferkiss described Populism as a relic of the agrarian past that was not adapted to the modern industrial world. However, in the 1960s, New Left historians and historians influenced by the republican paradigm (Rodgers) portrayed Populism as the swansong of a virtuous pre-industrial and republican past and Populists as tragic heroes sacrificed on the altar of modernisation (Lasch, Goodwyn, McMath). Livingston, on the contrary, saw them as comic heroes whose demise was necessary to modernise the country. Postel's revisionism rejects the idea of Populism as a tradition-oriented movement: he depicts the agrarian movement of the 1890s as a "vision" of progress. Nugent, like most historians of Progressivism (Edwards, Flanagan), highlights the continuity between Populism and Progressivism. The debate among historians actually echoes the disputes between advocates and opponents of Populism in the 1890s: Populist historians writing their own history (Dunning, Morgan, Garvin and Daws) denounced the condescension of intellectuals such as McVey who thought Populists were backward; see bibliography. For a more detailed analysis of the historiography of Populism, see Worth Robert Miller, "A Centennial Historiography of American Populism," *Kansas History: A Journal of the Central Plains* 16, no. 1 (1993): 54–69.

Texas Alliance posed in front of the cabin where their first formal meeting was held in 1877 in Pleasant Valley, Lampasas County, Texas.[4] How did a movement that started with a dozen farmers eventually mobilise millions of Americans? The article will examine the strategies, tools and institutions Alliances used to mobilise their constituency and study one militant group that was particularly galvanised into action – women. The political and intellectual history questions raised by the "agrarian uprising" – discussed most notably in Charles Postel's recent re-evaluation of Populism – will be considered from a double perspective: the sociology of social movements and book and periodical studies.[5] This paper thus contributes to a better understanding of the successes and limits of agrarian mobilisation.

Context of Grievances and Resource Mobilisation

The sociology of social movements provides a useful framework for understanding the strategies pursued by Farmers' Alliances to mobilise "the labouring class."[6] The farm crisis that hit the country in the late nineteenth century generated a context of grievances for the agrarian periphery. Farmers in the South and the Midwest suffered from droughts, bad crops, low prices, deflation, debt and unfair railroad rates. Farmers exported their cash crops, but monopolistic railroads had the power to fix rates and essentially controlled farmers' access to global markets: it was often cheaper to transport grain from Chicago to Liverpool

---

4 The cabin was dismantled and moved to Chicago where it was exhibited at the World's Columbian Exposition of 1893. It was then chopped up and the pieces were given out to Populist militants. "First Farmers Alliance." Image ID: 3397. Wisconsin Historical Society, https://www.wisconsinhistory.org/Records/Image/IM3397, accessed August 29, 2019.
5 "Agrarian uprising": Benjamin O. Flower, *Progressive Men, Women, and Movements of the Past Twenty-five Years* (Boston: The New Arena, 1914), 96.
6 According to Tilly, three criteria are necessary for a social movement: a campaign linking "claimants" and "object(s) of claims," "repertoires of collective action" that embody the campaign and "WUNC displays," in other work participants' demonstration of worthiness, unity, numbers and commitment in order to influence collective representations. Tarrow focuses on four variables: political struggle, resource mobilisation, cultural frames and a general context of grievances. McAdam et al. insist on three factors: political opportunities, mobilising structures and cultural framings. Charles Tilly, *Social Movements, 1768–2004* (Boulder, CO: Paradigm Publishers, 2004), 3–4; Sidney G. Tarrow, *Power in Movement: Social Movements and Contentious Politics* (Cambridge: Cambridge University Press, 1998), 16; Doug McAdam et al., *Comparative Perspective on Social Movements. Political Opportunities, Mobilizing Structures, and Cultural Framings* (Cambridge: Cambridge University Press, 1996), 6.

than getting it across two states.⁷ Traditional parties were unresponsive and left them only one option: to mobilise. Mobilising means transforming passive individuals into an active group in the pursuit of common goals, here rescuing the distressed agrarian world dependent on farmers' well-being through cooperatives, government regulation and inflationary monetary policy. However, this transformation did not emerge out of nothing: it built upon decades of grassroots organising efforts by the Greenback-Labor Party, which focused on antimonopoly and currency reform, the Knights of Labor, a labour federation, and the Grange, an agrarian fraternal organisation and advocacy group. These institutions had been declining: Farmers' Alliances seized the opportunity and took up the torch of reform and even radicalised their antimonopoly demands.⁸

Crises and political opportunities provided the incentive, but social movements also needed to mobilise resources to take political action. The movement did not suddenly develop because agrarians felt the same grievances at the same time. Instead, the organisational campaign devised notably by Charles Macune combined several organisations that led to massive mobilisation of ordinary Americans. According to Macune, farmers had to "employ the same professional and business methods that other commercial interests employed to gain political influence and bargaining strength in the national economy."⁹ He followed a policy of non-partisanship and mergers. He joined forces with other farmers and workers' organisations, such as the Arkansas-based Agricultural Wheel. He set up an office in Washington to direct the national lobbying efforts of the Alliance, oversaw the National Reform Press Association and edited the National Farmers' Alliance and Industrial Union's official paper, *The National Economist*, mailed to 100,000 weekly subscribers.¹⁰ Periphery agrarians wanted to integrate the new progressive national project. The explicit political horizon was national: like other professional organisations, the Alliance was centralised but the pyramidal structure did not mean that it was a top-down process. On the contrary, the central locus of the Alliance experience was the 40,000 sub-alliances across rural America. The national organisation, via county and state alliances, came only afterwards. With sometimes as few as half a dozen members, sub-alliances were

---

7 Hicks, *The Populist Revolt*, 61.
8 Worth Robert Miller, "Farmers and Third-Party Politics," *The Gilded Age: Essays on the Origins of Modern America*, ed. Charles W. Calhoun (1996) (Lanham, MD: Rowman & Littlefield Publishers, Inc., 2006), 283–306; Postel, *The Populist Vision*, 33; Goodwyn, *The Populist Moment*, 44.
9 Charles Postel, "Populist Origins – The Farmers' Alliance." *American Populism, 1876–1896* (Northern Illinois Digital Library), https://digital.lib.niu.edu/illinois/gildedage/populism, accessed August 29, 2019.
10 Postel, *The Populist Vision*, 37–40.

the fertile ground for what Goodwyn called a "movement culture," a "mass expression of a new political vision."[11]

Common Practices for a Common Vision

Mobilisation implied common practices: the "movement culture" involved frequent local Alliance meetings where members ate together to discuss cooperative efforts, meetings where the whole family came. They also provided socialisation opportunities and mutual assistance for sick or widowed neighbours. Social events cemented political ties.[12] County Alliance meetings were like spectacles. Trains of wagons trekked to camp meetings.[13] Picnics were organised where rank and file members talked among themselves about their vision for a fairer future, sang, listened to speeches given by Alliance lecturers but also by any "Member of the Order." Food and refreshments were shared or bought to finance Alliance literature.[14] Boston reformer, publisher and editor Benjamin O. Flower noted that agrarian peripheries were "electrified by political mass-meetings" and that "the campaign took on the aspect of a religious revival."[15] Flower financed realistic novelist Hamlin Garland's field study of the Kansas uprising. The result was serialised in Flower's radical magazine *The Arena* in 1892 and published afterwards in book form. Not only did the novel refute the image of Populists as "cranks" and reveal the "power of the people when once awakened," but its female protagonist explains how the "movement has come into [farmers'] lives like a new religion – the religion of humanity." Garland's book, Flower insisted, "should be read by every American farmer and every member of the Farmers' Alliance and Industrial Union."[16] The revivalist style

---

[11] *The Topeka Commonwealth*, "How to Organize an Alliance," February 8, 1881; Goodwyn, *The Populist Moment*, 33, 178.
[12] Ibid., 33–34.
[13] "Populist group, Dickinson County, Kansas." 1890s. Kansas Historical Society, https://www.kansasmemory.org/item/24949, accessed August 29, 2019.
[14] Dover Township Farmers' Alliance. "Farmers' Alliance picnic!" Darling & Douglass, Printers, Topeka, KS, August 28, 1889. Kansas Historical Society, https://www.kansasmemory.org/item/211923, accessed August 29, 2019.
[15] Flower. *Progressive Men*, 98.
[16] Hamlin Garland, *A Son of the Middle Border* (1917) (New York: Penguin Books, 1995), 329–344; *A Spoil of Office: A Story of the Modern West* (Boston: The Arena Publishing Company, 1892), 157; Flower, "Notes and Announcements. *A Spoil of Office*," *The Arena* 5 (1892): xliv–xlvii; "Books of the day. *A Spoil of Office*," *The Arena* 6 (1892): xli–xlvi.

and religious rhetoric should not blind us however to the fact that meetings were first and foremost political rallies.

Populist literature was meant to account for the unprecedented mobilisation in agrarian peripheries. Ordinary people were portrayed as actors of their own history. Their story was nonetheless told from the point of view of middle-class intellectuals such as Garland or Flower who, even if they were sympathetic and militant, silenced agrarians. Songs are a way for historians to recover the voice of the rank and file: "the people" can then be the actor and the author of their history. "Our Battle Song," for instance, rewrites the Civil War song "Hold the Fort." In 1864, Union troops had held a fort near Atlanta until Sherman's army rescued them. The incident became a song that was reprised by an evangelist who urged listeners to hold on until Jesus came back. It was published in sheet music, parodied by the British Transport Workers and imitated by the Knights of Labor who turned the defensive song into a call to "storm the fort" of "tyrant laws." The Populist version continued in the same vein: "brawn and brain" struggle against "injustice" and "the people" against "money kings"; the union of producers – Farmers' Alliances and Knights of Labor – echoes the Union of patriots during the Civil War. In the song, Populists carry on the Lincolnian struggle for emancipation ("Who would be a slave?"). They use a common trope among radicals: demanding profound changes in order to recapture the American promise. Populists re-appropriate the traditional form of patriotic songs but reframe it as a radical economic critique of the new "traitors" of the 1890s: monopolies and financiers.[17] What is unprecedented is not so much the form as the sense of agency it underscores, the discreet and unnoticed – but not insignificant – infrapolitical acts of resistance the rewriting reveals or, at least, the "insurgent definition" of their community it empowered agrarians to give.[18]

Alliance meetings reframed well-known repertoires of contention – revivalist rhetoric and patriotic songs – for their own political ends. Common practices forged a common militant culture and gave supporters a new "vision" of modernisation and fairness. Populists advocated large-scale bureaucratic organisation and centralisation as well as a stronger federal government. However, modern methods to rationalise markets and politics built upon traditional notions of

---

[17] "Our Battle Song." *Alliance Songster*. S.l.: s.n., circa 1890. Kansas Historical Society, https://www.kansasmemory.org/item/209682, accessed August 29, 2019. "Hold the Fort." S.l.n.d. Union Songs, https://unionsong.com/u511.html, accessed August 29, 2019.

[18] James C. Scott, *Domination and the Arts of Resistance: Hidden Transcripts* (New Haven: Yale University Press, 1990); Roger Chartier, "Le monde comme représentation," *Annales. Économies, Sociétés, Civilisations*, 44ᵉ année, no. 6 (1989): 1514.

agrarian justice, in particular the principles encapsulated in Thomas Jefferson's apocryphal maxim "equal rights to all, special privileges to none," then ubiquitous in Populist writings.[19] The significance of the movement lay in the mobilisation of millions of common working people with sunburnt necks to moralise and modernise capitalism and politics by ensuring fair access to the benefits of modernity. Mobilisation empowered them and gave them a sense of possibility and autonomy, "individual self-respect" and "collective self-confidence." They could conceive the idea of acting in "self-generated democratic ways – as distinct from passively participating in various hierarchical modes bequeathed by the received culture."[20] The two building blocks of Alliance mass democratic politics were education and cooperation.

Cooperatives

Cotton and wheat crops were sold on national and global markets: prices dropped but costs went up, in particular railroad rates and credit. Cooperatives were a way to attack an economic system skewed against farmers and to "organize as intelligently and solidly as the Standard Oil Company has," as Nelson Dunning, a Farmers' Alliance publicist and historian, put it.[21] Farmers responded to structural problems. First, they built self-help cooperative stores to get cheaper freight rates from railroad companies or to buy guano to fertilise their fields from South America but then they launched experiments in large-scale cooperatives such as The Texas Farmers' Alliance Exchange. The Alliance Exchange, organised in 1887 by Charles Macune, was meant to cut out middlemen and negotiate higher prices with purchasers in New Orleans, New York, Hanover and Liverpool. The Exchange would provide farmers with cheap credit and centralise purchasing of farm supplies and consumer goods, from cook stoves to ploughs. Alliance members viewed cooperatives as a "model for the future, combining modern technique, centralisation, and economies of scale to serve the marketing and credit

---

[19] Data mining in multiple databases shows that the maxim was rare in print culture before 1890 (Newspaper.com, Google Books, HathiTrust), even if secondary sources often attribute the sentence to Jefferson. In 1911, a Republican Congressman ironically observed that the sentence was a vague paraphrase, by an unknown source, of a passage from Jefferson's First Inaugural Address, probably "Equal and exact justice to all men." In the years around 1900, the maxim could be found everywhere in reforming circles and was invoked as a self-evident historical truth. *Congressional Record*, April 18, 1911, 365.
[20] Goodwyn, *The Populist Moment*, xix, 33.
[21] Dunning, *The Farmers' Alliance History*, 182.

needs" of larger and smaller farmers. However, the project failed. Almost all of the efforts to control and regulate markets "quickly succumbed to the combined pressures of poverty, the global market, and the organized opposition of merchants, and railroad managers." Farmers were too poor to invest enough capital in cooperatives and not mobilised enough to compete with railroad companies and corporations.[22] According to Goodwyn, cooperatives made mobilisation possible: "the subsequent experience of millions of farmers within their cooperatives proceeded to 'educate' them about the prevailing forms of economic power and privilege," thus radically altering their political consciousness. For other historians, the evidence does not support this confrontational vision. There were not enough cooperatives to involve many farmers, nor were they created in the sequence Goodwyn's theory demands. Farmers also did not need to create a unique subculture to know about democratic and currency reforms:

> [Farmers] responded to their adversity in a manner typical of a people with a long tradition of political participation. [...] With their political culture in place, and with a reform program inherited from the Greenback, antimonopoly, and labor movements readily available from the inception of their movement, the farmers arose in a great surge of political protest, a political prairie fire. [...] In their basically incremental approach they were similar to most other successful protest groups in America.[23]

The cooperative vision, whether it was part of a long tradition or an unprecedented mobilisation drive, did mobilise farmers who discussed "the cooperative commonwealth."[24] And discussion was central for Alliance mobilisation.

Print Culture

According to the *Kansas City Times*, "local alliances were the backbone of the movement." Organising them in networks and using large-circulation newspapers accounted for its success in Kansas. The official organ of the Alliance, the *Kansas Farmer*, together with *The Advocate*, calmly mobilised citizens through

---

22 Postel, "Populist Origins," online; *The Populist Vision*, 103–133.
23 Stanley B. Parsons et al., "The Role of Cooperatives in the Development of the Movement Culture of Populism," *Journal of American History* 69, no. 4 (1983): 868, 884–885.
24 The phrase had been central in reforming circles since Grönlund published *The Coöperative Commonwealth* in 1884; Laurence Grönlund, *The Coöperative Commonwealth in its Outlines: An Exposition of Modern Socialism* (Boston: Lee and Shepard, 1884).

the power of accurate figures and investigative journalism.[25] The key grassroots organisation was the sub-alliance and the key idea of the sub-alliance was empowerment through education. The Farmers' Alliance called itself "the most powerful and complete educator of modern times."[26] As one lecturer said, the "sub-alliance is a schoolroom" and neighbourhood organisations actually met in schoolhouses where members could learn about history, literature, scientific farming and political economy: commerce, regulation and monetary systems. Local intellectuals, such as ministers, teachers, doctors and newspaper editors, served as a cadre for the movement and mobilised both educated and practically illiterate members. Other institutions fed the demand for up-to-date knowledge: extensive lecturing circuits with more than 40,000 traveling lecturers who promoted discussion and questioning, a national network of hundreds of reform newspapers, large quantities of inexpensive books and pamphlets, lending libraries and book clubs.[27] Mobilising meant circulating reform literature. In 1890, Populists took control of the Kansas legislatures. In 1892, even more People's Party candidates were elected. In a cartoon, radical freethinking artist Watson Heston attributes this success to the "Alliance Circulating Library": reforming newspapermen, businessmen, workingmen and farmers are requesting publications from a female librarian, notably books on political economy and dystopias describing what would happen in the future if nothing was done to reform the country.[28] People began "to think as well as to throb," as one historian put it. In a novel, the narrator notes: "People commenced to think who had never thought before, and people talked who had seldom spoken. [...] Little by little they commenced to theorize upon their condition. Despite the poverty of the country, the books of Henry George, Bellamy, and other economic writers were bought as fast as the dealers could supply them."[29]

Grassroots members were readers: "communities of print" had made this "awakening of language" possible. Agrarians discovered "new and radical pow-

---

25 *Kansas City Times.* "How it was organized," reprinted in *The Advocate* [Meridien, KS], November 19, 1890, 11.
26 *National Economist.* "Alliance Education." November 11, 1890.
27 McMath, *American Populism*, 151. Goodwyn, *The Populist Moment*, xxi.
28 Heston also illustrated *The Bible Comically Illustrated* in 1900; Watson Heston, "The Campaign of Education," *American Nonconformist and Kansas Industrial Liberator* [Winfield, KS], July 9, 1891, 1. Newspapers.com, https://www.newspapers.com/image/366919553/, accessed August 29, 2019.
29 Comer Vann Woodward, *Tom Watson: Agrarian Rebel* (1938) (New York: Oxford University Press, 1963), 13; Elizabeth Higgins Sullivan, *Out of the West: A Novel* (New York and London: Harpers & Brothers, 1902), 133, 136.

ers in words."[30] More material factors were also at work: new printing technologies, cheaper paper, linotype machines for composition, rural free delivery of mail as well as low second-class mail rates (one cent a pound for printed matter disseminating information of a public character), the development of advertising that cut prices as well as "boilerplates," that is to say time- and money-saving partial printing plates received by mail and ready to print. A reformer only needed 150$ to start a paper, so most small towns had at least one local newspaper often edited, composed and printed by the same person. As a result, newspapers had grown exponentially.[31] Alliance papers used different textual and typographical strategies to shape their own "interpretive community" and influence their members' reading, what one historian calls the "mobilization of bias": clubbing offers to buy several Alliance newspapers, quoting and reprinting articles from other Alliance papers that made tenets of the movement viral.[32]

The 1890s also saw the advent of a "magazine revolution," a new generation of cheaper mass-circulation magazines relying on advertising revenue and adopting "a brisker, more personal, and more muscular style, promoting reading for awareness of the new, the timely, and the most progressive."[33] The network of local radical periodicals and the National Reform Press Association relayed the work of lecturers and cooperative organisers. National magazines, such as *The Arena*, gave a national voice to this political ferment. *The Arena* was more radical than all the other magazines, "a multiple-crusade magazine of general circulation" and the only Eastern magazine to support the agrarian revolt. It was its "textbook": Alliance members quoted *The Arena* in speeches and meetings

---

30 "Communities of print": Tarrow, *Power in Movement*, 50; "Awakening of language": Alan Trachtenberg, *The Incorporation of America: Culture and Society in the Gilded Age* (New York: Hill and Wang, 1982), 178.

31 McMath, *American Populism*, 148–150; *Data Visualization: Journalism's Voyage West*, "The Growth of Newspapers Across the U.S.: 1690–2011," Rural West Initiative, Bill Lane Center for the American West, Stanford University, http://web.stanford.edu/group/ruralwest/cgi-bin/drupal/visualizations/us_newspapers, accessed September 20, 2016.

32 Stanley Fish, *Is There a Text in This Class? The Authority of Interpretive Communities* (Cambridge & London: Harvard University Press, 1980), 97; E.E. Schattschneider in David Paul Nord, *Communities of Journalism: A History of American Newspapers and Their Readers* (Urbana & Chicago: University of Illinois Press, 2001), 248.

33 Richard Ohmann, "Chapter 6. Diverging Paths. Books and Magazines in the Transition to Corporate Capitalism," *A History of the Book in America. Volume 4. Print in Motion. The Expansion of Publishing and Reading in the United States, 1880–1940*, ed. Carl F. Kaestle and Janice A. Radway (Chapel Hill: University of Carolina Press, 2009), 108; Matthew Schneirov, *The Dream of a New Social Order: Popular Magazines in America, 1893–1914* (New York: Columbia University Press, 1994), 60.

and leaders of the movement wrote in the magazine.[34] Farmers' Alliances used local papers and *The Arena* to build an alternative political culture and circumvent mainstream media which, so they said, misrepresented the movement. Sociologists of social movements call this "framing," in other words "fashioning shared understandings of the world and of themselves that legitimate and motivate collective action," what Tilly also calls WUNC displays (worthiness, unity, numbers and commitment).[35] Displays of worthiness implied fighting against the ridicule heaped upon the Farmers' Alliance in mainstream media and political circles. Alliance members were not "cranks," as critics scornfully said then, but used the latest scientific data to support their arguments. Banners and songs signalled unity. Numbers were a regular feature of articles boasting about the development of the movement. Commitment was obvious: despite poverty, Alliance members bought newspapers and books and invested in cooperatives.

Thanks to cooperatives and the joint work of local papers, *The Arena* magazine and the National Reform Press Association, the Farmers' Alliance forged a direct link between grassroots organising and the new national forum where politics happened. Cooperatives united local farmers to compete on a national, and even global, market. Reform print linked local concerns and a national audience. Women, who were particularly mobilised, also connected homes to the national political arena.

A Case Study in Mobilisation: Women in Farmers' Alliances

Mobilising implies concrete places on top of print networks. "Grassroots settings," as Tilly calls them, facilitate and structure collective action: cooperatives, schoolhouses and also homes.[36] Women joined Farmers' Alliances in unprecedented numbers: 250,000 in 1890 only for the NFAIU. The second largest organisation, the Woman's Christian Temperance Union, boasted 160,000. Women joined for the same reasons men joined: they shared the work on the farm, experienced the same hardships and pressed for the same reforms to alleviate

---

34 Frank Luther Mott, *A History of American Magazines, Volume IV: 1885–1905* (Cambridge: Belknap Press of Harvard University Press, 1957), 408–410; Jean-Louis Marin-Lamellet, *Libérer et guérir: Benjamin Orange Flower ou les ambigüités du progressisme (1889–1918)* (Université de Lyon, PhD dissertation, 2016), https://tel.archives-ouvertes.fr/tel-01527128v2.
35 McAdam et al., *Comparative Perspective on Social Movements*, 6.
36 Tilly, *Social Movements*, 4.

rural poverty. Most farmers lived harsh lives in sod houses and sub-alliance meetings and newspapers focused on how to relieve the drudgery of daily chores by using modern methods and appliances. The better management of homes and gardens featured high in "home and garden" sections of newspapers. Improving living environments would also create better conditions for raising children: "in the idealized rural home women enjoyed the time and energy to attend to the moral and educational needs of the family."[37] However, it was difficult for women to live up to the ideal.

Farmers' Alliances also provided women with a means for advancement. They empowered activists who took part in the mobilising work. Only a few progressive political groups encouraged women to participate in politics: the Greenback party and the Union Labor party in the previous decades, Farmers' Alliances in the 1890s. Women also organised their own Alliance while working within the main organisation. For instance, women from Barton County in Kansas organised a Farmers' Alliance in July 1890. They travelled more than 10 miles, some even 18, to participate in the movement. Like men, they stood up for "equal rights to all [and] special privileges to none" and fought against political corruption and a "dangerous financial system, wherein the wealth of the country is fast passing from the hand of the many into the hands of the few." They explicitly pointed out to the common causes of mobilisation: "by such class legislation, not only are our brothers driven to poverty, but many of our own fair sex are driven to misery and woe, many are daily being driven from their homes." They also insisted on their rights as American citizens to take a stand and "assume a political character," even if traditional parties looked down on the move. Women saw their educational role within the movement as decisive and, even though they were "disfranchised," they were convinced they swayed elections: they had distributed 254 papers in the county and maintained a circulating library for the public and Alliance members (as in Watson Heston's cartoon). Although women were confined to the stereotypical roles of food provider in some groups, Barton County Farmers' Alliances members organised rallies with female speakers, a female chairman and a female reception committee, which showed what Populism could do in terms of political participation for women.[38] A good example of Alliance woman is the state secretary of the Nebraska Farmers' Alliance, Luna Kellie. She was the only leading woman of the Farmers' Alliance who spent her adult life on a rural homestead. In the

---

[37] Postel, *The Populist Vision*, 85, 76.
[38] *Proceedings of the Alliance Women's Association of Barton County, Kansas* (Great Bend, KS: Beacon Job Print, 1891), Kansas Historical Society, www.kansasmemory.org/item/207942, accessed August 29, 2019.

1920s, she wrote her memoirs on the back of old Farmers' Alliance certificates. She told about her hopes for a better future and about the mental and physical woes she endured on the farm. Kellie tirelessly corresponded, edited and set type: her rural home was the hub of a great network linking isolated farmers across the country.[39] Advocates of women's rights did not dissociate aspirations for equality from their demands for better homes: radical politics emerged from traditional places and family-friendly picnics.

Ordinary women were mobilised and became activists but Farmers' Alliances also attracted politically ambitious middle-class professionals, "a brilliant coterie of thoughtful and earnest ladies who have contributed so largely to the strength of the independent movement in the West," as reform editor Flower put it.[40] Eva McDonald-Valesh lectured for the Minnesota Farmers' Alliance and fought both for female farmers in the state and for female workers in Minneapolis and St Paul. She considered poverty to be a systemic problem affecting the "mortgage-cursed frontier" as much as big city tenements. McDonald-Valesh shows that, even though Alliances were farmers' organisations, there was no rural/urban divide but interdependent ecosystems and common interests between country and city dwellers.[41] Annie Diggs was a lawyer and writer who ran the National Reform Press Association and the Women's Alliance in Washington. She expounded the role of "women in the Alliance movement" in *The Arena*. Isolated farms were "recruiting stations" for "insane asylums" and political activism could wrest women from this debilitating life. Diggs also refuted "the frivolous theories of timorous or hostile objectors": "facts about women in politics" proved that this supposedly male activity did not "unsex" them.[42] Populist women terrified mainstream politicians and intellectuals because they challenged gender norms. A Kansas woman, Mary Elizabeth Lease – who, according to reporters, called on farmers to "raise less corn and more hell" – gained national prominence with her speeches that electrified audiences. Within the movement, mobilising worked in the same way for men and women. However, the perception of mobilisation differed. Of course, women, like men, were ridiculed because of their political and economic ideas but the most vicious attacks were reserved for the fact that not only did women mobilise (they had done so in abolitionist, temperance and suffrage movements), but they mobilised alongside

---

39 Luna Kellie, *A Prairie Populist: The Memoirs of Luna Kellie*, ed. Jane Nelsen Taylor (Iowa City: University of Iowa Press, 1992); Postel, *The Populist Vision*, 79–82.
40 Flower, "Notes and announcements. McDonald-Valesh," *The Arena* 5 (1892): li.
41 Eva McDonald-Valesh, "The Strength and Weakness of the People's Movement," *The Arena* 5 (1892): 726–731; "The Tenement House Problem in New York," *The Arena* 7 (1893): 580–586.
42 Annie L. Diggs, "The Women in the Alliance Movement," *The Arena* 6 (1892): 160–180.

men outside what were considered as female spheres. For example, despite Lease's militant calls for class warfare, it was her gender-role deviance that generated the vast majority of critics: Lease was portrayed as physically masculine and as an unfit mother. The simple fact of mobilising, in this context, defiled "true womanhood" and threatened the traditional social order.[43] In the satirical magazine *Puck*, female lecturers were compared to bearded ladies: they were a gender aberration to be relegated to freak shows.[44]

Although many women were leaders of the movement or lecturers for the cause, Farmers' Alliances did not fully live up to their promise of equality for ordinary women: it offered them visions of progress but, when they did not organise on their own, on their own terms, they were often "relegated to providing refreshments at Alliance meetings."[45] They thought about progress mostly in economic terms. Women's suffrage was not a priority within Farmers' Alliances and sparked off debates, but a vocal minority did campaign for the right to vote. For others, for instance Diggs, the question "pale[d] into relative inconsequence" when compared to economic issues and the "salvation of the imperilled homes of the nation."[46] They focused on women's "capacity for gainful employment," such as teachers or telephone operators, which was a way out of the drudgery of the farm. Mobilisation meant economic empowerment and, of course, education: "Educate your daughters that they may be independent," urged one Texas farmwoman.[47] In Hamlin Garland's novel about the agrarian revolt, *A Spoil of Office*, the Alliance lecturer Ida Wilbur exemplifies the empowered women within the movement. She electrifies the camp meeting at the beginning of the novel and she then acts as a guide for the hero, Bradley, in his political and sentimental journey. At the end, the newly-elected Congressman can challenge the corrupt capital thanks to her. In his review, Flowers explained that the book "should be read by every American woman" because it advocated "woman's absolute emancipation."[48] Ida Wilbur's analysis of the woman question highlights the debate within the Farmers' Alliance on the suffrage question:

> It is not a question of suffrage merely – suffrage is the smaller part of the woman-question – it is a question of equal rights. It is a question of whether the law of liberty applies to

---

[43] It also suggests that her opponents feared her strength in galvanising her audiences; Brooke Spear Orr, "Mary Elizabeth Lease: Gendered Discourse and Populist Party Politics in Gilded Age America," *Kansas History: A Journal of the Central Plains* 29, no. 4 (2006–2007): 256.
[44] *Puck's Library*. "Where Whiskers Go Better," no. 111, October 1896, unpaged.
[45] Postel, "Populist Origins," online.
[46] Diggs, "The Women in the Alliance Movement," 165.
[47] Postel, *The Populist Vision*, 71, 88.
[48] Flower, "Notes and Announcements. *A Spoil of Office*," xlv.

humanity or to men only. [...] The woman question is not a political one merely, it is an economic one. The real problem is the wage problem, the industrial problem. The real question is woman's dependence upon man as the bread-winner.[49]

Some reformers focused on economics; others thought suffrage was the key to raising women's status and power.

Farmers' Alliances later provided support for woman suffrage referenda. After the People's Party was created in 1892, Populist political mobilisation "did for woman suffrage reform what antislavery reform did for woman's rights in the 1830s: it provided a context that prepared and enabled white men to see the political exclusion of women as unjust." Both women and Populists were excluded by dominant parties and espoused egalitarian ideals. Thanks to Populists, the measure passed in Colorado (1893) and Idaho (1896) but failed in Kansas (1894) and California (1896). The suffrage movement became associated with Populism and suffered for more than a decade after 1896.[50] Even though Populist state governments helped women win the right to vote and Farmers' Alliances in the Midwest and West supported women's suffrage at the local and state level, some Populists, mainly in the South, opposed women entering politics. As a result of regional divisions and of the precedence of economic issues, the national Populist Party failed to include a woman suffrage plank in its platform. However ambivalent the movement may seem in hindsight, anti-suffragists nonetheless associated woman suffrage with "Populism of the most extravagant type."[51]

Conclusion: Successes and Limits

The revolt of periphery agrarians terrorised mainstream politicians and intellectuals. Farmers' Alliances were branded as "menacing socialism from the Western

---

49 Garland, *A Spoil of Office*, 142–143.
50 The next state victory did not come until 1910. By then, Populists' radical ideas had merged with western Progressivism and found mainstream support among middle-class urban Progressives; Suzanne M. Marille, *Woman Suffrage and the Origins of Liberal Feminism in the United States, 1820–1920* (Cambridge: Harvard University Press, 1996), 124–158, 155 (quote); Rebecca J. Mead, "The Woman Suffrage Movement in the United States," *Oxford Research Encyclopedia of American History*, March 28, 2018, Oxford University Press, https://oxfordre.com/americanhistory/view/10.1093/acrefore/9780199329175.001.0001/acrefore-9780199329175-e-17, accessed September 10, 2019.
51 Helen K. Johnson, *Woman and the Republic: A survey of the woman suffrage movement in the United States and a discussion of the claims and arguments of its foremost advocates* (New York: D. Appleton & Co, 1897), 102.

States" and belittled as "cranks." A *Judge* cartoon depicted Populists in a balloon literally filled with "hot air": reformers are spreading the word of "lunacy" and throwing out papers that read "government control of railroad and telegraph."[52] Measuring the success of mobilisation with distraught reactions does not however do justice to its internal dynamics. Even if they failed as an economic movement, Farmers' Alliances created a "movement culture" among the rural lower- and middle-class. They organised "parallel institutions where people could experiment with democratic forms": cooperation, education and spaces for ordinary citizens to think and act, a rupture in ordinary life where they could invent their own language of protest.[53] The initial piecemeal actions converted into sustained mobilisation because the movement faced powerful opponents, such as railroad companies, banks and unresponsive parties (in the Democratic South, Populism also faced intimidations and lynchings). Mobilisation was also based on "dense social networks and connective structures" and on a pattern of agrarian antimonopoly protest inaugurated after the Civil War.[54]

Farmers' Alliances mobilised women and African Americans.[55] They wanted to convince their members to vote for their economic interests and not according to their sectional, ethnic, gender and racial identities.[56] Mobilisation had to face sharp divisions though: between North and South, white farm owners and immigrant labourers, progressive and conservative members on the suffrage question, Whites and African Americans, and farmers and workers. As historian Laura Grattan notes: "Some [Populists] were open to building popular power across lines of race, gender, and class; others became exemplars of white supremacy,

---

[52] *The New York Times* ridiculed the agrarian movement, condemning the "essential crankiness of cranks." During his six-year term as U.S. Senator from Kansas between 1891–1897, Populist politician William Peffer kept scrapbooks of political cartoons deriding the agrarian mobilisation: https://www.kansasmemory.org/item/212843. "Menacing Socialism in the Western States," *Forum* 15 (1893): 322–342; "A Party of Patches," *Judge* 20, June 6, 1891, cover; *The New York Times*, "Socialism and Populism," August 2, 1896, 4.

[53] Lawrence Goodwyn, *Democratic Promise: The Populist Movement in America* (New York: Oxford University Press, 1976), 606.

[54] Tarrow, *Power in Movement*, 29.

[55] At least 250,000 African Americans were members of the Colored Alliance, even if estimates vary; Omar H. Ali, *In the Lion's Mouth: Black Populism in the New South, 1886–1900* (Jackson: University Press of Mississippi, 2010), 53.

[56] Garland's novel, *Jason Edwards*, was dedicated to Farmers' Alliances "whose high mission [was] to unite the farmer and the artisan, the north and the south, the blue and the gray under one banner, marching in a continent-wide battle-line against the denial of equal rights." Hamlin Garland, *Jason Edwards: An Average Man* (Boston: The Arena Publishing Company, 1892), dedication.

nativism and patriarchy."⁵⁷ Interracial mobilisation was effectively inhibited by the "separate but equal" theory. The Southern and Northern Alliances were white-only organisations. The Colored Farmers' Alliance was a "separate movement" with its own "leaders, organizations, demands and experiences." Instances of biracial coalitions did occur in Tom Watson's Georgia, in Grimes County, Texas, or in Wilmington, North Carolina, but they all ended tragically, respectively with disenfranchisement, murders and a coup.⁵⁸ The Colored Farmers' Alliance was "the largest movement of African Americans in the United States until the modern civil rights movement" but, because of the threat of an empowered black electorate in the South, especially in alliance with poor white farmers, Democrats extended segregation into virtually every aspect of southern life.⁵⁹ Or, were Farmers' Alliances instrumental in the creation of Jim Crow laws in the 1890s?⁶⁰ Were segregation and disenfranchisement the consequence of mobilisation or one of its premises? The paucity of sources complicates the history of black Populism and more research needs to be done.

Despite its limits in terms of interracial inclusiveness, mobilisation, as a process, was successful for both races. However, it did not necessarily translate into political change and policy reform. As a non-partisan organisation, the Alliance mobilised its members to use their vote to pressure major parties into pledging support for their demands. When it failed to reconnect political parties with ordinary citizens' grievances, grassroots mobilisation moved into electoral politics. The Colored Farmers' Alliance in particular saw a national party as a way out of violent regional politics. The failure of cooperatives also drew reforms toward political action. The different alliances eventually united and created an independent third party in 1892. Within the Farmers' Alliance, some refused to abandon non-partisanship. The question of "going into politics" divided the organisation. Populists were electorally successful at all levels though. Presidential candidate James Weaver won four states and got 8.5 per cent of the popular vote in 1892 and 22 electoral votes. However, when the party nominated Democratic

---

57 Laura Grattan, *Populism's Power: Radical Grassroots Democracy in America* (Oxford: Oxford University Press, 2016), 54.
58 The Southern Alliance also broke the 1891 black cotton pickers' strike to get a minimum wage; Thomas E. Watson, "The Negro Question in the South," *The Arena* 6 (1892): 540–550; Woodward, *Tom Watson: Agrarian Rebel*; Ali, *In the Lion's Mouth*, xiv, 142–144; Lawrence Goodwyn. "Populist Dreams and Negro Rights: East Texas as a Case Study," *The American Historical Review* 76, no. 5 (1971): 1435–1456.
59 Ali, *In the Lion's Mouth*, 10, 165–166.
60 Postel contends that they accepted racial separation because it was "an essential part of the New South doctrine of progressive development." Postel, *The Populist Vision*, 175.

candidate William Jennings Bryan in 1896, Democrats co-opted agrarian reform. Divisions between Populists who advocated fusion with the Democratic Party and those who wished to remain independent eventually killed the party. Mobilisation faltered when political principles clashed with questions of strategy (independent action or not).

However, even if the Farmers' Alliance and then the Populist Party disappeared, their grassroots strategies did reconnect the Democratic Party with mobilised periphery agrarians in the long term. The seeds of reform were planted and Democrats, which had traditionally been linked to limited government, became the party of government intervention. Populism also influenced the Progressive movement. For instance, President Wilson pushed for reforms first promoted by Farmers' Alliances. As Kazin contends, Populism, like socialism, changed the political climate: its "disruptive potential and moral critique" convinced "prominent politicians from both major parties to make a decisive break from the gospel of laissez-faire" and "helped powerful liberals reform the nation."[61] Sanders concurs:

> Agrarian movements constituted the most important political force driving the development of the American national state in the first half century before World War I. And by shaping the form of early regulatory legislation and establishing the centrality of the farmer-labor alliance to progressive reform and the Democratic Party, the agrarian influence was felt for years thereafter.[62]

Short-term victories – suffrage referenda and interracial coalition – quickly turned into failures. Even if mobilisation (as an outcome) failed, it nonetheless gave marginalised actors a sense of agency undreamed-of in a society that was growing beyond human scale. In 1914, Walter Lippmann opened his book, *Drift and Mastery*, on a quote by English professor Graham Wallas that captured the process that had been transforming the U.S. in the previous decades: "One effect of this transformation is a general change of social scale. Men find themselves working and thinking and feeling in relation to an environment, which, both in its worldwide extension and its intimate connection with all sides of human existence, is without precedent in the history of the world." Massive mobilisation was possible because agrarians' problems – and solutions – were na-

---

61 Michael Kazin. *American Dreamers: How the Left Changed a Nation* (New York: Alfred Knopf, 2011), 108, 110.
62 Sanders, *Roots of Reform*, 1.

tional and global in scope but also because the rapid development of print culture could connect this international arena to intimate experiences.[63]

Bibliography

Primary Sources

Congressional Record. April 18, 1911, 365.
Diggs, Annie L. "The Women in the Alliance Movement." *The Arena* 6 (1892): 160–180.
Dover Township Farmers' Alliance. "Farmers' Alliance picnic!" Darling & Douglass, Printers, Topeka, KS, August 28, 1889. Kansas Historical Society, https://www.kansasmemory.org/item/211923. Accessed August 29, 2019.
Dunning, Nelson A. *The Farmers' Alliance History and Agricultural Digest.* Washington, DC: The Alliance Publishing Company, 1891.
"First Farmers Alliance." Image ID: 3397. Wisconsin Historical Society, https://www.wisconsinhistory.org/Records/Image/IM3397. Accessed August 29, 2019.
Flower, Benjamin O. "Books of the day. *A Spoil of Office.*" *The Arena* 6 (1892): xli–xlvi.
Flower, Benjamin O. "Notes and announcements. McDonald-Valesh." *The Arena* 5 (1892): li.
Flower, Benjamin O. "Notes and Announcements. A Spoil of Office." *The Arena* 5 (1892): xliv–xlvii.
Flower, Benjamin O. *Progressive Men, Women, and Movements of the Past Twenty-five Years.* Boston: The New Arena, 1914.
Garland, Hamlin. *Jason Edwards: An Average Man.* Boston: The Arena Publishing Company, 1892.
Garland, Hamlin. *A Son of the Middle Border.* 1917. New York: Penguin Books, 1995.
Garland, Hamlin. *A Spoil of Office: A Story of the Modern West.* Boston: The Arena Publishing Company, 1892.
Garvin W.L., and S.O. Daws. *History of the National Farmers' Alliance and Co-operative Union of America.* Jacksboro, TX: J.N. Rogers & Co, 1887.
Grönlund, Laurence. *The Coöperative Commonwealth in its Outlines: An Exposition of Modern Socialism.* Boston: Lee and Shepard, 1884.
Heston, Watson. "The Campaign of Education." *American Nonconformist and Kansas Industrial Liberator* [Winfield, KS], July 9, 1891, 1. Newspapers.com, https://www.newspapers.com/image/366919553/. Accessed August 29, 2019.
"Hold the Fort." S.l.n.d. Union Songs, https://unionsong.com/u511.html. Accessed August 29, 2019.
Johnson, Helen K. *Woman and the Republic: A survey of the woman suffrage movement in the United States and a discussion of the claims and arguments of its foremost advocates.* New York: D. Appleton & Co, 1897.
Judge. "A Party of Patches," vol. 20, June 6, 1891, cover.

---

[63] Walter Lippmann. *Drift and Mastery: An Attempt to Diagnose the Current Unrest* (New York: M. Kennerley, 1914), 35–36 and epigraph.

Kansas City Times. "How it was organized," reprinted in *The Advocate* [Meridien, KS], November 19, 1890, 11.

Kellie, Luna. *A Prairie Populist: The Memoirs of Luna Kellie*, edited by Jane Nelsen Taylor. Iowa City: University of Iowa Press, 1992.

Lippmann, Walter. *Drift and Mastery: An Attempt to Diagnose the Current Unrest*. New York: M. Kennerley, 1914.

McDonald-Valesh, Eva. "The Strength and Weakness of the People's Movement." *The Arena* 5 (1892): 726–731.

McDonald-Valesh, Eva. "The Tenement House Problem in New York." *The Arena* 7 (1893): 580–586.

McVey, Frank. *The Populist Movement*. New York: Macmillan, 1896.

Morgan, W. Scott. *History of the Wheel and Alliance and the Impending Revolution*. Hardy, AR: published by the author; St. Louis: C.B. Woodward, 1891.

National Economist. "Alliance Education." November 11, 1890.

"Our Battle Song." *Alliance Songster*. S.l.: s.n., circa 1890. Kansas Historical Society, https://www.kansasmemory.org/item/209682. Accessed August 29, 2019.

Peffer, William. Scrapbooks. https://www.kansasmemory.org/item/212843. Accessed August 29, 2019.

"Populist group, Dickinson County, Kansas." 1890s. Kansas Historical Society, https://www.kansasmemory.org/item/24949. Accessed August 29, 2019.

Proceedings of the Alliance Women's Association of Barton County, Kansas. Great Bend, KS: Beacon Job Print, 1891. Kansas Historical Society, www.kansasmemory.org/item/207942. Accessed August 29, 2019.

Puck's Library. "Where Whiskers Go Better," no. 111, October 1896, unpaged.

Sullivan, Elizabeth Higgins. *Out of the West: A Novel*. New York and London: Harpers & Brothers, 1902.

The New York Times. "Socialism and Populism." August 2, 1896, 4.

The Topeka Commonwealth. "How to Organize an Alliance," February 8, 1881.

Tracy, F.B. "Menacing Socialism in the Western States." *Forum* 15 (1893): 322–342.

Watson, Thomas E. "The Negro Question in the South." *The Arena* 6 (1892): 540–550.

Secondary Sources

Ali, Omar H. *In the Lion's Mouth: Black Populism in the New South, 1886–1900*. Jackson: University Press of Mississippi, 2010.

Chartier, Roger. "Le monde comme représentation." *Annales. Économies, Sociétés, Civilisations*, 44ᵉ année, no. 6 (1989): 1505–1520.

Data Visualization: Journalism's Voyage West. "The Growth of Newspapers Across the U.S.: 1690–2011." Rural West Initiative, Bill Lane Center for the American West, Stanford University, http://web.stanford.edu/group/ruralwest/cgi-bin/drupal/visualizations/us_newspapers. Accessed September 20, 2016.

Edwards, Rebecca. *New Spirits: Americans in the Gilded Age, 1865–1905*. Oxford, New York: Oxford University Press, 2006.

Ferkiss, Victor C. "Populist Influences on American Fascism." *The Western Political Quarterly* 10, no. 2 (1957): 350–373.

Fish, Stanley. *Is There a Text in This Class? The Authority of Interpretive Communities.* Cambridge & London: Harvard University Press, 1980.

Flanagan, Maureen A. *America Reformed: Progressives and Progressivisms, 1890s-1920s.* New York: Oxford University Press, 2007.

Goodwyn, Lawrence. *Democratic Promise: The Populist Movement in America.* New York: Oxford University Press, 1976.

Goodwyn, Lawrence. "Populist Dreams and Negro Rights: East Texas as a Case Study." *The American Historical Review* 76, no. 5 (1971): 1435–1456.

Goodwyn, Lawrence. *The Populist Moment: A Short History of the Agrarian Revolt in America.* Oxford, New York: Oxford University Press, 1978.

Grattan, Laura. *Populism's Power: Radical Grassroots Democracy in America.* Oxford: Oxford University Press, 2016.

Hicks, John. *The Populist Revolt: A History of the Farmers' Alliance and the People's Party.* 1931. Lincoln, NE: University of Nebraska Press, 1961.

Hofstadter, Richard. *The Age of Reform: From Bryan to F.D.R.* New York: Vintage Books, 1955.

Kazin, Michael. *American Dreamers: How the Left Changed a Nation.* New York: Alfred Knopf, 2011.

Lasch, Christopher. *The True and Only Heaven: Progress and its Critics.* New York: W.W. Norton & Company, 1991.

Livingston, James. *Origins of the Federal Reserve System: Money, Class, and Corporate Capitalism, 1890–1913.* Ithaca: Cornell University Press, 1986.

Livingston, James. *Pragmatism, Feminism, and Democracy: Rethinking the Politics of American History.* New York: Routledge, 2001.

Marilley, Suzanne M. *Woman Suffrage and the Origins of Liberal Feminism in the United States, 1820–1920.* Cambridge: Harvard University Press, 1996.

Marin-Lamellet, Jean-Louis. *Libérer et guérir: Benjamin Orange Flower ou les ambigüités du progressisme (1889–1918). 2016.* Université de Lyon, PhD dissertation, https://tel.archives-ouvertes.fr/tel-01527128v2.

McAdam, Doug, et al. *Comparative Perspective on Social Movements. Political Opportunities, Mobilizing Structures, and Cultural Framings.* Cambridge: Cambridge University Press, 1996.

McMath, Robert C. *American Populism: A Social History, 1877–1898.* New York: Hill and Wang, 1993.

Mead, Rebecca J. "The Woman Suffrage Movement in the United States." *Oxford Research Encyclopedia of American History.* March 28, 2018. Oxford University Press. https://oxfordre.com/americanhistory/view/10.1093/acrefore/9780199329175.001.0001/acrefore-9780199329175-e-17. Accessed September 10, 2019.

Miller, Worth Robert. "A Centennial Historiography of American Populism." *Kansas History: A Journal of the Central Plains* 16, no. 1 (1993): 54–69.

Miller, Worth Robert. "Farmers and Third-Party Politics." *The Gilded Age: Essays on the Origins of Modern America*, edited by Charles W. Calhoun, 283–306. 1996. Lanham, MD: Rowman & Littlefield Publishers, Inc., 2006.

Mott, Frank Luther. *A History of American Magazines, Volume IV: 1885–1905.* Cambridge: Belknap Press of Harvard University Press, 1957.

Nord, David Paul. *Communities of Journalism: A History of American Newspapers and Their Readers.* Urbana & Chicago: University of Illinois Press, 2001.

Nugent, Walter. *Progressivism: A Very Short Introduction.* New York: Oxford University Press, 2009.

Ohmann, Richard. "Chapter 6. Diverging Paths. Books and Magazines in the Transition to Corporate Capitalism." In *A History of the Book in America. Volume 4. Print in Motion. The Expansion of Publishing and Reading in the United States, 1880–1940*, edited by Carl F. Kaestle and Janice A. Radway. Chapel Hill: University of Carolina Press, 2009.

Orr, Brooke Spear. "Mary Elizabeth Lease: Gendered Discourse and Populist Party Politics in Gilded Age America." *Kansas History: A Journal of the Central Plains* 29, no. 4 (2006–2007): 246–65.

Parrington, Vernon Louis. *Main Currents in American Thought: An Interpretation of American Literature from the Beginnings to 1920. Vol. 3. The Beginnings of Critical Realism in America: 1860–1920.* New York: Harcourt, Brace and Company, 1930.

Parsons, Stanley B. et al. "The Role of Cooperatives in the Development of the Movement Culture of Populism." *Journal of American History* 69, no. 4 (1983): 866–885.

Postel, Charles. *Equality: An American Dilemma, 1866–1896.* New York: Farrar, Straus and Giroux, 2019.

Postel, Charles. "Populist Origins – The Farmers' Alliance." *American Populism, 1876–1896.* Northern Illinois Digital Library, https://digital.lib.niu.edu/illinois/gildedage/populism. Accessed August 29, 2019.

Postel, Charles. *The Populist Vision.* Oxford; New York: Oxford University Press, 2007.

Rodgers, Daniel T. "Republicanism: The Career of a Concept." *The Journal of American History* 79, no. 1 (1992): 11–38.

Sanders, Elizabeth. *Roots of Reform: Farmers, Workers, and the American State, 1877–1917.* Chicago; London: University of the Chicago Press, 1999.

Schneirov, Matthew. *The Dream of a New Social Order: Popular Magazines in America, 1893–1914.* New York: Columbia University Press, 1994.

Scott, James C. *Domination and the Arts of Resistance: Hidden Transcripts.* New Haven: Yale University Press, 1990.

Tarrow, Sidney G. *Power in Movement: Social Movements and Contentious Politics.* Cambridge: Cambridge University Press, 1998.

Tilly, Charles. *Social Movements, 1768–2004.* Boulder, CO: Paradigm Publishers, 2004.

Trachtenberg, Alan. *The Incorporation of America: Culture and Society in the Gilded Age.* New York: Hill and Wang, 1982.

Wiebe, Robert. *The Search for Order, 1877–1920.* New York: Hill and Wang, 1967.

Woodward, Comer Vann. *Tom Watson: Agrarian Rebel.* 1938. New York: Oxford University Press, 1963.

Karine Rivière-De Franco
5 Women Speaking to Women?
Margaret Thatcher, Theresa May and the Female Electorate

Almost a century after Nancy Astor entered the House of Commons as the first woman MP – a consequence of the Representation of the People Act and the Parliament (Qualification of Women) Act passed in 1918[1] – Theresa May became the second woman Prime Minister of the United Kingdom. With Margaret Thatcher (Prime Minister from 1979 to 1990), they remain the exception in British political history. Over the course of the twentieth century the glass ceiling blocking women's progress in the political sphere has been cracked and women now practically constitute a "critical mass" in Westminster;[2] after the 2015 General Election, women represented 29 per cent of all Members of Parliament. However female politicians continue to face discrimination and sexism, as recent reports from the Inter-Parliamentary Union highlighted.[3] Sexist remarks from leading male politicians can still be heard in the Commons[4] and as the Fawcett Society – the United Kingdom's leading charity campaigning for women's rights – commented after the election, "the hardest gains for women in Parliament have yet to come, and it will become harder as we approach parity."[5]

Female politicians, as male ones, engage and communicate with voters in different ways. Political communication aims at persuading electors, convincing

---

[1] As an Irish Nationalist, Constance Markievicz, who was the first woman to be elected to Parliament in 1918, refused to sit.
[2] According to some theories, for women to have an impact on mainstream politics, they have to represent at least 30 per cent of all representatives; Sarah Childs, *Women and British Party Politics: Descriptive, Substantive and Symbolic Representation* (London: Routledge, 2008).
[3] *Sexism, harassment and violence against women parliamentarians*, 2016, https://www.ipu.org/resources/publications/issue-briefs/2016-10/sexism-harassment-and-violence-against-women-parliamentarians; *Sexism, harassment and violence against women in parliaments in Europe* (2018), https://www.ipu.org/resources/publications/issue-briefs/2018-10/sexism-harassment-and-violence-against-women-in-parliaments-in-europe, accessed April 6, 2020.
[4] "Calm down, dear" (David Cameron, 27/04/2011), "stupid woman" (Jeremy Corbyn, 19/12/2018), WATTS Joe, "Stupid woman: a mini history of sexism in Westminster, from Jeremy Corbyn to David Cameron", *The Independent*, 19/12/2018.
[5] The roots of the Fawcett Society are to be found in the London National Society for Women's Suffrage created in 1866 by Millicent Garrett Fawcett. It was relaunched as the Fawcett Society in 1953 and is considered as Britain's leading charity campaigning for women's rights, https://www.fawcettsociety.org.uk/blogs/blog/women-2015-general-election, accessed December 23, 2019.

wavering undecided and floating voters and mobilising supporters and party faithfuls. To make electioneering more effective, parties endeavour to adapt their messages to different subgroups of the electorate and what they believe are voters' main concerns. Targeting the electorate therefore constitutes a key element of modern campaigns[6] and women represent one of the categories that leaders may single out in their literature, speeches and statements.[7] This paper intends to analyse to what extent Margaret Thatcher and Theresa May, as the only female British Prime Ministers, attempted to address the female electorate and its priorities in their political communication, to mobilise these voters in favour of the Conservative Party and more generally to promote women's issues. The choice of these two politicians seems all the more relevant as political scientists have worked on the possible correlation between descriptive representation – the number of women represented at the different levels of power – and substantive representation – the defence of the specific interests of a particular group, the female population – to consider the impact that women may have on politics and to assess if female politicians do represent women's interests.[8]

The diachronic study covers two different periods of British politics: the 11 years of Thatcherism in the 1980s and Theresa May's brief premiership dominated by the consequences of the result of the referendum on British membership of the European Union in the second decade of the twenty-first century. In between these two eras, the United Kingdom underwent profound economic, social and cultural transformations, the role and status of women in society changed and gender expectations and prejudice evolved. Moreover, two male Prime Ministers decided to tackle one specific aspect of gender inequalities, women's political under-representation. Tony Blair implemented positive action measures to increase the number of female Labour MPs (All Women Shortlists), which led to

---

[6] For modern election campaigning, see Shaun Bowler and David M. Farrell (eds.), *Electoral Strategies and Political Marketing* (New York: St Martin's press, 1992); Dennis Kavanagh, *Election Campaigning. The New Marketing of Politics* (Oxford: Oxford University Press, 1995); Martin Rosenbaum, *From Soapbox to Soundbites. Party Political Campaigning in Britain since 1945* (London: Macmillan, 1997).
[7] Véronique Molinari, "Du 'vote des flappers' au 'vote à talons hauts': évolutions et constantes dans la mobilisation de l'électorat féminin par les partis politiques britanniques de 1920 à 2006", *Recherches féministes* 20, no. 1 (2007): 167–190.
[8] Sarah Childs, *Women and British Politics. Descriptive, Substantive and Symbolic Representation* (London: Routledge, 2008); Virginia Sapiro, "When are Interests Interesting," in *Feminism and Politics*, ed. Anne Phillips (Oxford: Oxford University Press, 1998), 161–192.

the historic number of 101 Labour women entering Parliament in 1997.⁹ When David Cameron – Theresa May's predecessor – won the Conservative Party leadership election, he launched a modernisation process. This included a feminisation of the party, in its membership as well as in its policy priorities.[10]

This chapter is based on a corpus of political and electoral sources: General Election manifestos – in particular the introductions written by party chiefs –, the speeches delivered by leaders at their party's annual conferences, Prime Ministers' answers during Question Time in the House of Commons (PMQT) and Acts of Parliament, the bills approved by MPs under their premierships.[11] After having examined the major characteristics of the female electorate and the historical relationship between the Conservative party, feminism and women, the communication of the two female British Prime Ministers will be analysed to determine if they attempted to mobilise female voters and address their concerns.

The Female Electorate and the Conservative Party

Women as a Target Group for Political Parties

Targeting voters is based on the assumption that different subgroups of the electorate – women but also ethnic minorities, young people, pensioners, Northerners or homeowners – may have specific interests, hold particular opinions and adopt distinct political attitudes. Shared experiences would thus lead to a belief in a common set of ideas and to a uniform homogeneous political behaviour.[12] Indeed, part of the reluctance to grant women the franchise was precisely the uncertainty over the way they would exercise such a power. The years after

---

9 The party landslide victory was also partly attributed to female voters, who had been wooed by New Labour. However, less than a third of all women was satisfied with the Labour government before the 2001 General Election; Véronique Molinari, op. cit.

10 In 2017 women represented 30 per cent of Conservative Party members, compared with 49 per cent in 1994; Tim Bell, Paul Webb and Monica Polletti, *Grassroots. Britain's party members: who they are, what they think and what they do* (Queen Mary University of London, 2018), https://esrcpartymembersprojectorg.files.wordpress.com/2018/01/grassroots-pmp_final.pdf, accessed April 8, 2020.

11 The corpus is made up of four General Election manifestos (1979, 1983, 1987, 2017), 14 conference speeches (1979–1990, 2016–2017), 244 PMQT (205 for 1979–1990, 39 for 2016–2017) and 618 Acts of Parliament (581 for 1979–1990, 37 for 2016–2017).

12 Lynda Lee Kaid, Dan Nimmo and Keith R. Sanders (eds.), *New Perspectives on Political Advertising* (Illinois: Southern Illinois University Press, 1986); Dennis Kavanagh, op. cit; Martin Rosenbaum, op. cit.

the franchise was first extended saw women's organisations try to create a women's bloc and to get organised as a distinct electoral force. At the same time, until the 1929 General Election, political parties specifically addressed the new electorate through public meetings, speeches and leaflets.[13] In the 1990s, attempts at mobilising women appeared, once again, to be a recurrent feature of election campaigns.[14]

It may prove more difficult for party leaders to address the female electorate in an effective way, as women are deemed to be less interested in politics than men. In 1979, 54 per cent of women declared some or a great deal of interest compared with 68 per cent of men, while 46 per cent of women claimed not much or no interest compared with 32 per cent of men. In 2017, 62 per cent of women reported some interest compared with 70 per cent of men.[15] Besides, the British Election Studies found that women were more likely to identify with the Conservatives than men (respectively 45 per cent and 38 per cent in 1964, 45 per cent and 42 per cent in 1987, 27 per cent and 25 per cent in 2005).[16] Party membership among women also tended to be higher in the Conservative Party (five per cent of all female party members belonged to the Conservative Party and two per cent to Labour in 1963, three per cent and one per cent in 1987),[17] even if it has declined since the 1990s (women represented 30 per cent of all members in 2017 compared with 49 per cent in 1994).[18]

---

[13] Véronique Molinari, op.cit.

[14] The Fawcett Society also highlighted the potential influence of the women's vote with the "Listen to my vote" campaign in 1996. Véronique Molinari, "Mobilisation des électrices et instrumentalisation de la différence: les campagnes électorales de 2004 et 2005 en Grande-Bretagne et aux Etats-Unis", in *Stratégies et campagnes électorales en Grande-Bretagne et aux Etats-Unis*, ed. Renée Dickason, David Haigron et Karine Riviere-de-Franco (Paris: L'Harmattan, 2009), 87–88.

[15] Ivor Crewe, Anthony Fox and Neil Day, *The British Electorate 1963–1992. A compendium of data from the British Election Studies* (Cambridge: Cambridge University Press, 1995), 153; Rosie Campbell, "The women's vote is a myth: the average voter is a female voter", 04/11/2019, https://www.kcl.ac.uk/news/the-womens-vote-is-a-myth-the-average-voter-is-a-female-voter, accessed April 6, 2020.

[16] Ivor Crewe, Anthony Fox and Neil Day, op. cit., 47–48. Robert Johns, *Gender and party identification: Another reason why affect versus cognition matters* (2006), 10, https://ecpr.eu/filestore/paperproposal/5ffde109-dd24-41c9-acbc-cc1b62ce995e.pdf, accessed 11/01/2020.

[17] Ivor Crewe, Anthony Fox and Neil Day, op. cit., 122.

[18] ESRC-funded Party Members Project, Queen Mary University of London and Sussex University, https://inews.co.uk/news/politics/conservative-party-members-tory-women-gender-balance-320515, accessed 11/01/2020.

As for gender (voting) gap,[19] women have tended indeed to have a voting behaviour that slightly differs from men's. Globally speaking, the gender gap has favoured the Conservatives: from 1979 to 2017, 39 per cent of women voted Conservative and 36 per cent Labour. Without female voters Labour would have won all elections between 1945 and 1979.[20] However the gap has evolved over the years. Whereas from 1979 to 1992 and from 2010 to 2015 most women were more supportive of the Conservatives than of Labour (+10 points), from 1997 to 2005, a majority of women turned to New Labour and Tony Blair (+7.5) and in 2017 the women's vote was evenly split (43 per cent each).[21] Therefore, in 2017 having a female leader did not prove an asset for the Conservatives as women did not disproportionately vote for the party as they had done in the 1980s. However, to understand women's voting behaviour, other variables, such as social class or ethnicity and, above all, age, have to be taken into account and studying a gender generational gap – a disproportionate percentage of younger women supporting Labour and of older women backing the Conservatives – may be more relevant.

To talk to the female electorate individually, parties rely on the assumption that this category of voters has specific concerns and priorities which differ from men's. Women's issues can be defined as policies whose direct and immediate consequences affect women more than men or subject matters which mostly concern women either for biological or social reasons.[22] The parties' electoral appeal would thus focus on these topics. Such a political strategy has been reinforced by the decline of the traditional class-based voting since the 1970s. Instead of demonstrating a social class-based pattern, voters tend to form a rational decision based on the comparison of the various political offers, the rational choice theory. Women's issues may therefore constitute one form of issue-based vot-

---

19 Joni Lovenduski and Pippa Norris, *Gender and Party Politics* (London: Sage Publications, 1993).
20 Pippa Norris quoted in Adrian Bingham, "Conservatism, Gender and the Politics of everyday life, 1950s-1980s", in *Rethinking right-wing women. Gender and the Conservative Party, 1880s to the Present*, edited by Clarisse Berthezène and Julie V. Gottlieb (Manchester: Manchester University Press, 2017), 157.
21 YouGov and Ipsos MORI in *The British General Election of 1979, 1983, 1987, 1992, 1997, 2001, 2005, 2010, 2015, 2017*, David Butler, Dennis Kavanath and Philip Cowley (London, Palgrave Macmillan).
22 Linda Trimble and Jane Arscott, *Still Counting: Women in Politics Across Canada* (Peterborough: Broadview Press, 2003); Azza Karam and Joni Lovenduski (eds.), *Women in Parliament: Beyond Numbers* (Stockholm: International IDEA, 1998).

ing.²³ Furthermore the defence of women's issues – substantive representation – represents one of the arguments in favour of a higher descriptive – numerical – representation of women in politics.²⁴ Among the different British political parties, the relationship of the Conservative Party with feminism and women's issues has evolved.

The Conservative Party and the "Woman Problem"

According to popular beliefs, feminism belongs to the left-wing of the political spectrum and the Conservative Party – with its defence of tradition, hierarchy, natural authority and suspicion of change – may not be considered as the best organisation to be interested in feminist debates, to recognise women as individuals with specific needs and to implement women-friendly policies. The concepts of feminist conservatism or conservative feminism may be considered as oxymora. Indeed second-wave feminism strongly rejected the patriarchal family and the traditional sexual division of labour, which appears in complete contradiction with the Conservative Party's long history of glorifying the family and in particular mothers, wives and housewives.²⁵ Feminist campaigners have been highly critical of Conservative policies and voters with feminist values tend to be disproportionately unlikely to vote for the party.

At the same time, the party has for a long time relied on women at the grassroots level. Women were first actively involved in the organisation of social functions and canvassing in the Primrose League, a group created in 1883 by Lord Randolph Churchill to spread Conservative principles.²⁶ Then once it was created

---

23 Hilde T. Himmelweit et al., *How Voters Decide. A Longitudinal Study of Political Attitudes and Voting Extending over Fifteen Years* (London: Academic Press, 1981); Bo Sarlvik and Ivor Crewe, *Decade of Dealignment. The Conservative Victory of 1979 and Electoral Trends in the 1970s* (Cambridge: Cambridge University Press, 1983); David Denver and Gordon Hands (eds.), *Issues and Controversies in British Electoral Behaviour* (New York: Harvester Wheatsheaf, 1992); V.O. Key, *The Responsible Electorate. Rationality in Presidential Voting* (Massachusetts: Harvard University Press, 1966); Paul F. Lazarsfeld, Bernard Berelson and Hazel Gaudet, *The People's Choice. How the Voter Makes up his Mind in a Presidential Campaign* (New York: Columbia University Press, 1968).
24 Anne Phillips, *The Politics of Presence* (Oxford: Clarendon, 1995).
25 G.E. Maguire, *Conservative Women. A History of Women and the Conservative Party, 1874 – 1997* (London, Palgrave Macmillan, 1998), 202.
26 Philippe Vervaecke, "The Primrose League and Women's Suffrage, 1883 – 1918" in Myriam Boussahba-Bravard (ed.), *Suffrage Outside Suffragism, Women's Vote in Britain, 1880 – 1914* (Houndmills: Palgrave Macmillan, 2007), 180 – 201.

they worked in the women's section of the party, the Central Women's Advisory Committee now called the Conservative Women's Organisation.[27] For many years they were expected to restrict their activities to being members, organisers, canvassers or candidates' wives, even if the first sitting female MP, Nancy Astor, a self-proclaimed feminist, was a Tory. However, from the 1960s onwards, Conservative women transformed their image of dutiful housewives into modern independent-minded and ambitious women who could also be at the forefront of politics and hold prominent functions. At the same time since women obtained the franchise, the party has tried to address its female supporters and members. In 1921 it launched a magazine entitled *Home and Politics*, which was published until 1930.[28] In the twenty-first century, a feminisation of the party was undertaken under David Cameron's leadership to get rid of the image of the "nasty party" and to attract the women who had supported New Labour. Increasing female representation within the party became a key element of its modernising agenda, even if it merely endorsed equality rhetoric and equality promotion, but did not go as far as implementing equality guarantees, to resort to Joni Lovenduski's categorisation.[29]

The complex relations between Conservatism and feminism explain the popular representation of a party having "a woman problem".[30] This negative image was still pointed out as a major difficulty for the party for the 2017 General Election by Fleur Butler, Chairman of the Conservative Women's Organisation for Yorkshire and Humber.[31] However the Conservative Party is the only major party to have twice elected women at its head. As the only female party leaders and Prime Ministers, to what extent did Thatcher and May address the female electorate and take women's issues into account in their political communication?

---

27 G.E. Maguire, op. cit., 150.
28 Véronique Molinari, "Du 'vote des flappers' au 'vote à talons hauts' : évolutions et constantes dans la mobilisation de l'électorat féminin par les partis politiques britanniques de 1920 à 2006", op. cit., 167–190.
29 Joni Lovenduski, *Feminizing Politics* (Cambridge, Polity Press, 2005), 146.
30 Sarah Childs and Paul Webb, *Sex, Gender and the Conservative Party. From Iron Lady to Kitten Heels* (London, Palgrave Macmillan, 2012), 1.
31 https://www.independent.co.uk/voices/conservative-party-feminism-women-carers-children-policy-economics-left-out-a8040081.html, accessed January 11, 2020.

Margaret Thatcher – The Refusal to Target the Female Electorate and a Traditional Vision of Women's Role in Society

Margaret Hilda Roberts came from a lower middle-class Methodist family. She studied chemistry at Oxford, before marrying Denis Thatcher and then qualifying as a barrister. She was elected as the MP for Finchley in 1959 and appointed as Secretary of State for Education by Edward Heath in 1974. The following year she became leader of the Opposition when she won the Conservative Party leadership election, and in 1979 she became Prime Minister. She broke new ground as the first woman Prime Minister, led the party into three General Election victories and became the longest serving Prime Minister in modern history. Did she attempt to mobilise the female electorate in her political communication?

In 1979, 1983 and 1987, the party manifestos conformed to the tradition of a personalised foreword by the party chief. However, Thatcher never directly referred to women voters.[32] The female electorate was included in larger groups, such as "country" (1979, 1983), "nation" (1979), "society" (1979), "people" (1979, 1983, 1987), "families" (1987) or simply "us" (1979) and "we" (1987). Women were never singled out while she explicitly mentioned other categories, such as "the old and the sick and the disabled" (1983). The titles of the various chapters of the programmes ("parents", 1979. "families", 1983), as well as the number of occurrences of the terms "woman" and "women" (eight out of 13,000 words on average, most of which were non-specific), clearly indicated that the Conservatives did not identify women as a specific group with particular interests and expectations from the government. During a press conference in 1987, Margaret Thatcher explicitly justified the lack of policies aimed at female voters ; when a journalist observed that other parties had addressed women in their programmes, she answered that "you do not have a policy especially for women [...] Policies are for all the people. I respectfully point out that we really do not live in wholly separate compartments."[33] When the manifestos did directly address women's issues, they mainly reflected the priorities of housewives and mothers (prices, 1983, housing, 1983).Women were portrayed as distinct individuals only twice, in relation with the development of cervical cancer screening (1987) and the number of

---

[32] The term "woman" appears once in the 1983 manifesto but along with the word "man" ("Every thinking man and woman wants to get rid of nuclear weapons").
[33] Press conference, 10/06/1987, https://www.margaretthatcher.org/document/106882, accessed January 13, 2020.

self-employed workers (1983). The 1980s manifestos revealed both the lack of attention paid to the female electorate and a very traditional vision of women in society, which did not reflect the reality of the British society of the time. Women's labour force participation had increased significantly (60 per cent in 1979, 66 per cent in 1987, 74 per cent in 2017)[34] and housewives no longer represented the majority of female voters. The roles of housewife and mother had become less appealing and "left the language of domesticity looking decidedly old-fashioned to younger generations."[35]

As party leader, Margaret Thatcher delivered 12 speeches at the Conservative Party annual conference. This form of oral communication is aimed both at the party delegates attending the event and through media coverage at the whole British population. A third of Margaret Thatcher's speeches included no remark about women, while the others contained a very low number of references (an average of 2.25 occurrences of "woman" and "women" per speech out of an average of 4,702 words), most of which happen to be general ("men and women"). She mainly took into account women's marital and family status ("wives", "widows", "families", "parents") and she developed topics of interest for housewives, such as food prices (1980) and the difficulty of balancing the family budget (1983). Women were also presented as victims, either of the Irish Republican Army (1981, 1989) or of the miners' strike (1984). She nevertheless felt proud that as Prime Minister she had saved a women's hospital (1986), abolished taxation on the pensions of war widows (1979) and reformed taxation so that married women were taxed separately from their husbands (1989). Margaret Thatcher's vision of women in her conference speeches relies on the traditional division between gendered public and private spheres. In the whole of her political communication, she spoke to women "as a traditional and conventional woman to another",[36] praised women's common sense and presented to voters the image of a perfect housewife, pictured with her children, shopping, cooking or making her husband's breakfast.

As Prime Minister Margaret Thatcher had to answer questions from members of the House of Commons twice a week for 11 years during Prime Minister's Ques-

---

[34] https://www.ons.gov.uk/economy/nationalaccounts/uksectoraccounts/compendium/economicreview/april2019/longtermtrendsinukemployment1861to2018#womens-labour-market-participation, accessed January 13, 2020.
[35] Adrian Bingham, "Conservatism, Gender and the Politics of everyday life, 1950s-1980s", in Clarisse Berthezène and Julie V. Gottlieb (eds.), op. cit., 165.
[36] Wendy Webster, *Not a Man to Match her. The Marketing of a Prime Minister* (London: The Women's Press, 1990), 101.

tion Time.³⁷ This parliamentary activity may be used to draw attention to certain topics or to address specific groups of the electorate. However, she did not use PMQT to delve into female subject matters or to mention her government's action in favour of women (the words "woman" and "women" were uttered in less than five per cent of the sessions).³⁸ She once referred to women's health (breast and cervical cancers, 26/02/1987) and to women's pensions (8/03/1983), but she maintained that mothers' primary duty was to bring up children (23/01/1990) and she did not use International Women's Day and the election of a female leader in Nicaragua (8/03/1990) as an opportunity to reflect on the enduring sexual inequalities in the United Kingdom. She always denied the existence of discrimination and she believed that the existing legislation provided equality of opportunities ("there is nothing more you can do by changing the law [...] I don't think there's been a great deal of discrimination against women, for years, you've been able to come into Parliament, you've been able to be Ministers, you've been able to do many, many things").³⁹ She set herself up as a role model, a woman who had succeeded thanks to hard work, merit and qualifications, an individualistic "queen bee".⁴⁰

However, during Thatcher's PMQT, the Opposition denounced the consequences of the government's policies on women as a homogeneous category. Labour MPs criticised the impact of the economic policy of the Conservatives on British women. Margaret Thatcher was accused of "crucifying the women of this country" (8/03/1990), making them "suffer" (13/03/1990) and endangering their healthcare through cuts in the NHS budget (12/07/1983). Helen McElhone even blamed her for having "misled women at the last General Election by her confidence trick of portraying herself as an ordinary housewife and mother", whereas "mothers are suffering because of her policies" (17/02/1983). When she answered her critics, Margaret Thatcher rejected any new legislation to tackle violence against women (17/02/1987) and she pretended not to have heard a question about her nearly all-male Cabinets (30/01/1990). In her rhetoric, Mar-

---

37 Until 1997, PMQT used to take place twice a week for a quarter of an hour. Since 1997, it has occurred every Wednesday for half an hour. Corpus of 205 PMQT (1979, 1990 as well as the two General Election years of 1983 and 1987), https://www.margaretthatcher.org/search, accessed January 9, 2019.
38 Average of 4.68 per cent. Two occurrences in 1979, eight in 1990, two in 1983, one in 1987.
39 Interview, Thames TV Afternoon Plus, 06/01/1981, https://www.margaretthatcher.org/document/104546, accessed January 13, 2020.
40 R. Rowland, "Women Who do and Women Who don't Join the Women's Movement"; Jane Pilcher, "The Gender Significance of Women in Power. British Women Talking about Margaret Thatcher", *The European Journal of Women's Studies* 2, no. 4 (1995).

garet Thatcher disregarded women as a collective entity and "the chief silence, the chief absence from Mrs Thatcher's convictions [...] concerns gender."[41] Besides, the negative assessment made by Labour politicians was shared by feminists who condemned the disproportionate impact of public sector cuts on women and, as years went by, the first priority of some feminists became to "vote Thatcher out".[42]

Among the Acts of Parliament passed from May 1979 to November 1990[43], a tiny minority (3 per cent) affected women more than men. The 1985 Sexual Offences Act created new offences regarding prostitution and increased the maximum penalty for attempted rape. The same year the Prohibition of Female Circumcision Act criminalised the practice and the Surrogacy Arrangements Act banned commercial surrogacy arrangements. In 1987 the Social Fund (Maternity and Funeral Expenses) Act provided exceptional welfare benefits to pregnant women. Moreover, to conform to European legislation, the British Parliament voted the Sex Discrimination Act in 1986 to fight against sexual discrimination in employment.[44] During the same period, a dozen laws related to marriage, divorce and family. Margaret Thatcher prioritised the family as a social and economic entity over women as individuals in their own right with specific needs.

The refusal to single out women among the electorate and the portrayal of women as primarily mothers and housewives appeared as regular features of Margaret Thatcher's political and electoral communication. Even if she had acknowledged the role of the suffragettes,[45] she strongly disapproved of the Women's Liberation Movement[46] and rejected any association with feminism. She had declared in 1978: "I am not a feminist".[47] Moreover, her record on women's issues contrasted with her male predecessor's. Edward Heath had established the Cripps committee to investigate the legal discrimination faced by women and

---

41 Wendy Webster, op. cit., 3.
42 Laura Beers, "Feminist responses to Thatcher and Thatcherism", in Clarisse Berthezène and Julie Gottlieb (eds.), op.cit., 185.
43 581 Public General Acts, www.legislation.gov.uk, accessed June 12, 2014.
44 http://www.eurofound.europa.eu/emire/UNITEDpercent20KINGDOM/SEXDISCRIMINATIO NACT1986SDA1986-EN.htm, accessed July 18, 2014.
45 Speech, 3/07/1978, https://www.margaretthatcher.org/document/103725, accessed January 13, 2020.
46 Interview, Thames TV CBTV, December 13, 1982, https://www.margaretthatcher.org/document/105071, accessed January 13, 2020.
47 Interview, *Horsney Journal*, 21/04/1978, https://www.margaretthatcher.org/document/103662, accessed January 13, 2020.

many of its recommendations were later implemented.⁴⁸ Paradoxically, once a woman became leader, the concern of the Conservative Party for women's equal rights declined. Margaret Thatcher's ideology was also rooted in a very individualistic conception of liberal competitiveness, which was incompatible with the recognition that women had collective interests. The situation was clearly different 40 years later.

Theresa May – A Self-proclaimed Feminist Willing to Tackle Women's Issues in a Context Dominated by Austerity Measures and Brexit

Before she succeeded David Cameron as Prime Minister, Theresa May had been the first chairwoman of the Conservative party, the first female Conservative Minister for Women and Equalities and the first female Conservative Home Secretary. Her appointment as Minister for Women and Equalities in 2010 first attracted criticisms because of her previous parliamentary voting record on gay rights. However, she supported shared parental leave, mandatory gender pay gap reporting and legislation to eradicate violence against women.⁴⁹ As Prime Minister, in what way was her political discourse different from her female predecessor on gender and equality issues and did she choose to talk to female voters?

In the introduction to the 2017 Conservative Party manifesto, Theresa May did not directly appeal to the female electorate. In a general way, she addressed the whole British population and women were encompassed in global terms such as "people", "everyone" and "all of us". Even if references to women in the rest of the programme were few (13 occurrences of "woman" and "women" out of about 30 000 words), it included specific paragraphs dedicated to women's issues. In the section entitled "Gender pay gap", the Conservatives promised to reduce wage inequalities between men and women, to promote flexible employment, to improve shared-parental leave and make return to work easier, and to work for parity in public appointments and higher representation on boards. In the part about "Preventing domestic violence", they announced a Domestic Violence and Abuse bill and pledged to enshrine a definition of domestic violence and abuse in law and to create a domestic violence and abuse commis-

---

48 1970 Matrimonial Proceedings and Property Act, 1973; Guardianship Act. G.E. Maguire, op. cit., 159–163.
49 Rosa Prince, *Theresa May. The Enigmatic Prime Minister* (London: Biteback Publishing, 2017), 212.

sioner. The will to fight gender inequalities in the United Kingdom was accompanied by a commitment to act abroad ("Leading the world in development"): to develop girls' education, put an end to 'the subjugation and mutilation of women" and tackle "sexual violence in conflict". Even though subject matters which mostly affect women did not constitute a key part of the party programme, the document reflected a certain concern for women as individuals in their diverse identities – married and single women, mothers and workers – and raised some women's issues – economic inequalities, under-representation and violence – a characteristic which was completely missing from the 1980s manifestos. However, the debates about discrimination and inequalities have evolved since the 1980s and the lexical field itself has changed, from the fight against sexual discrimination to the battle for gender equality.

Theresa May's 2016 and 2017 Conservative Party conference speeches did not address the female electorate much nor did they delve much into women's issues. Only rare mentions of "women" could be noted (seven occurrences out of 7,176 words in 2016, nine out of 7,169 in 2017), many of which did not prove gender-specific. Significant portions focused on pressing or tragic issues, Brexit, the Grenfell Tower fire and the Manchester Arena bombing. However, the speeches were based on the key notions of "justice", "fairness" and "opportunities" (2016) and "the British Dream" (2017) and she wished to create a society working for "people", "everyone", "every person", "us all" (2016). While she addressed "ordinary working-class people" on numerous occasions and mentioned briefly other groups ("parents", "people living in rural areas", the "struggling younger generation"), she did not directly talk to female voters. Furthermore, her condemnation of discrimination and inequalities concentrated on "racial disparities" only.

Nevertheless, in Theresa May's conference speeches women were indeed listed as one category of the population when she highlighted the need for the unity of all British people ("Men and women, young and old, black and white, Muslim, Christian, Sikh, Hindu, Jew", 2017). She also alluded to her female predecessor ("Men – and of course one woman", "Lady Thatcher who taught us we could dream great dreams again", 2016) and denounced the inaction of Jeremy Corbyn to confront "misogyny" within the Labour Party ("this is a politician who lets anti-Semitism, misogyny and hatred run free, while he doesn't do a thing to stop it", 2017). She proudly reported on the government's record on female employment ("More women in work than ever before", 2017), stressed the importance of girls' education in developing countries ("UK Aid is helping to educate women and girls in parts of Asia", 2017) and referred to her own achievements as Home Secretary ("I introduced the first ever Modern Slavery Act", 2016).[50]

During the annual gathering of the Conservative Party, Theresa May did not talk much about and to women, but her remarks reflected a modern vision of the rights and status of women, who should be free from discrimination and prejudice and have an equal access to education and employment. These remarks sound modest compared with her previous public statements on women's rights and explicit feminist commitments. Indeed during the 2002 party conference, as chairwoman of the Conservative Party, she had strongly attacked her own party for its under-representation of women; she had blamed it for having "more men in the shadow Cabinet called David than there are women" and described it as "male, pale and stale".[51] She had also been pictured wearing the t-shirt of the Fawcett Society, reading "This is what a feminist looks like", and for Trevor Phillips, former head of the Equality and Human Rights Commission, "Theresa May [...] is just as aggressive as Harriet Harman was on women's equality".[52]

As Prime Minister Theresa May faced MPs every Wednesday for half an hour during PMQT. During these parliamentary exchanges, she referred to women in more than half of her answers (60 per cent),[53] resorted to a rich lexical field ("women", "girls", "mother", "female", "domestic violence", "gender"...) and broached numerous topics which directly affected the female electorate. She praised several successful persons who represent role models for others. She celebrated the contribution of women in the armed services (Women's Royal Naval Service, 13/12/2017), in leading organisations (Ruth Cooke as head of the Clarion Housing Group, 13/12/2017) and in politics (Sarah Clarke as the Lady Usher of the Black Rod, 25/10/2017). She also expressed her wish for "more young women and women to be able to see this House as a place they actively want to come to" (25/10/2017), explicitly supporting a higher numerical representation of women in the political sphere. Before becoming Prime minister, not only had she criticised the low number of women in the Conservative Party

---

[50] The Modern Slavery Act passed in 2015 was meant "to make provision about slavery, servitude and forced or compulsory labour and about human trafficking, including provision for the protection of victims; to make provision for an Independent Anti-slavery Commissioner; and for connected purposes", http://www.legislation.gov.uk/ukpga/2015/30/introduction/enacted, accessed April 6, 2020.
[51] http://www.ukpol.co.uk/theresa-may-2005-speech-on-women-2-win, accessed January 15, 2020.
[52] Quoted in Rosa Prince, op. cit., 178.
[53] Corpus of 39 PMQT (2016–2017), https://www.parliament.uk, accessed January 30, 2019. She mentioned the terms "woman" or "women" in 24 sessions.

but she had founded with Anne Jenkin an organisation aimed at promoting more female Conservative candidates.[54] Women2win intended to ensure that the party "fairly represents women at all levels of politics" through "identifying, training and mentoring female candidates for public office". As a result, the number of Conservative women MPs increased from 17 to 67 between 2005 to 2017.[55] Theresa May explained that she was aware that she might herself be an inspiration for aspiring female politicians (20/07/2016) and on several occasions she mocked the Labour Party for its all-male leadership (20/07/2016, 22/11/2017, 13/12/2017).[56] However, she did not appoint a gender-balanced government as could have been expected and women made up a quarter of her first Cabinet (however an increase compared with David Cameron's 2010 Cabinet which included less than 20 per cent of female members).[57] Many references to female issues were related to VAWG (Violence Against Women and Girls). She reiterated her will to tackle domestic violence, which had been one of her priorities as Home Secretary ("I worked hard on it as Home Secretary and I continue to do so as Prime minister", 8/02/2017, 20/07/2016, 07/09/2016, 22/02/2017, 8/03/2017, 13/12/2017). She strongly condemned "so-called honour-based violence" as "violence and a criminal act – pure and simple" (20/07/2016) and she vowed to continue "the pursuit of eradicating modern slavery" (2/11/2016). Her commitment to VAWG predated her premiership, since as shadow spokesperson for Schools, Disabled People and Women she had criticised forced marriages and as shadow Women and Equalities Minister she had denounced the gender pay gap and sex trafficking.[58] Moreover, as Home Secretary she had initiated the Modern Slavery Act against Sex Trafficking in 2015.

However, during PMQT Labour leader Jeremy Corbyn accused Theresa May of having let women down by compelling many "to give up work to care for loved ones" (08/02/2017) and he held her responsible for the closures of "two thirds of women refuges" (07/09/2016). Moreover, the Prime Minister was blamed for the austerity measures implemented by the 2010 – 2015 Coalition government

---

[54] Véronique Molinari, "Women2Win et la féminisation du Parti conservateur: les coulisses d'un débat," *Observatoire de la société britannique*, no. 6 (2008), https://journals.openedition.org/osb/449, accessed January 16, 2020.
[55] https://www.women2win.com, accessed January 16, 2020.
[56] The Labour Party never elected a woman as leader. Harriet Harman was deputy leader and acting leader for a few months after Gordon Brown's resignation in 2010.
[57] She appointed Amber Rudd as Home Secretary, Liz Truss as Secretary of State for Justice, Justine Greening as Secretary of State for Education and Andrea Leadsom as Secretary of State for the Environment, Food and Rural Affairs.
[58] Rosa Prince, op. cit., 191.

of which she had been a prominent member as Home Secretary. The policies, such as the pension reform, were deemed to have had a disproportionate impact on women and some feminists developed a "gendered austerity critique".[59]

Under Theresa May's premiership,[60] Westminster adopted the Preventing and Combating Violence against Women and Domestic Violence (Ratification of Convention) Act (2017), which constituted the ratification by the United Kingdom of the Council of Europe Convention on Violence against Women. Moreover, the Policing and Crime Act (2017) included a provision for the anonymity of victims of forced marriages. Compared to her previous action as Home Secretary, the absence of a more extensive women-friendly legislation may be seen as far from satisfactory. However, as *The Economist* explained, "as Brexit has dominated, the rest of the government's agenda has withered",[61] and therefore women's rights and many other issues have been neglected.

Theresa May, a self-styled feminist, acknowledged gender specificities in her political rhetoric and tackled issues of importance to modern active women, such as the gender-pay gap, childcare or the under-representation of women in high positions. Her work on violence against women as Home Secretary was also praised. However, her record as Prime Minister was denounced by some feminists as disappointing and insufficient as far as women were concerned.

Conclusion

Addressing female voters can constitute an electoral strategy aimed at gaining or regaining the votes of this specific electorate and/or reflect a personal commitment to and interest in women's issues, especially in the case of women leaders. As Prime Ministers, Margaret Thatcher and Theresa May had the power to defend women's rights and to improve women's social and economic conditions. While they belonged to the same party, the two female Prime Ministers adopted a very different approach to the question of the female electorate and women's issues in general. As the first female Prime Minister, Margaret Thatcher benefitted from no role model and had to prove that she was the right man for the job. She pub-

---

59 Scottish National Party MP Anne McLaughlin, 19/10/2016, 1/02/2017, 19/09/2017. The reform has also been contested by WASPI, Women Against State Pension Inequality, an organisation founded in 2015. Rosie Campbell and Sarah Childs, "The (feminized) Conservative Party", in Clarisse Berthezène and V. Julie Gottlieb (eds.), op. cit., 194.
60 The corpus is made up of two Public General Acts for 2016 and 35 for 2017.
61 "An absent agenda", *The Economist*, January 24, 2019.

licly ignored women's priorities and did not address female voters. At the same time through her personal image and her political discourse, she projected a very traditional vision of women. Theresa May reflected the interests and priorities of women, raised awareness on equality issues and acted to increase female political representation and to tackle violence against women.

Both of them were the targets of strong criticisms from feminist groups and political opponents, especially as feminist groups have traditionally been associated with the Labour party. As academic Sylvia Bashevkin remarked, "the agenda of Britain's first female Prime Minister appeared, ironically, to collide head-on with many feminist priorities"[62], and for sociologist Jane Pilcher, "Thatcher is a reminder that it is not merely sufficient for women to gain positions of public political power in order for pro-women policies to be enacted".[63] Sophie Walkers, the leader of the Women's Equality Party – a feminist party created in 2015 – deplored the inaction of Theresa May's government on pay transparency, childcare and social care. For her Theresa May's silence on women's issues was "deafening",[64] a standpoint shared by Labour MP Harriet Harman for whom Theresa May was no better than her female predecessor ("like Margaret Thatcher before her, Theresa May is no supporter of women").[65]

The two female Prime Ministers resorted to different styles of political communication and diverged on their conception of the electorate and how to connect with voters. Bearing in mind that some male leaders (Edward Heath, Tony Blair, David Cameron) attempted to tackle some equality issues, targeting women and implementing a women-friendly agenda depends more on personality, personal convictions and political strategy than on gender. The correlation between descriptive representation and substantive representation proves complex and shared experience does not guarantee good representation.[66] Besides, the evolution of society and mentalities, as well as feminist pressure groups, affect political leaders and their discourse. From the 1980s to the twenty-first century, the language of politicians on gender as well as their stance on equality issues have evolved. The Conservative party, which used to promote an individual

---

62 Sylvia Bashevkin, "Tough Times in review. The British Women's Movement during the Thatcher years", *Contemporary Political Studies* 28, no. 4 (1996): 52.
63 Jane Pilcher, "The Gender Significance of Women in Power. British Women Talking about Margaret Thatcher", op. cit., 506.
64 https://www.theguardian.com/lifeandstyle/2016/nov/27/theresa-may-silence-womens-issues-sophie-walker-equality-party, accessed February 6, 2019.
65 https://blogs.spectator.co.uk/2016/09/labour-women-attack-theresa-may-no-sister-un-feminist, accessed April 24, 2017.
66 Sarah Childs, *Women and British Politics*, op. cit.

conception of rights, has partly endorsed a vision of collective interests. Indeed the 2008 report of the Conservative Women's Policy Group (*Women in the World Today*) read "more like a feminist publication than a traditionally Conservative one".[67]

Among the hundreds of fringe events which were organised during the 2019 Conservative Party conference, two panels focused on women voters ("The Gender Voting Gap: How can political parties better respond to female voters' concerns?" and "Where has the female vote gone?"), in particular on how "to better engage and respond to female voters".[68] These meetings represented another illustration of the long-term concern of the party to mobilise various categories of the electorate.

Bibliography

Bashevkin, Sylvia. "Tough Times in Review. The British Women's Movement during the Thatcher Years." *Comparative Political Studies* 28, no. 4 (1996).

Berthezène Clarisse, and Julie V. Gottlieb, eds. *Rethinking right-wing women. Gender and the Conservative Party, 1880s to the Present*. Manchester: Manchester University Press, 2017.

Bowler Shaun, and David M. Farrell, eds. *Electoral Strategies and Political Marketing*. New York: St Martin's press, 1992.

Boussahba-Bravard, Myriam, ed. *Women's Vote in Britain, 1880–1914*. Houndmills: Palgrave Macmillan, 2007.

Campbell Rosie, Sarah Childs and Joni Lovenduski. *Women at the top 2005, Changing Numbers, Changing Politics?* Hansard Society, 2005.

Childs, Sarah. *Women and British Politics. Descriptive, Substantive and Symbolic Representation*. London: Routledge, 2008.

Childs, Sarah, and Paul Webb. *Sex, Gender and the Conservative Party. From Iron Lady to Kitten Heels*. London: Palgrave Macmillan, 2012.

Crewe, Ivor, Anthony Fox and Neil Day. *The British Electorate 1963–1992. A compendium of data from the British Election Studies*. Cambridge: Cambridge University Press, 1995.

Denver, David. *Elections and Voting Behaviour in Britain*. Deddington: Philip Allan, 1994.

Equal Opportunities Commission. *Sex and Power: Who Runs Britain?* London: EOC, 2011.

Karam, Azza M., ed. *Women in Parliament: Beyond Numbers*. Stockholm: International IDEA, 1998.

Kavanagh, Dennis. *Election Campaigning. The New Marketing of Politics*. Oxford: Oxford University Press, 1995.

Kavanagh, Dennis. *Politics and Personalities*. London: Macmillan, 1990.

Lovenduski, Joni. *Feminizing Politics*. Cambridge: Polity Press, 2005.

---

[67] Timothy Heppel and David Seawright (eds.), *Cameron and the Conservatives. The Transition to Coalition Government* (Basingstoke: Palgrave Macmillan, 2012), 155.

[68] https://conservativepartyconference.com/printallfringeevents/all, accessed January 14, 2020.

Lovenduski Joni, and Vicky Randall. *Contemporary Feminist Politics: Women and Power in Britain*. Oxford: Oxford University Press, 1993.

Maguire, G.E. *Conservative Women. A History of Women and the Conservative Party, 1874–1997*. London: Palgrave Macmillan, 1998.

Molinari, Véronique. "Mobilisation des électrices et instrumentalisation de la différence: les campagnes électorales de 2004 et 2005 en Grande-Bretagne et aux Etats-Unis". In *Stratégies et campagnes électorales en Grande-Bretagne et aux Etats-Unis*, edited by Renée Dickason, David Haigron and Karine Riviere-De Franco, 84–105. Paris: L'Harmattan, 2009.

Molinari, Véronique, "Du 'vote des flappers' au 'vote à talons hauts': évolutions et constantes dans la mobilisation de l'électorat féminin par les partis politiques britanniques de 1920 à 2006". *Recherches féministes* 20, no. 1 (2007): 167–190.

Nunn, Heather. *Thatcher, Politics and Fantasy. The Political Culture of Gender and Nation*. London: Lawrence & Wishart, 2002.

Phillips, Anne. *The Politics of Presence*. Oxford: Clarendon, 1995.

Ridge, Sophie. *The Women Who shaped Politics*. Great Britain: Coronet, 2017.

Rosenbaum, Martin. *From Soapbox to Soundbites. Party Political Campaigning in Britain since 1945*. London: Macmillan, 1997.

Rowland, R. "Women Who do and Women Who don't Join the Women's Movement". In Jane Pilcher, "The Gender Significance of Women in Power. British Women Talking about Margaret Thatcher". *The European Journal of Women's Studies* 2, no. 4 (1995).

Steinberg, Blema S. *Women in Power. The Personalities and Leadership Styles of Indira Gandhi, Golda Meir and Margaret Thatcher*. London: McGill-Queen's University Press, 2008.

Part 3: **Digital Mobilisation: Revolutionising Politics in the Twenty-first Century?**

Géraldine Castel
6 Digital Politics and Mobilisation in the UK

The Elusive Silver Bullet

Introduction

The use of information and communication technology in the political sphere is no longer a novelty. As early as 1969 in the United States, Ross Perot, a salesman for IBM in his youth and founder in 1962 of a company called Electronic Data Systems, formed a project to try and consult Americans on a variety of issues by marking computer cards and then mailing them to tabulating centres so that politicians would be made aware of the opinions and expectations of the citizens they aimed to represent. In 1992, when he became candidate to the American Presidential election, Perot reiterated his belief in using technology to implement electronic town halls meant to usher in a more direct form of democracy.

Since then, the capacity of technology to significantly influence democracy, political institutions and practices has been the object of much discussion, as illustrated for instance by Grossman's *Electronic Republic: Reshaping American Democracy for the Information Age*,[1] as opposed to Margolis and Resnick's *Politics as Usual: the Cyberspace "Revolution"*[2] or Matthew Hindman's *Myth of Digital Democracy*.[3]

Beyond U.S. borders, scholars have also painted a complex image of the interaction between ICTs and politics be it, among others, in France,[4] Poland and Norway,[5] Portugal,[6] Sweden,[7] Iran[8] or Australia.[9] In the British context, extensive work

---
[1] Lawrence Grossman, *Electronic Republic: Reshaping American Democracy for the Information Age* (Penguin Books, 1995).
[2] Michael Margolis and David Resnick, *Politics as Usual: The Cyberspace "Revolution"* (Sage, 2000).
[3] Matthew Hindman, *The Myth of Digital Democracy* (Princeton University Press, 2009).
[4] Éric George, "Des relations entre démocratie et TIC: quelques enseignements issus de travaux récents", *Interin* 4 (2007).
[5] Ilona Biernacka-Ligięza, "ICT and Local Governance – E-¬government in the Local Public Sphere in Poland and Norway", *Central European Journal of Communication* 4, no 2 (2011): 293–313.

has been conducted too on the potential, practices and impact of ICTs on politics from a broad range of perspectives. Gibson and Ward have been very active in this area[10] and other significant work has been published: Goodchild, Oppenheim and Cleeve[11] for instance evaluated the content and usability of MPs' sites, while Wills and Reeves[12] studied the use of Facebook as a political weapon and Graham, Broersma, Hazelhoff and Haar[13] analysed Twitter interactions on political topics. Moss and Coleman[14] focused on e-democracy devices and initiatives such as online forums, e-petitioning platforms or crowdsourcing tools while Fenton and Barassi[15] compared individual and collective forms of participation on social media.

---

6 Gustavo Cardoso, Cunha Carlos and Nascimento Susana, "Bridging the e-democracy gap in Portugal: MPs, ICTs and political mediation", *Information, Communication and Society* 9, no. 4 (2006): 452–472.
7 Magnus Lindh and Miles Lee, "Becoming Electronic Parliamentarians? ICT Usage in the Swedish Riksdag", *Journal of Legislative Studies* 13, no. 3 (2007): 422–440.
8 Yahya Kamalipour, "Communication Media and Globalization: an Iranian Perspective", *Global Media and Communication* 13, no. 3 (2007): 340–342.
9 Will Grant, Moon Brenda and Grant Busby Janie, "Digital Dialogue? Australian Politicians' use of the social network tool Twitter", *Australian Journal of Political Science* 45, no. 4 (2010): 579–604.
10 Rachel Gibson and Ward Stephen, "On-Line and on Message? Candidate Websites in the 2001 General Election", *British Journal of Politics and International Relations* (2003); Rachel Gibson and Ward Stephen, "The First Internet Election? UK Political Parties and Campaigning in Cyberspace", in J. Bartle, I. Crewe and B. Gosschalk, *Political Communications: The General Election Campaign of 1997* (London: Frank Cass Publishers, 2012), 83–112; Rachel Gibson and Stephen Ward, "U.K. Political Parties and the Internet: Prospects for Democracy" (USIR, 1997); "U.K. Political Parties and the Internet: "Politics as Usual" in the New Media?", *International Journal of Press/Politics* (1998); "Party Democracy On-line: UK Parties and new ICTs", *Information, Communication & Society* 2, no. 3 (1999): 340–367; "On-Line and on Message? Candidate Websites in the 2001 General Election", *British Journal of Politics and International Relations* (2003).
11 Lauren Goodchild, Charles Oppenheim and Marigold Cleeve, "MPs online: an evaluative study of MPs' use of web sites", *Aslib Proceedings* 59, no. 6 (2007): 565–587.
12 David Wills and Stuart Reeves, "Facebook as a Political Weapon: Information in Social Networks", *British Politics* 4, no. 2 (2009): 265.
13 Todd Graham, Marcel Broersma, Karin Hazelhoff and Guido Van't Haar, "Between Broadcasting Political Messages and Interacting with Voters," *Information, Communication and Society* 16, no. 5 (2013): 692–716.
14 Giles Moss and Stephen Coleman, "Deliberative Manoeuvres in the Digital Darkness: E-Democracy Policy in the UK", *The British Journal of Politics and International Relations* 16, no. 3 (2014): 410–427.
15 Natalie Fenton and Barassi Veronica, "Alternative Media and Social Networking Sites: The Politics of Individuation and Political Participation", *The Communication Review* 14 (2011): 179.

In a context of rapidly changing tools and approaches and controversy over outcome, this article proposes to build on an extensive set of primary and secondary sources to look back on the gradual adoption of digital technology in British politics, more specifically in relation to mobilisation and engagement purposes from the introduction of Excalibur in 1994 by Tony Blair's team to the general election of 2019. The meaning of those two concepts is however not self-evident and an attempt to define their most recent manifestations meets with the same limits encountered by Van Deth about political participation, i.e. the "dilemma of using either a dated conceptualization excluding many new modes of political participation or stretching their concept to cover almost everything".[16] This article will thus focus more particularly on the capacity for UK parties to use technology to reach out to the public and encourage involvement with its activities, be it at the organisational level of parties themselves or for mobilisation of voters for electoral purposes. It will first provide an overview of the evolution of platforms, actors, tools, contents and objectives over the period under consideration and then move on to address issues pertaining to the impact of such technological development on election results, parties and democracy more broadly.

In 1992, reflecting on Perot's "electronic town hall" project, James Howard wrote: "There aren't any shortcuts to democracy. It's messy, contentious, inconsistent and often unpleasant. Mr. Perot cannot order it to behave."[17] This overview aims to demonstrate that in Britain too, politicians and parties' attempts at harnessing digital technology to try and control various aspects of the political process have met with mitigated results. The growing number and complexity of the tools available has not made it possible for parties to design a dependable formula for success in mobilisation and engagement capable of turning elections and democracy more generally into a technically predictable and dependable endeavour.

---

[16] Van Deth, Jan, "What is Political Participation?", *Oxford Research Encyclopedias* (2016).
[17] Howard, James, "Perot's 'Electronic Town Hall' Wouldn't Work, letter to the editor", *New York Times*, June 7, 1992.

An Overview of Digital Politics for Engagement Purposes

Context

Drawing a clear-cut picture of the evolution of political engagement in the UK over the last decades is in itself a challenge. Metrics do exist but fail to paint an unequivocal image. Indeed, every year since 2004, the Hansard Society has released an audit of political engagement. In its 2019 instalment, its authors state that "Core indicators of political engagement remain stable but beneath the surface, the strongest feelings of powerlessness and disengagement are intensifying."[18] Such results are obviously affected by contextual factors related to the turbulence of British politics in recent years but trends over the 15 years the audits have been published also point to a lack of homogeneity: in 2019, 47 per cent of respondents "feel that they have no influence at all over national decision-making, a new high for the audit series" while "32 percent say they do not want to be involved 'at all' in local decision-making, a rise of 10 points in a year". Yet since 2004, the number of people who feel that getting involved is effective has fallen by only 5 per cent (37 per cent to 32 per cent) while over the same period, certainty to vote has increased (51 per cent to 61 per cent) as have knowledge of politics (42 per cent to 51 per cent), and interest in politics (50 per cent to 53 per cent).

Turnout figures for General Elections do not make for unequivocal reading either. While participation in the last two decades never reached the 83 per cent of 1950 and even fell down to 59 per cent in 2001, figures have been increasing since with a turnout of 68.7 per cent at the 2017 election.[19] And if demographic and sociological considerations play a part in discrepancies in the answers provided, one must be wary of generalisations. For instance, while young people (18 to 24) declare themselves far less likely to vote than those over 65 (47 per cent to 71 per cent), their interest in politics is similar (50 per cent for both); they believe themselves to be more knowledgeable about politics than their elders (44 per cent to 41) and they feel getting involved is more effective (35 per cent to

---

[18] Joel Blackwell, Brigid Fowler and Ruth Fox, "Audit of Political Engagement", *Hansard Society* 16, no. 3 (2019), https://www.hansardsociety.org.uk/publications/reports/Audit-of-political-engagement-16, accessed April 1, 2019.
[19] "General Election Turnout 1945–2019", UK Political Info, 2019, http://www.ukpolitical.info/Turnout45.htm, accessed April 1, 2019.

27 per cent). Likewise, if social class is very clearly correlated to a propensity to vote or interest in politics, the difference between the DE group and the C1 one in terms of efficiency of involvement is less marked (29 per cent to 35 per cent). As far as parties are concerned, figures from the 2019 Audit also point to a contrasted evolution. While 34 per cent of respondents still consider themselves "a 'very' or 'fairly' strong supporter of a political party" with stable answers in that respect since 2004, 50 per cent say "the main parties do not care about people like them".

When it comes to party membership, figures need to be taken with a certain degree of caution as parties have no official obligation to publish them in Britain and the definition of membership is itself disputed. Yet the *Membership of UK Political Parties* briefing paper from the House of Commons library released in 2019 points to a steep decline since the 1950s for Labour, the Conservatives and the Liberal Democrats. And although parties partially recovered from the historic low of 2013, combined membership of the three major parties in 2019 only reached 1.7 per cent of the whole electorate and none has managed to rise over 1 per cent individually since the 1990s.[20]

While those figures make for complex interpretation, various initiatives from major parties over the last decades nonetheless suggest decline in party membership and, more broadly, anxiety over their capacity to connect and engage significantly with British citizens have been cause for concern. This has been the case of structural reforms introduced by Labour leaders such as Tony Blair[21] or Ed Miliband, or David Cameron's re-branding[22] of the Tory party building on Theresa May's 2002 speech to the Conservative conference while she was its chairwoman:

> We have to face a deeply uncomfortable truth. [...] The public are losing faith in politics. Politicians are seen as untrustworthy and hypocritical. We talk a different language. We live in a different world. [...] While the parties shout at each other, no one outside the Westminster village pays attention to any of it. People just switch off. [...]

---

20 Lukas Audickas, Noel Dempsey, Richard Keen and Philip Loft, "Membership of UK Political Parties", *House of Commons Library Briefing Paper*, July 20, 2019, https://researchbriefings.parliament.uk/ResearchBriefing/Summary/SN05125, accessed April 1, 2019.
21 Cf. initiatives in Blair's Sedgefield constituency in the early 1990s to lower membership fees and encourage social events in communities or the 1993 conference decision to allow One Member One Vote for leadership elections.
22 Cf. Castel, "David Cameron and the Web: The Parallel Evolution of Two Newcomers in the Run-up to the 2010 Election", *LISA* XII, no. 8 (2014).

There's a lot we need to do in this party of ours. Our base is too narrow and so, occasionally, are our sympathies.[23]

Vince Cable as leader of the Liberal Democrats also emphasised the need for his party to breathe new life into their relationship with voters and British citizens more generally, stating in 2018: "I want to work with our party to transform the way we work with people so that we engage more actively with the millions of voters who currently share our values but feel disenfranchised".[24]

Platforms and Media

The emergence of a growing range of digital media provided parties with an opportunity to try and bridge the gap between themselves and the public. In the run up to the 1997 General Election, all three main parties in the UK had a website. But the use of ICTs within British political parties was still mostly experimental and subsidiary. Digital elements were introduced in the years leading up to the 2001 General election but were essentially limited to emails to share artwork or other campaign material. James Crabtree, the author of an extensive analysis of David Cameron's use of ICTs released in *Wired Magazine*, recalls: "Even in 2005, the [Conservative] party had no web strategy, nor a team to implement it. This was a time, one adviser recalls, when "the person who ran the website was also the same person you rang up if your Outlook broke".[25] In the run-up to the 2005 General Election, half the population still had no Internet access and of those who did, almost half used it less than weekly.[26]

The period between the 2005 and 2010 General elections then witnessed the rise of blogs such as the 2006 one detailing Cameron's trip to India but also the *Blue Blog* for the Conservatives from 2008 or *Labour List* launched in 2009. In the same period were created Facebook, YouTube and Twitter which then became

---

[23] Theresa May, "Conference Speech", *The Guardian*, October 7, 2002, https://www.theguardian.com/politics/2002/oct/07/Conservatives2002.Conservatives1, accessed April 1, 2019.
[24] Vince, "Building a Liberal Democrat Movement", Liberal Democrat Website, September 7, 2018, accessed April 1, 2019, https://www.libdems.org.uk/building-a-liberal-democrat-movement.
[25] James Crabtree, "David Cameron's battle to connect", *Wired*, March 24, 2010, https://www.wired.co.uk/article/david-camerons-battle-to-connect, accessed April 1, 2019.
[26] Office for National Statistics, "Internet access – households and individuals, Great Britain: 2018", 2018, https://www.ons.gov.uk/peoplepopulationandcommunity/householdcharacteristics/homeinternetandsocialmediausage/bulletins/internetaccesshouseholdsandindividuals/2018, accessed April 1, 2019.

and still are the main vehicles for party communication, even though other networks such as Instagram or Snapchat have also been put to use more recently.

While Tony Blair for instance still very much relied on newspapers and television to convey his message to the public and therefore worked hard to obtain the support of Rupert Murdoch, owner of *The Sun* and the information network Sky, the Conservatives had Google's CEO as key speaker at their 2006 conference and David Cameron invited Mark Zuckerberg of Facebook to Downing Street in 2010. Politicians progressively realised the potential of the Internet for communication, with the main benefits of broadcasting by those means being immediacy, comprehensiveness of contents and minimal mediation between the source and the target.

Contents

Those contents also evolved over the period under consideration. The website for the Liberal Democrats for the 1997 election for instance offered information on party policies and representatives, a history of the movement and a list of news stories mentioning the party, which were typical features for the 1990s in a clearly top-down broadcasting of mostly textual contents. Prior to the 2001 election, the Labour site introduced an interactive map of "Labour achievements" as well as audio and video contents (podcast of interviews with ministers, videos of supporters explaining their decision to join Labour) pointing to a diversification of communication material. Labour's Dave the Chameleon campaign for the 2006 local elections was built around a blue cartoon chameleon on a bike, representing David Cameron and his alleged facility for shifting position on various issues. It illustrated the parties' growing willingness to explore with a dedicated website, downloadable posters, ringtones and video episodes of a short series. For the 2010 election, the Conservatives designed a Wheel of Misfortune mock gaming site to make fun of what they considered a lack of consistency on Nick Clegg's part. They also organised an online consultation for the draft of their health manifesto and accepted an invitation from Mumsnet to take part in their online chat, just like Gordon Brown and Caroline Lucas, among others.

By 2017, the growing influence of social media was visible in the report of the electoral commission on campaign spending, which revealed a sharp increase in digital advertising from 0.3 per cent of total advertising spending for parties in 2011 to 42.8 per cent in 2017[27] (Electoral Commission 2018, 6).

---

27 Electoral Commission, "Digital Campaigning: Increasing Transparency for Voters", June

The same document also provided useful information on the type of contents being broadcast digitally with, for Labour in 2017, 40 per cent animation and 19 per cent user-generated contents, which included the "I'm voting Labour" Snapchat image filter viewed 7.6 million times and which drove 1.2 million views to a Labour-built site that helped voters locate their polling station.[28] Memes also proved particularly popular, like the cover of Dickens' novel *Oliver Twist* with "Breaking News! The Conservative Manifesto Revealed" at the top or a picture of Theresa May alongside another one of mushrooms and the caption: "If Theresa May is so against drugs, why did she cut her hair like a magic mushroom?" (White 2017).[29] The fact that political ads (15 per cent) and party election broadcasts (5 per cent) were relegated far behind this type of contents shows a marked difference with the first digital campaigns which gave them priority.

Organisation

However, communication was not the only aspect of engagement facilitated by digital technology. Recruitment of members and activists and coordination of their work were also affected. The sites for the 1997 election usually comprised a Join Us feature. In 2001, Labour for instance added a calendar of coming events and the possibility to sign up to receive a newsletter. In 2005, the frontpage of their site opened on a form entitled "I support Labour's pledges" for users willing to be informed of upcoming events to give their contact details. Then, a donate icon was on display as well as a feature called "Ask the Prime Minister" and one to sign a "Keep the NHS Free" petition. An "action centre" page offered the possibility for volunteers to participate in the campaign and sign up for training, and for members to upload material. For the 2010 election, on the site's menu, out of the seven tabs, four were meant to encourage engagement and recruitment (Campaign, Support, Tools and Membersnet).

Membersnet is representative of the platforms implemented by UK parties to facilitate coordination of both online and offline actions and of an increasing

---

2018, https://www.electoralcommission.org.uk/who-we-are-and-what-we-do/changing-electoral-law/transparent-digital-campaigning, accessed April 1, 2019.

28 SevenVentures, "5 Marketing lessons from 2017 UK Election", *Therestlesscmo*, July 19, 2017, accessed April 1, 2019, http://therestlesscmo.com/post/5-marketing-lessons-from-2017-uk-election.

29 Charles White, "The memes that decided the outcome of the General Election", *Metro*, June 11, 2017, https://metro.co.uk/2017/06/11/the-memes-that-decided-the-outcome-of-the-general-election-6701277/, accessed April 1, 2019.

range of digital tools made available to them. Launched in 2006 and updated several times since, its access is significantly not restricted to members but opened up to "supporters" too. It offers party campaigners tools for organising events such as interactive maps and calendars of upcoming activities like meetings or leaflet delivery. It comprises an online and secure chatting platform for members and provides constituency parties with site templates as well as templates for posters, leaflets etc. to be adapted to local circumstances or voters' profiles.

Such a platform thus assists with traditional campaigning activities like canvassing for example. Before volunteers knock on doors, they are given the names and profiles of the person they are likely to meet, but also answers to previous visits such as voting intentions or areas of concern so as to customise their approach. The person in charge of the canvassing session provides this information from a tablet or printout, and more recently, apps like the Labour Doorstep one, so that each volunteer can access the data directly from their phone and crucially also feed the data collected back into the party database. Momentum, the group behind most of Labour's digital strategy in the 2017 and 2019 General elections, also designed the Calling for Corbyn phone canvassing app, which allowed volunteers to work from home, and the My Nearest Marginal online map to connect members of the public willing to get involved with the campaign and direct them to the closest key constituency, even going as far as helping them to reach their destination via Carpool Momentum.[30] For phone banks, volunteers are also provided via a tool called Dialogue with the contact details of voters as well as scripts of points to mention during the conversation according to local criteria or voters' profiles.

The parties collect information on volunteers themselves too so as to optimise campaigning activities according to criteria like skills, location or areas of interest. More recently, Constituency Labour Parties have been encouraged to use a platform called Organise to prevent resignation of members or lapse in their subscriptions via customised email templates and classification of members' emails according to their membership status and renewal date.

Since 2013, Membersnet has been supplemented by Nation Builder, the software used by the Obama campaigns and in the UK by the Liberal Democrats, the SNP and the Conservatives too. This software enables parties to broadcast contents simultaneously on several outlets (emails, text messages, social media posts...) following a pre-established schedule from a single platform and gives

---

30 Hughes, Casper, "How Momentum delivered Labour's stunning election result – and how the Tories are trying to copy it", *The Independent*, July 19, 2017.

them an overview of broadcasting over all media, a history of past actions and analytics to track progress.

Objectives

In the last decade, and more specifically in the context of the 2017 and 2019 General Elections, Labour has demonstrated a capacity superior to its rivals in designing contents more likely to be shared by users with their friends on social media in order to achieve free, more efficient "organic" reach as opposed to paid-for advertising. Evidence from the digital campaigning guide made available to Labour candidates by party headquarters suggests that using such formats was actively and deliberately encouraged. This document states:

> People share content that elicits Humour, Urgency (Breaking news, immediate election results, "revealed", exposé-style content), Pride (Labour's heritage and history, our achievements, statements on our values), Action (Convert peoples' passion over an issue into action: share the facts, sign this petition, join our rally...). Always think HUPA![31]

And indeed, such a strategy was one of the key strengths of Labour in 2017. For Mathew Walsh:

> By achieving very high levels of organic reach, Labour managed to target undecided voters in marginal constituencies, energise voters who had drifted away from the party, and mobilise the young. [...] The Labour party simply produced more content than its competitors, it posted more frequently and the content was more engaging.[32]

Over the six-week election period, one in three Facebook users watched an entire Momentum video while on election day, Labour reached 400,000 voters using a "cascade", "a people-powered messaging tool via WhatsApp"[33] so as to remind them to vote. Though less successful in terms of organic reach than Labour, the Conservatives also designed material meant for such dissemination, such as for

---

[31] Labour Party, "Digital Campaigning Guide", 2017, http://scottishLabour.org.uk/wp-content/uploads/2018/05/10008_17-Digital-Campaigning-Guide_v10.pdf, accessed April 1, 2019.

[32] Matt Walsh, "Understanding Labour's ingenious campaign strategy on Facebook", LSE Blogs, November 10, 2017, https://blogs.lse.ac.uk/politicsandpolicy/explaining-Labours-facebook-success/, accessed April 1, 2019.

[33] Momentum, "2017 General Election", 2018, https://peoplesmomentum.com/2018/01/12/2017-general-election/, accessed April 1, 2019.

example the *This man is only six seats away from being Prime Minister* video focused on Jeremy Corbyn's background, viewed eight million times.

To promote the broadcasting of contents, parties have been making use of search engine optimisation with an expert hired by the Conservatives as early as 2007. They also tested Google ads in that period and other parties have caught up since. In 2017 for example, both Labour and the Conservatives bought the phrase "Dementia Tax"[34] which was used to criticise the Conservative proposals regarding the care of the elderly. Consequently, beside the search results for the phrase could be found a link to Labour's objections to these proposals and another directing viewers to the part of the Conservative manifesto devoted to this issue so as to try and counter the detrimental effect of this label on their policy. In 2017, the Conservatives paid Google £500,000, Labour £210,000 and the Liberal Democrats £170,000 for such ads but also for advertising on YouTube.[35]

But if connecting with as many voters as possible remains a goal of such initiatives, the main development of the last decade has been the increasing willingness and capacity of parties to reach individuals and groups, fewer in number but deemed essential to electoral victory. Resources have thus been focused on marginal seats or so-called "swing" voters, who could positively alter election results and who were deemed more likely to be influenced by advertising and engagement messages. For instance, Dominiczak reports in 2015, for the Conservatives:

> Fewer than 100,000 votes in a handful of marginal constituencies – mostly currently held by the Liberal Democrats – are the key to a Conservative victory in this week's election, David Cameron's advisers believe.
>
> The Conservatives have a list of 23 target seats, disclosed for the first time, which strategists are focusing their efforts on in the final days before the vote.[36]

Since the first experiments in the 1990s, the evolution of technology has made such targeting much easier by increasing the volume of information available but also by providing more sophisticated tools to analyse such vast quantities of data.

---

[34] In Google's advertising system, advertisers bid on certain keywords in order for their clickable ads to appear in Google's search results.
[35] Joey D'Urso, "Who spent what on Facebook during 2017 election campaign", *BBC News*, March 31, 2018, https://www.bbc.com/news/uk-politics-43487301, accessed April 1, 2019.
[36] Peter Dominiczak, "Tories targeting fewer than 100,000 voters for victory", *The Telegraph*, May 3, 2015, https://www.telegraph.co.uk/news/politics/david-cameron/11580533/Tories-targeting-fewer-than-100000-voters-for-victory.html, accessed April 1, 2019.

The first experiment in that respect began in 1994 for Labour with a database called Excalibur aimed at gathering information on key issues and rivals to help achieve fast response at election times. It was then planned to extend the prototype to store data on members and voters but the project was abandoned for budgetary reasons. The concept was however reintroduced following the 2005 General election as technology had evolved. The current Labour database puts together all the data the party holds over its voters, members, activists and anyone who took part in a party-related activity, even if only to sign up for a newsletter or to donate money once. All parties now possess such databases. The Conservative system was called Vault from 2005, then Merlin and Votesource more recently.

Parties have thus built massive databases with the information collected by their members to which they added data from the electoral register but also from the property sales register, census statistics, phone companies, online retailers, loyalty cards etc., containing information such as names of voters in a specific constituency, age, gender, income, charities supported, occupation, house ownership.[37]

Private operators like Nation Builder or data brokers have also been selling data to parties to feed their databases:

> In 2018, one such company, Acxiom, claimed to be able to provide information on up to 10,000 attributes on some 2.5 billion consumers, including on religion, socioeconomic status, relationship status, housing situation, and internet habits. For example, Acxiom segments were used together with Facebook data as part of the Conservative party campaign in the 2015 general election.[38]

In the 2015 and 2017 General elections as well as the Brexit referendum in 2016, the use of such targeting rose significantly with the Conservatives as the main spenders in this area[39]:

> For example, one Facebook message targeted female UKIP waverers with the slogan: "We're building a brighter, more secure future for our children and grandchildren. A vote for UKIP,

---

37 Information Commissioner's Office, "Democracy disrupted? Personal Information and Political Influence", July 11, 2018, accessed April 1, 2019, https://ico.org.uk/media/2259369/democracy-disrupted-110718.pdf.
38 Privacy International, "How the UK Conservative Leadership Race is Latest Example of Political Data Exploitation", June 18, 2019, https://privacyinternational.org/long-read/3019/how-uk-Conservative-leadership-race-latest-example-political-data-exploitation, accessed April 1, 2019.
39 Mark Ward, "Facebook becomes key tool in parties' political message", *BBC News*, June 2, 2017, https://www.bbc.com/news/election-2017-40119962, accessed April 1, 2019.

or any party other than the Conservatives, would let in Labour and the SNP – and risk everything we've achieved together over the last five years."

Attached was a short video about the economic recovery:

> [...] Homing in on these marginal constituencies and targeting older, less politically engaged users on Facebook (as opposed to younger, more politically savvy users on Twitter), appeared to pay off big time for the Conservatives.[40]

Because their canvassing operation is less strong than Labour's, technology provided the Conservatives with an alternative to gather data on voters for targeting purposes. This was also true for the movements involved in the EU referendum which could not rely on party databases. Vote Leave for instance spent 40 per cent of its total budget, or £2.7 million, on the services of a company specialised in social media targeting and advertising.[41]

In 2017, Labour introduced software called Promote, which links their huge database to social media profiles so that, for instance, someone mentioning worries about taxation during canvassing or a phone call from a volunteer would then find content on the party's programme on this topic on their Facebook page. The procedure for Promote is meant to be straightforward: the member identifies targets on the party database, lists them, creates ad content, specifies how long he/she wants their ad to run for and the budget available and Promote automatically posts the ad to the Facebook page of the targeted voters. This functions in connection with a tool called Contact Creator which contains voter data classified according to a variety of criteria aimed at targeting communication like social media posts or emails so as to, for instance, send a message on school policies to couples with children in a certain area. One of the functionalities offers the possibility to track whether emails or links within emails were opened or not so as to assess reach and efficiency of specific content. Nation builder can also help identify people on social media who have interacted with a post via a "like" for instance so as to send them further information in the future.

---

[40] Net Imperative, "Politics case study: How smart social media targeting helped Conservatives with the UK election", January 28, 2016, http://www.netimperative.com/2016/01/politics-case-study-how-smart-social-targeting-helped-Conservatives-win-the-uk-election/, accessed April 1, 2019.

[41] Dan Sabbagh, "Rise of Digital Politics: Why UK Parties Spend Big on Facebook", *The Guardian*, March 23, 2018.

Impact

Voting Behaviour and Electoral Outcome

Since the 1990s, British parties have therefore refined their digital tools and methods. However, the impact of the various digitally-induced modifications described above on mobilisation and election outcomes is complex to assess given that voting behaviour is the result of a multiplicity of factors and how difficult it is to isolate one from the others. Yet research from Liberini, Redoano, Russo, Cuevas and Cuevas on the 2016 American election concludes:

> Online political campaigns targeting Facebook users by gender, location and political allegiance significantly increased support for Republican candidate Donald Trump. The micro-targeted campaigns exploiting Facebook's profiling tools were highly effective both in persuading undecided voters to support Mr Trump, and in persuading Republican supporters to turn out on polling day.[42]

While Mark Ward for the BBC reports the following opinion of Dominic Cummings, director of the Vote Leave campaign in 2016 and current advisor to Boris Johnson:

> [Vote Leave] put 98 percent of its cash into digital adverts. Over the course of 10 weeks it served about one billion targeted ads – most of which were despatched via Facebook.
> Mr Cummings said the campaign went through a well-managed process of refining the adverts to make sure they reached the right people at the right moments.
> "Many big-shot traditional advertising characters told us we were making a huge error," Mr Cummings has said of that campaign. "They were wrong. It is one of the reasons we won."[43]

But how far can "one of the reasons" be a decisive one? On the one hand, although the difference made by ICTs at election time may be limited, both the 2016 U.S. presidential election and the Brexit referendum were decided by relatively low margins, suggesting that in such tight contests, even a limited influence can be sufficient to tip the balance, with serious consequences. While a similar approach to the one described by Cummings seemed to pay off for the

---

42 Federica Liberini, Redoano Michela, Russo Antonio, Cuevas Angel and Cuevas Ruben, "Politics in the Facebook Era: Evidence from the 2016 US Presidential Elections", *CAGE Working Papers* 389 (2018): 2.
43 Mark Ward, "Facebook becomes key tool in parties' political message", BBC News, June 2, 2017, https://www.bbc.com/news/election-2017-40119962, accessed April 1, 2019.

Conservatives in 2015, it did not prevent however the highly disappointing results for the party at the 2017 election. Although they spent much more than Labour for digital advertising and reached 80 per cent of voters in their targeted seats thanks to Facebook ads,[44] they still lost their majority in parliament.

Similarly, in 2019, on Facebook, Twitter and Instagram, Jeremy Corbyn was firmly ahead of Boris Johnson both in terms of engagement with his posts and number of new followers and the same was true at party level too.[45] Moreover, between the 2017 and 2019 elections, Labour had perfected its targeting tools and its platform designed to optimise its campaign on the ground – My Campaign Map – was said to be the most elaborate ever. It offered a more refined use of data to identify allegedly key constituencies and much more flexibility to send volunteers not just to their nearest marginal, as in 2017, but to the constituency where help was the most needed. Yet Labour not only lost the marginals but was also heavily defeated in its traditional heartlands, which questions the notion of safe seats, the role of technology in facilitating the targeting described above as well as the relevance of high social media engagement for electoral victory.

Asked about Barak Obama's 2008 campaign, hailed for its use of digital technology for mobilisation purposes, Conservative party chairman Eric Pickles in 2009 concluded:

> It was not a case of the traditional "it was the *Sun* what won it" being replaced by "it was Google that got it". [...] To believe that the online campaign was a silver bullet that if replicated will guarantee electoral success [...] risks us kidding ourselves into a complacency that getting our web presence right guarantees a win. Obama won because he [...] spoke directly to the American public increasingly frustrated and disillusioned by the political process. Obama gave them hope, a vision of the future and importantly offered Leadership they "could believe in."[46]

This is an opinion shared by Joe Todd, the press and communications officer of Momentum, the group in charge of Labour's digital strategy in 2017 and 2019: "If you don't have the political programme or the vision that mobilises people and

---

44 Mark Ritson, "How to Win an Election in Seven Complex Steps", Marketing Week, June 5, 2017, https://www.marketingweek.com/mark-ritson-how-win-election/, accessed April 1, 2019.
45 David Berretta, "Introducing the Pulsar/89up Social Election Tracker", *Pulsar*, December 5, 2019, https://www.pulsarplatform.com/blog/2019/introducing-the-pulsar-uk-election-social-index/, accessed April 1, 2019.
46 Tim Montgomerie, "The Conservative Party is streets ahead of the opposition when it comes to online campaigning, claims Eric Pickles", *Conservativehome*, March 14, 2009, https://Conservativehome.blogs.com/torydiary/2009/03/the-conservat-1.html, accessed April 1, 2019.

makes them enthusiastic and passionate, the technology's useless."[47] However effective the bullet, it is thus only one element in a complex chain reaction involving factors and forces only partially within the remit of party control.

Instability and Control for Parties

In a variety of cases, the adoption of digital technologies has actually introduced a higher degree of unpredictability and instability for parties, as exemplified for instance by the resignation from the Labour Shadow Cabinet of Emily Thornberry in 2014 in the context of the Rochester and Strood by-election after she tweeted a controversial picture of a white van in front of a house with English flags displayed on its front, in keeping with Gibson, Nixon and Ward's 2003 belief that "The internet has come to be seen as both saviour and executioner of political parties."[48]

The type of tightly managed campaigning with strict party control over message run by Alastair Campbell on behalf of Tony Blair for instance now seems to belong to a by-gone era with the multiplication of communication channels with low barriers for access and the potential for viral reach encouraged by digital technologies. With their potential unsurprisingly came new complications for parties. The 2010 campaign among others can attest to this phenomenon. Mere hours after the official launch of the Conservative "We Can't Go on Like This" poster series, templates were available on the web to design parodies with functionalities for immediate sharing on social networks, thus ruining the effect of a carefully prepared and highly expensive campaigning effort as the satirical versions ended up more commented both online and offline than the originals. In 2015, web users were also quick to point out that the peaceful landscape used as a background to the "Let's stay on the road to a stronger economy" Conservative poster was in fact a picture of a German countryside while UKIP's #WhyI'mVotingUkip hashtag for the 2014 elections to the European parliament was highjacked by opponents posting tweets such as "#WhyImVotingUkip Because in a country built by Angles, Saxons, Normans and Germans, the last

---

[47] Thomas Zagoria and Schulkind Rudy, "How Labour activists are already building a digital strategy to win the next election", New Statesman, July 18, 2017, https://www.newstatesman.com/politics/elections/2017/07/how-Labour-activists-are-already-building-digital-strategy-win-next, accessed April 1, 2019.

[48] Steven Ward, Rachel Gibson and Paul Nixon, *Political Parties and the Internet: Net Gain?* (London: Routledge, 2003), 1.

thing we need is immigrants" or "#WhyImVotingUkip because 60 years of peace in Europe is crippling my share options in B.A.E."⁴⁹

Conveying political messages and designing campaigning material with the help of templates or accessible editing software have thus been significantly facilitated, but the organisation of campaigning itself and the mobilisation of supporters have evolved too. Within parties, effort to introduce such technologies has sometimes been met with internal resistance, emphasising the notion that digital tools do not operate in a void away from contextual interference but depend for their impact on a multiplicity of factors beyond strictly technological ones. For example, the use of ICTs by the Cameron team to try and modernise the Conservative party from 2005 was repeatedly hindered from within the party itself. The reluctance to adopt tools such as Merlin or MyConservatives.com, the equivalent of Membersnet, was directly related to a general context of suspicion toward headquarters fuelled by episodes such as the drafting in 2006 of a priority list meant to enable more women and minority candidates to stand for elections but seen as a threat to local interests and autonomy.

Concurrently, while platforms as elaborate as Membersnet are still the monopoly of parties, activists loosely affiliated with them or independent from them have been making use of tools such as Slack for collaborative work via direct messaging, file sharing, task assignation or progress notification, but also WhatsApp for communication or Facebook groups to coordinate action.

Official campaigns are therefore joined by other, ad-hoc, informal groups, which Dommett and Temple refer to as "satellite campaigns", i.e "campaigns originating beyond party structures and control",⁵⁰ a phenomenon echoed in the change in terminology adopted by the Hansard Audit in 2009, which substituted "politically active" for "political activist", using the following argument to account for their decision: "The definition "politically active" is new in this audit – the indicator previously referred to "political activist" but following a review, we have determined that the latter term may misrepresent the focus of the indicator question for it is possible to be politically active without being an activist as traditionally understood in the context of party politics."⁵¹ The Grime4Corbyn

---

49 James Crisp, "Twitter Hashtag Backfires on UKIP Ahead of Elections", Euractiv.Com, May 21, 2014, https://www.euractiv.com/section/uk-europe/news/twitter-hashtag-backfires-on-ukip-ahead-of-elections/, accessed April 1, 2019.
50 Katharine Dommett and Luke Temple, "Digital Campaigning: The Rise of Facebook and Satellite Campaigns", *Britain Votes* (2017): 189–202, 195.
51 Ruth Fox, Virginia Gibbons and Matt Korris, "Audit of Political Engagement 7: the 2010 Report", Hansard Society, 2010, https://assets.ctfassets.net/rdwvqctnt75b/4utWyL6rVuIgIMmkY

movement in 2017 exemplifies this trend. Musicians from that electronic and dance music scene launched several initiatives in support of the Corbyn campaign and voting more generally. They set up a website, organised fundraising concerts and discussion panels on issues such as urban poverty. The hashtag #grime4Corbyn on Twitter came to overtake #LabourManifesto.

The degree of integration of such satellites into the main campaign varies and can transform over time. Momentum for instance started as a pro-Corbyn grassroot group in 2015 but its new constitution introduced in 2017 made membership of the Labour party compulsory for its participants. As for grime4Corbyn, while it claimed independence from the party, borders were not waterproof as AJ Tracey's video on the official Twitter page of Labour attests. Thus, digital technologies contributed to a blurring of the boundaries circumscribing political organisations and of the definition of insiders and outsiders to such bodies.[52]

For Chadwick and Stromer-Galley, this trend is rather positive: "Parties are being renewed from the outside in, as digitally enabled citizens breathe new life into an old form by partly remaking it in their own participatory image. Particularly on the left, the overall outcome might prove more positive for democratic engagement and the decentralization of political power than many have assumed".[53] Yet, they also state: "The role of digital media practices in reshaping political parties and election campaigns is driven by a tension between control and interactivity but the overall outcome for the party organizational form is highly uncertain".[54]

The relationship between insiders with a grasp of digital technology ranging from proficiency to unambiguous dismissal and digitally literate outsiders at best loosely constrained by party rules and procedures is part of this uncertainty, as well as the capacity of party headquarters to mobilise such a disparate force to serve its political objectives. Significantly, the Grime4Corbyn movement refused to campaign for Labour in 2019, with most of the artists involved feeling abandoned by the party and the candidate once the 2017 election was over.[55]

---

geEMI/1db7d836a1beb27bffd953da65a56848/Audit_of_Political_Engagement_7__2010_.pdf, accessed April 1, 2019.

52 Géraldine Castel, "The Evolution of UK Parties in the Web 2.0 and Post-Spin Era", in *New Technology, Organizational Change and Governance*, ed. E. Avril et C. Zumello (London: Palgrave, 2013).

53 Andrew Chadwick and Jennifer Stromer Galley, "Digital Media, Power, and Democracy in Parties and Election Campaigns: Party Decline or Party Renewal?", *International Journal of Press/Politics* 21, no. 3 (2016): 283–293.

54 Ibid.

55 Bakare Lanre, "Grime4Corbyn Artists Step Back from New Campaign for Labour", *The Guardian*, November 10, 2019.

They preferred to get involved with other initiatives such as the Fck Boris street parties in an evolution reminiscent of that of campaigners involved in 2010 in the Facebook page "We got Rage Against the Machine to n°1, We can get the Lib Dems into Office!" who drifted off to join other campaigns after the election rather than participate in the day to day activities of the party they had supported.

With the stepping down of Jeremy Corbyn following the results of the 2019 General Election, such a migration has started for Momentum activists as well, a trickle while the leadership contest is still ongoing but which could turn into a flood with the defeat of Rebecca Long-Bailey, the candidate supported by the movement, for the position of party leader. An en masse departure of the most digitally skilled activists of the party would deprive it of a powerful asset for future campaigning and organisation, highlighting the risk in entrusting the party's digital strategy to a group attached to a candidate and a set of causes rather than to the party itself. However, even if the exodus does not happen, the situation still remains complex. Gerbaudo evokes Momentum's "younger militants, who have been politicised by events such as the 2010 student protests, the Occupy movement, and Corbyn's election as Labour leader. These people tend to be suspicious of delegate democracy, of the heavy intermediation that it involves, and of the cadres who carry out these tasks. They [...] believe that all members should be empowered to participate directly in important decisions whenever possible."[56] Digital technologies provide tools to help advance towards such an objective, like for instance the My.momentum platform (https://my.peoplesmomentum.com/) intended to help run consultations on various issues or draft proposals for the party's Democracy review.[57]

Yet, what then when those activists clash with party insiders, as Momentum has been doing with parts of Labour, and more particularly with the Parliamentary Labour Party and deputy leader Tom Watson from 2015 to 2019? What when the same movement launches a nationwide campaign to replace some of their party's democratically elected sitting MPs under its new trigger ballot system

---

[56] Paolo Gerbaudo, "Momentum, Labour and the Rise of the Platform Party" (Pluto Press, 2018), https://www.plutobooks.com/blog/momentum-Labour-online-digital-activism-social-media-party/, accessed April 1, 2019.
[57] The Democracy Review refers to a series of meetings held with thousands of Labour party members, CLPs, MPs etc. to gather views and ideas to enhance the democratic functioning on the party: "At Democracy Review events we have asked members what further changes we should make to reconnect people with politics – how we can develop a people powered policy-making process, how we ensure that all sections of our diverse society are involved in our structures" (Labour Party, 2018).

as Momentum did in July 2019? What happens then if the effort of parties to engage and mobilise generates an influx of motivated, innovative and influential individuals whose objectives eventually turn out to be different from those of the leadership or the majority of party members? Who is the legitimate voice of a party? How should its representatives be chosen? What form should internal democracy take? Such questions are nothing new within parties but technological evolution has generated both innovation and renewed interrogations on those issues.

Mixed Pointers for Democracy

Beyond parties too, the introduction of ICT has resulted in a contrasted picture. For Hoff, Horrocks and Tops in the introduction to *Democratic Governance and New Technology:*

> The focus of this book is the relationship between new forms of information and communication technology (ICT) and the current restructuring and redefinition of many of the fundamental relations within the political systems of Western European countries. The basic claim of the book is that ICT plays an important role in this process of restructuring and redefining. Evidence is brought forward of this relationship: that ICT has become part and parcel of different new 'visions' or models of democracy. However, the book concludes that the extent to which these developments offer solutions to concerns about crises of democracy that have been a feature of Western democracies since the 1960s is questionable.[58]

In terms of engagement more specifically, Koc-Michalska and Lilleker's 2017 issue of *Political Communication* entitled "Digital Politics: Mobilization, Engagement, and Participation" also offers mixed conclusions:

> Democracy is said to rest on the power of people, coming together to solve collective problems or, more typically, selecting representatives who develop mutually acceptable solutions for their societies. The question is the extent to which this model is being challenged in the digital era: *if* more deliberative and engaging forms of politics are emerging in online and offline public spaces and *how* people are encouraged to become active. The public displays of political opinions, attitudes, and preferences feed into a complex communicative ecosystem within which a range of messages circulate, some seen by millions some seen by

---

[58] Jens Hoff, Ivan Horrocks and Pieter Tops, "Democratic Governance and New Technology: Technologically Mediated Innovations in Political Practice in Western Europe", *Routledge/ECPR Studies in European Political Science* 9, no. 2.

a small few. Some messages lead to action, some do not; some people are empowered, some are not.[59]

Indeed, if ICT in politics can help foster engagement for the broader benefit of parties and democratic institutions, they can also bring about the opposite effect at the levels of campaigning, internal organisation or strategy mentioned before. Even as early as the 1990s, and while Perrot's "electronic town hall" had never actually been implemented, its limits were already visible to some observers and quoted in Kelly's 1992 *New York Time*'s article:

> Will Marshall [the director of the Progressive Policy Institute], and many who study the relationship between the public and public policy fear that Mr. Perot's idea would make worse the very ills it proposes to correct. It is, they say, an awkward, unworkable hybrid – New England town hall meets Brave New World – founded on a series of false assumptions, and likely to push a process already characterized by superficiality, special-interest biases and demagoguery further in that direction.[60]

Those terms still echo decades later as the 2018 Hansard Audit showed that 49 per cent of respondents think social media is making political debate more divisive, and 46 per cent that it is making political debate more superficial.[61]

Besides, findings from various reports, such as the one released in 2018 by the Electoral Commission entitled *Digital Campaigning: Increasing Transparency for Voters*, but also from charities and NGOs like Tactical Tech, reveal serious concerns over the impact of the spreading of so called "fake news" via social media. The document released in 2019 by the House of Commons Digital, Culture, Media and Sport committee on disinformation and fake news stated:

> We have always experienced propaganda and politically-aligned bias, which purports to be news, but this activity has taken on new forms and has been hugely magnified by information technology and the ubiquity of social media. In this environment, people are able to accept and give credence to information that reinforces their views, no matter how distorted or inaccurate, while dismissing content with which they do not agree as "fake news". This has a polarising effect and reduces the common ground on which reasoned debate, based on objective facts, can take place. Much has been said about the coarsening of public de-

---

[59] Karolina Koc-Michalska and Darren Lilleker, "Digital Politics: Mobilization, Engagement, and Participation", *Political Communication* 34, no. 1 (2017): 1–5, 4.
[60] Michael Kelly, "The 1992 Campaign: Third-Party Candidate; Perot's Vision: Consensus by Computer", *The New York Times*, June 6, 1992.
[61] Joel Blackwell, Brigid Fowler and Ruth Fox, "Audit of Political Engagement 15: the 2018 Report", *Hansard Society* 13 (2018).

bate, but when these factors are brought to bear directly in election campaigns then the very fabric of our democracy is threatened.[62]

A study by researchers from King's College demonstrated that two years after the Brexit referendum, the majority of UK voters still believed the "we send the EU £350 m a week – let's fund our NHS instead" message conveyed by the Leave Campaign to be true, despite recurrent, documented assertions to the contrary from journalists and experts then and since. A fake statement which, according to the Vote Leave campaign director, nonetheless played a key role in tipping the vote in favour of Brexit in 2016.[63] As mentioned in this quotation, fake news in politics is no novelty in itself but its conveying via social media makes it visible to a much wider audience, and confers to it a veneer of reliability thanks to the organic, peer-to-peer nature of its dissemination, with the potential for repeat messaging chipping away at initial disbelief. Moreover, algorithms behind influential social platforms such as Facebook or YouTube have been shown to favour more radical contents[64] but also quantity over quality, with the most watched contents being given priority over factually accurate ones, a trend made even more alarming as such variables can be altered artificially for a cost. A 2017 Trend Micro report thus reveals how 100 comments on a YouTube video can be bought for $2.6 on the Russian dark web, while making a video appear on YouTube's main page for two minutes costs $621. An elaborate online campaign to discredit a public figure is estimated at $55,000 and helping instigate a street protest at $200,000.

Yet, despite warnings following the 2016 Brexit and U.S. presidential campaigns, fake news remained prominent in the 2019 UK General Election. First Draft, a verification and investigation non-profit, highlighted for instance how thousands of misleading Conservative ads side-stepped scrutiny and reached voters thanks to Facebook's decision to cancel fact-checking on political ads.[65]

---

[62] Culture, media and sport committee, "Disinformation and Fake News" report, UK Parliament, February 18, 2019, https://publications.parliament.uk/pa/cm201719/cmselect/cmcumeds/1791/179103.htm, accessed April 1, 2019.
[63] Jonathon Read, "Half of UK still believes £350 m message plastered on side of Vote Leave's bus", *The New European*, October 28, 2018.
[64] Tufekci Zeynep, "Youtube: The Great Radicalizer", *The New York Times*, March 10, 2018; Nicas Jack, "How YouTube Drives People to the Internet's Darkest Corners", *Wall Street Journal*, February 7, 2018.
[65] Reid Alastair and Dotto Carlotta, "Thousands of misleading Conservative ads side-step scrutiny thanks to Facebook policy", *First Draft*, December 6, 2019.

Conversely, a report by the think tank Demos paints a more encouraging picture regarding social media more specifically:

> We are living through a radical shift in the nature of political engagement. [...] Social media builds bridges between people and institutions, and at a scale and with an ease that has never before been possible. [...] A large majority (72 percent) of people who used social media for political purposes reported that they felt more politically engaged, in one way or another, as a direct result.[66]

Such a report, in keeping with research from Karpf[67] or Halupka[68] for instance, goes against the belief reflected in the coining of the word "slacktivism"[69] that most forms of online activism are meant to boost the ego of the participants rather than contribute meaningfully to the advancement of causes. Based on answers to an Ipsos Mori poll, it states that "People who used social media for political activity were also more likely to act on their political convictions as a direct result of it" and that "Social media is engaging some of those disengaged with politics", the young in particular. This is a conclusion which itself fits with the 55 per cent of respondents to the 2018 Audit of political engagement who think social media help broaden political debate by giving a voice to people who would not normally take part, and 40 per cent that social media help break down barriers between voters, politicians and political parties.[70]

Conclusion

So, for all its potential sophistication, has digital technology forced democracy to conform to the goals of strategists who make use of its potential to help parties connect with voters and citizens and achieve results in terms of electoral success and engagement? An analysis of the last two decades in the UK, while highlighting significant changes in tools, contents, methods and strategy, has not made it possible to provide a definite answer as opposite trends seem at play, the intro-

---

66 Carl Miller, The Rise of Digital Politics, Demos, 2016, 13, https://www.demos.co.uk/wp-content/uploads/2016/10/Demos-Rise-of-Digital-Politics.pdf, accessed April 1, 2019.
67 David Karpf, "Online Political Mobilization from the Advocacy Group's Perspective: Looking Beyond Clicktivism", *Policy and Internet* 2, no. 4 (2010).
68 Max Halupka, "Clicktivism: A Systematic Heuristic", *Policy & Internet* 6, no. 2 (2014).
69 Monty Phan, "On the Net, 'Slacktivism' / Do-gooders flood in-boxes", *Newsday*, February 26, 2001.
70 Ibid., 30.

duction of digital elements in the political sphere having been neither neutral in its influence nor a providential silver bullet.

Under the terms of the Fixed-term Parliaments Act, the next General Election in the UK should take place in 2024, eons in technological terms so rapidly do tools and practices evolve. What the digital landscape will look like then is today an enigma. In the meantime, while bulwarks protecting democracy, from MPs to public servants, from the media to the Supreme Court, are being eroded, one might hope that digital technology in the future might help to strengthen the defences more than it contributes to the assault.

Bibliography

Anonymous. "General Election Turnout 1945–2019". *UK Political Info*, 2019. http://www.ukpolitical.info/Turnout45.htm.

Audickas, Lukas et al. "Membership of UK Political Parties". *House of Commons Library Briefing Paper*. July 20, 2019. https://researchbriefings.parliament.uk/ResearchBriefing/Summary/SN05125.

Bakare, Lanre. "Grime4Corbyn Artists Step Back from New Campaign for Labour". *The Guardian*, November 10, 2019.

Berretta, David. "Introducing the Pulsar/89up Social Election Tracker". *Pulsar*, December 5, 2019. https://www.pulsarplatform.com/blog/2019/introducing-the-pulsar-uk-election-social-index/.

Biernacka-Ligięza, Ilona. "ICT and Local Governance – E-government in the Local Public Sphere in Poland and Norway". *Central European Journal of Communication* 4, no. 2 (2011): 293–313.

Blackwell, Joel, Brigid Fowler and Ruth Fox. "Audit of Political Engagement" 15. *Hansard Society*, 2018. https://assets.ctfassets.net/rdwvqctnt75b/iHWHYym8BquqsMQ64oaEC/5c151f5dc7302f37633977500f68c104/publication__hansard-society-audit-of-political-engagement-15–2018.pdf

Blackwell Joel, Brigid Fowler and Ruth Fox. "Audit of Political Engagement" 16. *Hansard Society*, 2019.
https://www.hansardsociety.org.uk/publications/reports/Audit-of-political-engagement-16.

Cable, Vince. "Building a Liberal Democrat Movement". Liberal Democrat Website, September 7, 2018. https://www.libdems.org.uk/building-a-liberal-democrat-movement.

Cardoso, Gustavo, Carlos Cunha and Susana Nascimento. "Bridging the e-democracy gap in Portugal: MPs, ICTs and political mediation". *Information, Communication and Society* 9, no. 4 (2006): 452–472.

Castel, Géraldine. "The Evolution of UK Parties in the Web 2.0 and Post-Spin Era". In *New Technology, Organizational Change and Governance*, edited by E. Avril et C. Zumello. London: Palgrave, 2013.

Castel, Geraldine. "David Cameron and the Web: The Parallel Evolution of Two Newcomers in the Run-up to the 2010 Election". *LISA* XII, no. 8 (2014). http://lisa.revues.org/6970.

Chacko, Ben. "Jeremy Corbyn: the big interview". *Morning Star*, December 23, 2015. https://morningstaronline.co.uk/a-f97d-jeremy-corbyn-the-big-interview-1.

Chadwick, Andrew, and Jennifer Stromer Galley. "Digital Media, Power, and Democracy in Parties and Election Campaigns: Party Decline or Party Renewal?" *International Journal of Press/Politics* 21, no. 3 (2016): 283–293.

Crabtree, James. "David Cameron's battle to connect". *Wired*, March 24, 2010. https://www.wired.co.uk/article/david-camerons-battle-to-connect.

Crisp, James. "Twitter Hashtag Backfires on UKIP Ahead of Elections". *Euractiv.Com*, May 21, 2014. https://www.euractiv.com/section/uk-europe/news/twitter-hashtag-backfires-on-ukip-ahead-of-elections/.

Culture, media and sport committee. "Disinformation and Fake News" report, UK Parliament, February 18, 2019. https://publications.parliament.uk/pa/cm201719/cmselect/cmcumeds/1791/179103.htm.

D'Urso, Joey. "Who spent what on Facebook during 2017 election campaign". *BBC News*, March 31, 2018. https://www.bbc.com/news/uk-politics-43487301.

Dominiczak, Peter. "Tories targeting fewer than 100,000 voters for victory". *The Telegraph*, May 3, 2015. https://www.telegraph.co.uk/news/politics/david-cameron/11580533/Tories-targeting-fewer-than-100000-voters-for-victory.html.

Dommett, Katharine, and Luke Temple. "Digital Campaigning: The Rise of Facebook and Satellite Campaigns". *Britain Votes* (2017): 189–202.

Electoral Commission. "Digital Campaigning: Increasing Transparency for Voters". June 2018. https://www.electoralcommission.org.uk/who-we-are-and-what-we-do/changing-electoral-law/transparent-digital-campaigning.

Fenton, Natalie, and Veronica Barassi. "Alternative Media and Social Networking Sites: The Politics of Individuation and Political Participation". *The Communication Review* 14 (July 2011): 179–196.

Fox, Ruth, Virginia Gibbons and Matt Korris. "Audit of Political Engagement 7: the 2010 Report". Hansard Society, 2010. https://assets.ctfassets.net/rdwvqctnt75b/4utWyL6rVulgIMmkYgeEMI/1db7d836a1beb27bffd953da65a56848/Audit_of_Political_Engagement_7__2010_.pdf.

Gerbaudo, Paolo. "Momentum, Labour and the Rise of the Platform Party". *Pluto Press*, 2018. https://www.plutobooks.com/blog/momentum-Labour-online-digital-activism-social-media-party/.

George, Éric. "Des relations entre démocratie et TIC: quelques enseignements issus de travaux récents". *Interin* 4, 2007.

Gibson, Rachel, and Stephen Ward. "On-Line and on Message? Candidate Websites in the 2001 General Election". *British Journal of Politics and International Relations*, 2003.

Gibson, Rachel, and Stephen Ward. "The First Internet Election? UK Political Parties and Campaigning in Cyberspace". In *Political Communications: The General Election Campaign of 1997*, edited by J. Bartle, I. Crewe and B. Gosschalk, 83–112. London: Frank Cass Publishers, 2012.

Gibson, Rachel, and Stephen Ward. "U.K. Political Parties and the Internet: "Politics as Usual" in the New Media?". *International Journal of Press/Politics*. 1998.

Gibson, Rachel, and Stephen Ward. "U.K. Political Parties and the Internet: Prospects for Democracy". *USIR*, 1997.

Gibson, Rachel, and Stephen Ward. "Party Democracy On-line: UK Parties and new ICTs". *Information, Communication & Society* 2, no. 3 (1999): 340–367.

Goodchild, Lauren, Charles Oppenheim and Marigold Cleeve. "MPs online: an evaluative study of MPs' use of web sites". *Aslib Proceedings* 59, no. 6 (2007): 565–587.

Graham, Todd, Marcel Broersma, Karin Hazelhoff and Guido van't Haar. "Between broadcasting, Political Messages and Interacting with voters". *Information, Communication & Society* 16 (2013): 692–716.

Grant, Will, Brenda Moon and Janie Busby Grant. "Digital Dialogue? Australian Politicians' use of the social network tool Twitter". *Australian Journal of Political Science* 45, no. 4 (2010): 579–604.

Grossman, Lawrence. *Electronic Republic: Reshaping American Democracy for the Information Age*. Penguin Books, 1995.

Gu, Lion, Kropotov Vladimir and Fyodor Yarochkin. "The Fake News Machine". *Trend Micro*, 2017.

Halupka, Max. "Clicktivism: A Systematic Heuristic". *Policy & Internet* 6, no. 2 (2014).

Hindman, Matthew. *The Myth of Digital Democracy*. Princeton: Princeton University Press, 2009.

Hoff, Jens et al. *Democratic Governance and New Technology: Technologically Mediated Innovations in Political Practice in Western Europe*. New York: Routledge, 2000.

Howard, James. "Perot's 'Electronic Town Hall' Wouldn't Work, letter to the editor". *New York Times*, June 7, 1992.

Hughes, Casper. "How Momentum delivered Labour's stunning election result – and how the Tories are trying to copy it". *The Independent*, July 19, 2017.

Information Commissioner's Office. "Investigation into the use of data analytics in political campaigns". November 6, 2018. https://ico.org.uk/media/action-weve-taken/2260271/investigation-into-the-use-of-data-analytics-in-political-campaigns-final-20181105.pdf.

Information Commissioner's Office. "Democracy disrupted? Personal Information and Political Influence". July 11, 2018. https://ico.org.uk/media/2259369/democracy-disrupted-110718.pdf.

Kamalipour, Yahya. "Communication Media and Globalization: an Iranian Perspective". *Global Media and Communication* 13, no. 3 (2007): 340–342.

Karpf, David. "Online Political Mobilization from the Advocacy Group's Perspective: Looking Beyond Clicktivism". *Policy and Internet* 2, no. 4 (2010).

Kelly, Michael. "THE 1992 CAMPAIGN: Third-Party Candidate; Perot's Vision: Consensus by Computer". *The New York Times*, June 6, 1992.

Koc-Michalska, Karolina, and Darren Lilleker. "Digital Politics: Mobilization, Engagement, and Participation". *Political Communication* 34, no. 1 (2017): 1–5.

Labour Party. "Digital Campaigning Guide". 2017. http://scottishLabour.org.uk/wp-content/uploads/2018/05/10008_17-Digital-Campaigning-Guide_v10.pdf.

Labour Party. "Engagement and Retention in your CLP". 2019. https://Labour.org.uk/wp-content/uploads/2019/10/Engagement-and-Retention-in-your-CLP.pdf.

Liberini, Federica, Michela Redoano, Antonio Russo, Angel Cuevas and Ruben Cuevas. "Politics in the Facebook Era: Evidence from the 2016 US Presidential Elections". *CAGE Working Papers* (2018): 89.

Lindh, Magnus, and Lee Miles. "Becoming Electronic Parliamentarians? ICT Usage in the Swedish Riksdag". *Journal of Legislative Studies* 13, no. 3 (2007): 422–440.

Margolis, Michael, and David Resnick. *Politics as Usual: The Cyberspace "Revolution"*. New York: Sage, 2000.

May, Theresa. "Conference Speech". *The Guardian*, October 7, 2002. https://www.the guardian.com/politics/2002/oct/07/Conservatives2002.Conservatives1.

Merrick, Jane. "Jeremy Corbyn to 'bring back Clause IV': Contender pledges to bury New Labour with commitment to public ownership of industry". *The Independent*, August 9, 2015.

Miller, Carl. The Rise of Digital Politics". *Demos*. 2016. https://www.demos.co.uk/wp-content/uploads/2016/10/Demos-Rise-of-Digital-Politics.pdf.

Momentum. "2017 General Election". 2018. https://peoplesmomentum.com/2018/01/12/2017-general-election/.

Montgomerie, Tim. "The Conservative Party is streets ahead of the opposition when it comes to online campaigning, claims Eric Pickles". *Conservativehome*. March 14, 2009. https://Conservativehome.blogs.com/torydiary/2009/03/the-conservat-1.html.

Moss, Giles, and Stephen Coleman. "Deliberative Manoeuvres in the Digital Darkness: E-Democracy Policy in the UK". *The British Journal of Politics and International Relations* 16, no. 3 (2014): 410–427.

Net Imperative. "Politics case study: How smart social media targeting helped Conservatives with the UK election". January 28, 2016. http://www.netimperative.com/2016/01/politics-case-study-how-smart-social-targeting-helped-Conservatives-win-the-uk-election/.

Nicas Jack. "How YouTube Drives People to the Internet's Darkest Corners". *Wall Street Journal*. February 7, 2018.

Office for National Statistics. "Internet access – households and individuals, Great Britain: 2018". 2018. https://www.ons.gov.uk/peoplepopulationandcommunity/house holdcharacteristics/homeinternetandsocialmediausage/bulletins/internetacces shouseholdsandindividuals/2018.

Phan, Monty. "On the Net, "Slacktivism' / Do-gooders flood in-boxes". *Newsday*, February 26, 2001.

Privacy International. "How the UK Conservative Leadership Race is Latest Example of Political Data Exploitation". June 18, 2019. https://privacyinternational.org/long-read/3019/how-uk-Conservative-leadership-race-latest-example-political-data-exploitation.

Read, Jonathon. "Half of UK still believes £350 m message plastered on side of Vote Leave's bus". *The New European*, October 28, 2018.

Reid, Alastair, and Carlotta Dotto. "Thousands of misleading Conservative ads side-step scrutiny thanks to Facebook policy". *First Draft*, December 6, 2019.

Rentoul, John. "Politics explained: 'How Momentum grew up, from Corbyn fan club to policy powerhouse'". *The Independent*, May 19, 2019.

Ritson, Mark. "How to Win an Election in Seven Complex Steps". *Marketing Week*, June 5, 2017. https://www.marketingweek.com/mark-ritson-how-win-election/.

Sabbagh, Dan. "Rise of Digital Politics: Why UK Parties Spend Big on Facebook". *The Guardian*, March 23, 2018.

SevenVentures. "5 Marketing lessons from 2017 UK Election". *Therestlesscmo*, July 19, 2017. http://therestlesscmo.com/post/5-marketing-lessons-from-2017-uk-election.

Stamp, Gavin. "Decoding Jeremy Corbyn's Speech". *BBC News*, September 29, 2015. https://www.bbc.com/news/uk-politics-34389321.

Tufekci, Zeynep. "Youtube: The Great Radicalizer". *The New York Times*, March 10, 2018.

Van Deth, Jan. "What is Political Participation?". *Oxford Research Encyclopedias*, 2016.
Walsh, Matt. "Understanding Labour's ingenious campaign strategy on Facebook". LSE Blogs, November 10, 2017. https://blogs.lse.ac.uk/politicsandpolicy/explaining-Labours-facebook-success/.
Ward, Mark. "Facebook becomes key tool in parties' political message". *BBC News*, June 2, 2017. https://www.bbc.com/news/election-2017-40119962.
White, Charles. "The memes that decided the outcome of the General Election". *Metro*, June 11, 2017. https://metro.co.uk/2017/06/11/the-memes-that-decided-the-outcome-of-the-general-election-6701277/.
Wills, David, and Stuart Reeves. "Facebook as a Political Weapon: Information in Social Networks". *British Politics* 4, no. 2 (2009): 265–281.
Zagoria, Thomas, and Rudy Schulkind. "How Labour activists are already building a digital strategy to win the next election". *New Statesman*, July 18, 2017. https://www.newstatesman.com/politics/elections/2017/07/how-Labour-activists-are-already-building-digital-strategy-win-next.

Marion Douzou
7 Mobilising the Right(-wing) voters
The Tea Party's Use of Technology

Introduction

> "It does not take a majority to prevail, but rather an irate, tireless minority keen to set brush fires of freedom in the minds of men." Samuel Adams

This quote from one of the Founding Fathers is repeatedly used by Tea Party activists who identify with this idea of the "tireless minority fighting for freedom." Paradoxically, they are convinced that most people agree with them but stay silent. One of the events that led to the creation of many Tea Party groups was a viewing party of Glenn Beck's show. The goal was to get people to see that they were not alone and that in fact they were part of the silent majority.[1] The hope was that it would empower people to "get off the couch and stop yelling at the TV,"[2] to act and to work to elect the right kind of politicians.[3]

Scholars have shown that the Tea Party movement appeared as a reaction to Barack Obama's election and the policies he started putting in place shortly after his election.[4] Many Tea Party activists explain that in November 2008, they felt like a frog who had been dropped in boiling water and would jump out imme-

---

[1] Glenn Beck's website – The 9–12 project: "Do you watch the direction that America is being taken in and feel powerless to stop it? Do you believe that your voice isn't loud enough to be heard above the noise anymore? Do you read the headlines everyday and feel an empty pit in your stomach... as if you're completely alone? If so, then you've fallen for the Wizard of Oz lie. While the voices you hear in the distance may sound intimidating, as if they surround us from all sides—the reality is very different. Once you pull the curtain away, you realize that there are only a few people pressing the buttons, and their voices are weak. The truth is that they don't surround us at all. We surround them", http://www.glennbeck.com/content/articles/article/198/21018/?utm_source=glennbeck&utm_medium=contentcopy_link, accessed June 17, 2019.
[2] This expression is constantly used by Tea Party activists in interviews to explain their initial involvement in the movement.
[3] Dick Armey and Matt Kibbe, *Give Us Liberty: A Tea Party Manifesto* (William Morrow, 2010).
[4] Kate Zernike, *Boiling Mad: Inside Tea Party America* (Times Books, 2010); Theda Skocpol and Vanessa Williamson, *The Tea Party and the Remaking of Republican Conservatism* (Oxford University Press, 2013); Christopher Parker and Matt Barretto, *Change They Can't Believe In: The Tea Party and Reactionary Politics in America* (Princeton University Press, 2013).

https://doi.org/10.1515/9783110710403-008

diately to save its life. This description shows that fear about the future of the country initially led to Tea Party mobilisation. In her book *Strangers in Their Own Land*, Arlie Hochschild explains Tea Party mobilisation in Louisiana as a reaction to the belief that the American dream Tea Party activists had been waiting for was now out of reach because government programs benefited immigrants and minorities.[5] When one looks at early Tea Party slogans, the worry of seeing the U.S. become a socialist country and of losing the country constantly transpires: "Let's take our country back," "Give me liberty, not debt", "Stop spending OUR money," "Push back America, no socialism," "Stop taxing us to death," "Stop indebting my children." One way of ensuring that Obama could not implement his policies was to get people to the polls in the 2010 midterms to prevent Democrats from winning other elections. However, as Theda Skocpol and Vanessa Williamson show in their book *The Tea Party and the Remaking of Republican Conservatism*,[6] very early on, another demand emerged: activists were deeply unhappy with Republicans in name only – or RINOs as they called them – who were elected to promote conservative values but gave up on these values once elected.[7] Negative emotions such as fear or anger have been shown to push activists to act[8] and in this case the anger and frustration Tea Party activists felt towards these politicians allowed the coordinators of grassroots groups to create an "emotion culture"[9] which led them, like other movements before them, to launch a movement to change the Republican Party from within. They threatened incumbents with primary challengers, found more conservative candidates willing to run for office and kept elected officials under scrutiny. One of the slogans that is found in one of the earliest demonstra-

---

[5] Arlie Hochschild, *Strangers in Their Own Land: Anger and Mourning on the American Right* (The New Press, 2016).

[6] Theda Skocpol and Vanessa, Williamson, *The Tea Party and the Remaking of Republican Conservatism* (Oxford University Press, 2013).

[7] Purging moderate republicans from the Republican Party is not a new development. George Kabaservice showed the struggles between moderates and conservatives from the 1960s to the Tea Party movement. See Geoffrey Kabaservice, *Rule and Ruin: The Downfall of Moderation and the Destruction of the Republican Party, From Eisenhower to the Tea Party* (Oxford University Press, 2013).

[8] Deborah Gould, *Moving Politics: Emotions and ACT UP's Fight against AIDS* (University Chicago Press, 2009); James Jasper, "Emotions and Social Movements: Twenty Years of Theory and Research", *Annual Review of Sociology* 37 (2011): 285–303. On the Tea Party movement specifically, see Holloway Sparks, "Mama Grizzlies and Guardians of the Republic: The Democratic and Intersectional Politics of Anger in the Tea Party Movement", *New Political Science* 37 (2015): 25–47.

[9] Arlie Hochschild, *The Managed Heart: Commercialization of Human Feeling* (University of California Press, 1983).

tions is: "Politicians are like diapers: they need changing regularly." This rhetoric constantly comes back in all the interviews I conducted. Activists depict themselves as a minority fighting a corrupt Republican Party which has lost its way.

This chapter aims at showing that one of the main objectives of the Tea Party movement was to educate people about conservative principles, turn like-minded citizens out to vote and increase conservative mobilisation. To fight their battle – both against the Democrats and the Republican Party – and to build their movement, Tea Party activists relied heavily on the Internet. New technologies played a key role in their mobilisation from the early days to the later phases of the movement. In recent years, many researchers have studied social movements' interaction with the Internet: in their book *Digitally Enabled Social Change*, Jennifer Earl and Katrina Kimport argue that "a new digital repertoire of contention" has emerged.[10] In her book *The Revolution That Wasn't: How Digital Activism Favors Conservatives*,[11] Jen Schradie shows that the use conservatives have made of the Internet is a lot less visible than progressive social movements like #Metoo or #BlackLivesMatter. Scholars who have written about the Tea Party movement and its use of the Internet have tended to focus on new technologies as a tool to mobilise more participants in the beginning of the movement. For instance, Deana A. Rohlinger and Jesse Klein showed the importance of "Internet Communication Technology" in the mobilisation of the Tallahassee Tea Party and their attempts to frame their concerns in a way that would attract the most people.[12] In this case, their study focused on a local online forum moderated by a leader. Although this approach is important to the study of social movements and emotions, it fails to include the broader frame of the Tea Party galaxy and its use of new technologies.

This chapter will examine the new technologies Tea Party activists relied on by looking at the various types of tools they used – Twitter, Meetup, Facebook, YouTube etc – and what impact they had on the movement during its various stages. In order to do that, researchers need to carefully study their websites and their daily habits online but also conduct interviews about the way they see these tools and the place they hold in Tea Party mobilisation. This chapter is based on a fieldwork carried out in Pennsylvania. It relies on interviews

---

10 Jennifer Earl and Katrina Kimport, *Digitally Enabled Social Change: Activism in the Internet Age* (The MIT Press, 2011).
11 Jen Schradie, *The Revolution that Wasn't: How Digital Activism Favors Conservatives* (Harvard University Press, 2019).
12 Deana A. Rohlinger and Jesse Klein, "From Fervor to Fear: ICT and Emotions in the Tea Party Movement", in *Understanding the Tea Party Movement*, ed. Nella Van Dyke and David Meyer (Ashgate, 2014).

with Tea Party activists and elected officials done in 2014–2015[13] and in the summer of 2018. We argue that Tea Party activists' relationship to digital activism is hard to understand because it is not always organised at the national level by very top-down organisations which are easy to track because of their hierarchical structure. An army of grassroots activists also used it regularly to fight for their cause. Therefore, this chapter raises the question of the relationship between the grassroots and more top-down organisations and their ability to work together through digital activism.

The goal is to wonder how transformative digital activism was to the social movement experience of Tea Party activists. Firstly, we will see how the movement came about and how it organised itself. Understanding how the Tea Party galaxy works is key to establishing the use the various groups made of the Internet. Then, we will focus on the importance of new technologies on this movement and see how it sometimes even created new mobilisation tactics. Finally, we will analyse how beyond these new strategies, Tea Party groups used the traditional social movement repertoire and tried to make some of its tactics more efficient by using new technologies.

The Tea Party Nebula: Mobilising Conservatives to Take their Country and Party Back

In 2009, what caught the media's attention were the first Tea Party rallies which were organised throughout the country and in Washington, D.C. These demonstrations were often set up by conservative organisations which existed before the creation of the movement such as Americans For Prosperity or FreedomWorks, two groups linked to the millionaire Koch brothers.[14] They were also sponsored by Tea Party Patriots, for instance, a national organisation created in 2009. Its goal was to work as an umbrella group for all the local Tea Parties that were popping up all around the country and whose members were attending these demonstrations.

Therefore, very early on, the Tea Party movement was often described as having two branches that worked hand in hand: the grassroots branch and the top-down branch. In their book *The Tea Party and the Remaking of Republican Conservatism*, political scientists Theda Skocpol and Vanessa Williamson added another branch to this description of the movement: the media. Indeed, they argue

---

13 This fieldwork was made possible by a scholarship from the Georges Lurcy Foundation.
14 Jane Mayer, "Covert operations," *The New Yorker*, August 23, 2010.

that from its very beginning, the movement benefited from constant coverage by Fox News but also, more surprisingly, by more mainstream channels like CNN.[15] Unlike most social movements who often struggle to be heard, the Tea Party had no trouble reaching a conservative as well as a mainstream audience. Political scientists Tina Fetner and Brayden King also introduced a third layer to the movement which would work as an intermediary between a group of wealthy donors that financed the movement's grassroots.[16]

This fieldwork in Pennsylvania was done in 2014–2015, after Barack Obama's 2012 re-election, at a time when the Tea Party movement was no longer in the limelight. It was difficult to reconcile the vertical representations of this two or three-branch movement with what the present author was witnessing and what activists were saying in interviews. We argue that a better way of representing the Tea Party movement is to think of it as a galaxy of organisations and groups that can work together from time to time but most of the time work independently towards a somewhat similar goal. In many ways the Tea Party movement functions as a very horizontal movement. Its members refuse all leaders and are very wary of people who speak in the name of the movement. They welcome the help of outside organisations such as the ones mentioned earlier but also from conservative universities like *Grove City College*, think tanks like *The Heritage Foundation* or *The Commonwealth Foundation* or from talk-radio hosts both at the national level with Glenn Beck and at the local level with Dom Giordano or Rose Tennent and Jim Quinn.[17] These other groups that make up the Tea Party galaxy help them train grassroots activists, bring attention to a particular bill that is about to pass, or help them organise events. In the case of talk-radio hosts, they also ensure that emotions of outrage, anger and frustration that led to grassroots mobilisation are stoked daily and therefore almost guarantee continued activism for Tea Party members.

Representing the Tea Party movements in such a way allows us to understand its historical roots. Indeed, conservative media and conservative universities pre-date the movements and belong to a conservative network that was slowly built over time. To give a very striking example, some of the members of the John Birch Society, an anti-communist organisation founded in 1958, attend Tea Party meetings, just like members of militia groups such as the Oath-

---

15 Skocpol and Williamson, op. cit, 131.
16 Tina Fetner and Brayden King, "Three-Layer Movements, Resources and the Tea Party," in *Understanding the Tea Party Movement*, ed. Nella Van Dyke and David Meyer (Ashgate, 2014).
17 Dom Giordano is the host of "Dom Giordano Show" on WPHT 1210 AM radio in Philadelphia and Rose Tennent and Jim Quinn were the hosts of "The War Room" on WPGB in Pittsburgh.

keepers,[18] Christian-Right organisations,[19] or libertarian-leaning groups[20] do. Grassroots Tea Party groups bring together people who had never been involved in politics before and seasoned activists from prior conservative movements.

The concerns of grassroots Tea Party groups may vary from one group to the next because one might choose to focus on school board elections when another will make immigration its number one priority. However, one of the goals they have in common is to reclaim power over their elected officials and to take control of the Republican Party. To get organised to fulfil this goal and to keep in touch with the various participants in this Tea Party galaxy, technology plays a crucial role. It works as the link between all these groups and allows grassroots activists to mobilise.

The Power of Digital Activism in Tea Party Grassroots Mobilisation

Communication in a social movement is crucial. Activists need to communicate to supporters, to the general public – that is to potential supporters – and to its target – in our case, elected officials. Most of the time, mass media play this role. As David Meyer explains, mass media was often used as: "a medium of transmission of information to reach others. Activists want media to (a) report on their concerns; (b) cover their activities; (c) publicize their organisations; (d) convey a profile that emphasizes strength, seriousness, and legitimacy and effectiveness to supporters and potential supporters."[21] There is no denying that the Tea Party movement relied heavily on mass media, especially in the coverage of early dem-

---

[18] The Oathkeepers was created in 2009 by Steward Rhodes. According to their website, it is a "non-partisan association of current and formerly serving military, police, and first responders, who pledge to fulfill the oath all military and police take to "defend the Constitution against all enemies, foreign and domestic." That oath, mandated by Article VI of the Constitution itself, is *to the Constitution*, not to the politicians, and Oath Keepers declare that they will not obey unconstitutional orders, such as orders to disarm the American people, to conduct warrantless searches, or to detain Americans as "enemy combatants" in violation of their ancient right to jury trial". https://oathkeepers.org/about/, accessed on June 19, 2019.

[19] To give but one example, the Freedom and Faith Coalition sometimes has speakers talk to Tea Party groups.

[20] In Pennsylvania, the Valley Forge Revolutionaries which came out of the 2008 Ron Paul campaign participated in the first Tea Party demonstrations. Citizens for Liberty was another one of these libertarian groups which organised meetings on libertarian issues.

[21] David Meyer, *The Politics of Protest: Social Movements in America*, 2nd edition (Oxford University Press, 2015), 127.

onstrations in 2009–2010. However, the Internet allowed activists to build tools that made it possible for them to reach their supporters directly. It was especially crucial in the beginning of the movement.

The Launch of a Leaderless Mobilisation

Pinpointing the beginning of the Tea Party movement is not as easy as one may think. Some point to February 19, 2008, when CNBC presenter Rick Santelli went on a rant saying that Americans were tired of paying for their neighbour's mortgage and called for the organisation of a Chicago Tea Party in July:

> Rick Santelli: This is America! How many of you people want to pay for your neighbor's mortgage? (...) We're thinking about having a Chicago Tea Party in July. All you capitalists that want to show up to Lake Michigan I'm going to start organizing.
>
> The journalist: What are you dumping?
>
> Rick Santelli: Dumping in some derivative securities what do you think about that?[22]

The video went viral and it gave Conservatives' growing discontent a name as well as a momentary spokesperson. Others see the start of the Tea Party in the story of Keli Carender, a blogger from Seattle, who had expressed frustration on her blog a month before and had planned a demonstration three days before Santelli's rant.[23] In both these cases, the use of blogs and the ability to share this video quickly to a wide number of individuals were crucial. They put people in touch with one another and allowed a collective reaction. Robert Putnam warns against the tendency to "exaggerate the role of individual heroes and to understate the importance of the collective effort."[24] In this case, the use of the Internet transformed an individual rant which could have gone unnoticed into a spark that could set fire to the frustration conservatives had been experiencing for years. This obviously does not mean that every rant, every spark, is as widely shared or is able to mobilise people as effectively. One of the reasons it worked for the Tea Party movement was that some pre-existing groups like *FreedomWorks* were already in place and ready to help turn this discontent into a movement. To do so, they started a website called "ImwithRick.com" which, according

---

22 Rick Santelli's rant on CNBC: https://www.youtube.com/watch?v=bEZB4taSEoA.
23 Kate Zernike, *Boiling Mad: Inside Tea Party America* (Times Books, 2010), 13–19.
24 Robert Putman, *Bowling Alone: The Collapse and Revival of American Community* (Simon & Schuster International), 2001, 22.

to them, got tens of thousands of visitors in the first couple of days.[25] Many newcomers to politics asked for help to organise rallies and *FreedomWorks* put at their disposal various tools to mobilise such as a map which showed all the events organised by activists so individuals could find the closest group and a platform to communicate with other soon-to-be activists.

Simultaneously, the website *MeetUp* became a tool for grassroots groups to organise and plan their meetings. Each page gives a brief description of the group and what they stand for. It gives information about the coming events. People can join the group as they do on other platforms like Facebook. They can talk to one another, they can comment on events and they can be kept up to date about the next meeting. These groups create a kind of online community that then spreads to other platforms like Facebook when activists add one another as friends and continue their conversation on this new medium. Sites like MeetUp and Facebook were crucial in building the online community Tea Party groups relied on. It created a space for them to get to know one another and to fine-tune their ideological positions.

Building New Platforms and Training Activists

On Facebook, activists share articles, videos and pictures they find interesting or shocking. This usually leads to a long conversation – which can get pretty heated – either with people who disagree with the movement or with activists themselves. Facebook very quickly became a place where activists would get ideological training from a wide variety of sources. These organisations were starting to get the conservative message out through new channels as they deemed the existing ones too biased against their ideas. Jen Schradie explains that: "Conservative grassroots, professional, and media groups were unified in believing they needed to replace so-called fake news with their own political information online."[26] Indeed, for most Pennsylvania Tea Party activists, TV channels are not their primary sources of information but they claim to get most of their information online.

The documents activists share often come from conservative media such as *The Drudge Report*, *Glenn Beck's show*, *Breitbart.com* or *The Daily caller*. They rely on content that comes from organisations that pre-dated the movement as well

---

25 Dick Armey and Matt Kibbe, op.cit, 27.
26 Jen Schradie, op. cit, 8.

as new online right-wing opinion sites.[27] To take but one example, in the beginning of the movement, Glenn Beck's show on progressivism was widely shared. It showed the Fox News host in front of a blackboard explaining the history and the evils of progressivism in the U.S..[28]

Glenn Beck is far from being the only example. The desire to get ideological training leads groups to attend conferences at conservative universities like Grove City College which did a series on the Founding Fathers. These lectures highlight founders and presidents who they deem to have been forgotten or misjudged by liberal elites. One of these figures is Calvin Coolidge, whose presidency is presented as a golden age when the federal government intervened far less in citizens' lives and when unemployment was very low.[29] These conferences aim at creating a common vision of American history with its conservative heroes and values. It allows activists to see their mobilisation as part of a wider historical frame. The video of this conference is then shared online and on Facebook for activists who could not attend to watch.

Furthermore, new groups emerged to satisfy this desire to get ideological training and acquire historical arguments and examples. It led to the creation of websites like *Prager University*. Dennis Prager, a long-time talk-radio host, started this online "university" in 2011. They create five-minute videos on a wide range of topics that allow activists to learn the superficial conservative position on these issues. One of the videos entitled "JFK: republican or democrat?" explains how JFK would have been a Republican today.[30] Another video from Caroline Kitchens, from *The Enterprise Institute*, a conservative think tank created at the end of the 1930s, asserts that rape culture does not exist on college campuses.[31] The importance of the electoral college or the debate around abortion are also tackled in numerous videos. This university often relies on conservative "experts" who work for conservative think tanks to make conservative positions accessible to a wider audience.

The impact of such training can be seen in the interviews, in Facebook posts, and in the monthly meetings Tea Party groups hold. Indeed, the examples given

---

[27] *The Drudge report* was created in 1995, *Glenn Beck's show* in 2006, *Breitbart.com* in 2007. *The Daily caller* appeared in 2010, that is after the beginning of the Tea Party movement.

[28] "Glenn Beck on Progressivism Part 1", youtube.com, March 20, 2010, https://www.youtube.com/watch?v=tP5epjCTW0Q, accessed June 18, 2019.

[29] L. John Van Til, "*Thoughtful Cal, the Founders & the Progressives*", March 30, 2010, https://www.visionandvalues.org/2010/03/2010-thoughtful-cal-the-founders-and-the-progressives/, accessed June 18, 2019.

[30] https://www.youtube.com/watch?v=H-Qg_4zqpDI, accessed June 18, 2019.

[31] https://www.youtube.com/watch?v=K0mzqL50I-w&vl=en, accessed June 18, 2019.

by activists and the reasoning they use is often the same word for word even when they don't live in the same area. It is very likely to be the result of the same training – most of which is done online and on one's own. Such a training builds up the confidence of activists to communicate with the rest of the world and especially with their elected officials.

Keeping Politicians Accountable

New technologies play a key role in the tactics top-down groups and grassroots activists use. Indeed, as Jennifer Earl and Katrina Kimport explain, before the Internet, participation in social movements required spending hours with other people and even sometimes putting oneself in harm's way. With the Internet, there has been a "dramatic drop in participation costs (which) means that participants are able to easily and quickly respond to the calls for well-designed e-tactics."[32] Reliance on these "rushes of participation"[33] is a common tactic in the Tea Party movement. Indeed, one of the main goals of the Tea Party is to make sure Republican officials follow conservative principles – fiscally and socially speaking. For instance, they want to make sure that they vote against any bill that would directly or indirectly raise taxes or increase government spending. This leads them to keep a close eye on the way their elected officials vote. To help them keep politicians accountable, top-down groups like *Heritage Action* created scorecards that give grades to each elected official to assess how truly conservative they are. On *Heritage*'s website,[34] activists have access to all the votes an elected official has taken against *Heritage*'s position and therefore against conservative positions. When elected officials are about to vote on a bill, activists call, e-mail or go see them to put pressure on them to do the "right" thing. Because it is sometimes hard to follow when a bill is being voted on or what is really in the bill, top-down organisations and grassroots groups send alerts to mobilise activists and tell them to call their elected officials. *Americans For Prosperity* even created a "Twitter brigade" that is a team of stay-at-home moms who don't necessarily have time to go to rallies or to go see their elected officials but who will send a message or a tweet to their relatives and friends through Twitter, Facebook or e-mail. As one member of the "Twitter Brigade" explained: "The reason I got involved was through Katy Abram's Twit-

---

32 Jennifer Earl and Katrina Kimport, op.cit, 184.
33 Ibid., 184.
34 https://heritageaction.com/scorecard, accessed June 18, 2019.

ter brigade because I could sit on my sofa and tweet at somebody or post something on Facebook, I was doing that anyway. But I worked during the day so it wasn't likely that I was going to show up for a rally."[35] This tactic could be seen as no more than "slacktivism"[36] except the elected officials I interviewed in Pennsylvania said it was an efficient technique to show how much their constituents cared about an issue.

This tactic is not new and has been used by other organisations such as unions for years. What is surprising, in the case of the Tea Party, is that such a horizontal and decentralised movement that does not have official members who pay dues is able to use this strategy effectively. New technologies play a big part in making such tactics available to these new types of mobilisations. However, as we have seen, pre-existing organisations such as *Heritage Action* or *Americans For Prosperity* are key in making the grassroots' use of the Internet more efficient. Jen Schradie finds that leaderless movements are less likely to use the Internet: "Digital activism takes work, and work takes organisation. The social movement groups with the capacity to do digital work had more complex organisational infrastructure. It takes this infrastructure to develop, and especially maintain, digital use and participation." However, in the case of the Tea Party, the work that is required to make digital activism effective can take place thanks to the help of top-down organisations but also thanks to the activism of grassroots activists who can mobilise around an issue that is particularly important to them and might not even be supported by the top-down organisations they occasionally work with.[37] Grassroots Tea Party activists put in the work, spend hours online, updating their websites, writing newsletters, posting comments or messages on Facebook groups, writing to their elected officials or debating online.

---

35 Interview with an activist who was part of the "Twitter Brigade" before she started working for *Americans For Prosperity*, at the coffee shop Little Amps in Harrisburg on February 2, 2015.
36 "Slacktivism" is a combination of the words "slacker" and "activism". The Cambridge Dictionary defines slacktivism as an "Activity that uses the internet to support political or social causes in a way that does not need much effort, for example creating or signing online petitions: such forms of advocacy, particularly those related to social media, are often derisively referred to as "slacktivism" or "armchair activism". For more on slacktivism, see David Karpf, "Slacktivism as optical illusion", Oxford University Press' Blog, November 19, 2014, http://blog.oup.com/2014/11/slacktivism-optical-illusion-political-activism/, accessed March 18, 2020.
37 This was the case with SB-76, a bill that would have eliminated the property tax in Pennsylvania. Tea Party groups supported the bill and put pressure on elected officials through different tactics, including some digital ones. However, groups like *Americans For Prosperity* refused to take an official position on the issue and did not help in the mobilising effort at all.

However, if new technologies and the Internet make it easier for such movements to mobilise, it does not mean that the tactics they use to mobilise activists and voters have been revolutionised. Indeed, many tactics remain the same but their efficiency seems to have increased.

Using New Technologies to Increase the Efficiency of the Traditional Social Movement Repertoire

Many of the tactics used by Tea Party activists had already been used by prior social movements. For instance, to get their message out to the rest of the population, they hold monthly meetings during which they invite speakers to talk about a particular bill which is about to pass or, a month before election day, they organise candidates' forums. In such events they invite candidates for governor, Congress, but also state representatives and senators and candidates to very local races like county commissioner or coroner. They also organise marches or honk and wave rallies where they stand at a busy intersection with signs and wait for drivers to show a sign of support to their cause. These gatherings aim at showing that it is acceptable to hold conservative views – which activists say was particularly important during the 2016 election – and at making activists feel that they are supported by people outside of their group.

These tactics can usually be traced back to prior social movements from the left as well as from the right. Indeed, activists themselves identify some tactics as coming from the social movement repertoire of community organiser Saul Alinsky. They often boast that they are using the left wing's tactics against itself. One of the cornerstones of Saul Alinsky's method is to put pressure on elected officials: "It is not enough just to elect your candidates. You must keep the pressure on. Radicals should keep in mind Franklin D. Roosevelt's response to a reform delegation, 'Okay, you've convinced me. Now go on out and bring pressure on me!' Action comes from keeping the heat on. No politician can sit on a hot issue if you make it hot enough."[38] Making an issue hot enough that politicians have no choice but to take action is one of the cornerstones of Tea Party activism.

While keeping constant pressure on their elected officials, Tea Party activists also spend a lot of time looking for conservative candidates to run for office or

---

[38] Saul Alinsky, *Rules for Radicals: A Practical Primer for Realistic Radicals* (Random House, 1972), 34.

run themselves. This tactic has been used by prior right-wing movements like the Christian Right whose activists ran for school board or other local positions so they could take control of these institutions and influence policy on education and abortion.³⁹ In some counties, some of these Christian Right activists were still in power when Tea Party activists got elected to these positions. The ultimate goal of this tactic is to take control of the GOP and its endorsement process which is seen as biased against newcomers to politics who could be principled conservatives and replace corrupt politicians. This strategy is not new but technology has made it much easier.

Historian Lisa McGirr wrote about the mobilisation of Suburban Warriors, conservative women who became politically active in the 1960s in Orange County.⁴⁰ From what she describes, it is easy to see how maintaining contact among activists was not as easy as it is for Tea Party activists who, as we explained, use Facebook to continue the conversations they started in their monthly meetings. Even more so, new technologies have made it easier to coordinate strategies statewide or even countrywide. For instance, top-down groups send toolkits to activists all over the country to explain what to post on social media, who to call and what events to organise to get elected officials to vote a certain way on a bill.

The best example of what new technologies have brought to the Tea Party can be found in the way they contact voters, be it through doorknocking, texting, or calling. Let's focus here on door knocking. This tactic has long been used by many social movements and politicians to bring out the vote. However, in the Tea Party movement, top-down organisations lent a hand to grassroots activists (and vice versa) by giving them access to the data on voters they compiled over several years. This data is made up of party affiliation, voting records from prior elections, but also consumer data which means that the person knocking on doors already knows what type of voters they are going to speak to. The firm that specialises in this field is the I360 organisation which came out of the McCain Campaign and is funded by the Koch network.⁴¹ Its aim was to become the best voter contact platform in the world. All the data collected is updated to tablets and each door knocker is given a tablet with all the information on the next person they are going to go talk to. This makes doorknocking campaigns

---

39 See Melissa Deckman, *School Board Battles: The Christian Right and Local Politics* (Georgetown University Press, 2004); and Clyde Wilcox, *Onwards Christian Soldiers? The Religious Right in American Politics* (Westview Press, 2010).
40 Lisa McGirr, *Suburban Warriors, The Origins of the New American Right* (Princeton, NJ: Princeton University Press, 2001).
41 Mike Allen and Kenneth Vogel, "Inside the Koch data mine", *Politico.com*, December 8, 2014.

much more efficient while preserving human contact which is still the gold standard among getting voters to the poll. It allows activists to do several rounds of door knocking. Two months before their election, they might knock on the doors of people who haven't voted for years or are registered as independents. Then, a month before, they might reach out to Republicans who didn't vote in the last election and a week before to solid Republicans who they want to see turn out. Each time they talk to someone, they feed more information to the platform whose data becomes even more accurate.

As Tea Party activists are not always versed in new technologies, *Americans For Prosperity* organises training sessions during which they talk about every little detail and explain what the activist should do, how they should talk to the person whose door they are knocking on. The trainers usually tell many anecdotes about their experience dealing with disgruntled Democrats or Republicans who are annoyed at the way the GOP has treated them. Food, drinks and t-shirts are provided to each participant which creates a feeling of community. This army of volunteers then goes off doorknocking with the tablets lent by *Americans For Prosperity*.

This tactic is the most striking example of a very old tactic that was radically transformed by new technologies and the fight over voter and consumer data. It is even all the more noteworthy that it shows two sides of the movement working hand in hand, both benefiting from their momentary association. *Americans For Prosperity* needs the grassroots to cover as much ground as possible and to acquire more precise data for future elections, and the grassroots need them to make their canvassing more efficient.

Conclusion

Technology played a huge part in the Tea Party movement, both in its early mobilisation and in its under the radar activism, from 2013 to 2016. First, because Tea Partiers had a wider repertoire of contention at their disposal. Indeed, activists were able to use new tactics from a "new digital repertoire" such as flash activism to stop a particular bill from being voted on. At the same time, they could increase the efficiency of some of the tactics of Charles Tilly's modern repertoire[42] such as doorknocking or putting pressure on their elected officials. As Jennifer Earl and Katrina Kimport explain:

---

42 Charles Tilly, "Getting It Together in Burgandy", *Theory and Society*, no. 4, 479–504.

> We are arguing that technologies never just do one thing, or perhaps more appropriately, that technologies themselves never *do* anything. Technologies offer opportunities for people to do new things as well as to do old things in new ways, and the mix of uses they are put toward typically heterogeneously combines the mundane with the ingenious.[43]

The mix of digital tactics Tea Party activists and top-down organisations used to mobilise the grassroots were especially fruitful as they relied on the "ephemeral, sporadic and episodic character of some Web activism."[44] Some activists laid dormant until a national group or their local group urged them to become active and tweet or e-mail their representatives. This type of tactic made it easy for Tea Party activists to continue being active and appear more numerous past their peak in 2010–2012.

Secondly, in many ways the rise of new technologies has allowed for the appearance of this horizontal movement. Daniel Kreiss in his book *Prototype Politics* argues that: "The use of new technologies among activists has decreased or eliminated the need for any kind of formalized or centralized leadership in many contemporary social movements."[45] This proves true in the case of the Tea Party but also in the case of many other social movements like Occupy Wall Street or even more recently the Indivisible movement in the U.S. or the Yellow Vests movement in France. However, we must be careful not to exaggerate what new technologies bring to social movements. In the case of the Tea Party, for instance, the presence of tech-savvy top-down groups, of the conservative media echo chamber – be it talk radio hosts or TV hosts – and of a galaxy of think tanks and conservative universities able and ready to provide content on demand was equally important to the Tea Party experience.

Furthermore, as Jen Schradie explains, digital activism can require centralisation and infrastructure. In the case of the Tea Party, the digital tactics which required centralisation in the use of the Internet did not match the movement's philosophy of total independence and were therefore either abandoned or put in place at a local level. For instance, *The Precinct Project* – an organisation active in many states that tries to organise the takeover of the Republican Party from the ground up – did not get the results they could have hoped for partly because of the refusal of Tea Party groups to lose their independence. To achieve this, activists would have needed to coordinate at the state level and find candidates for all the lowest level positions to run. The fact that this

---

[43] Jennifer Earl and Katrina Kimport, op.cit, 191.
[44] Ibid, 185.
[45] Daniel Kreiss, *Prototype Politics: Technology-Intensive Campaigning and the Data of Democracy* (Oxford University Press), 3.

strategy only worked in some counties but not at the state or national level should not be seen as a failure as it was counter to the desire of grassroots groups to remain independent. This shows that new technologies are just one of the many tools that Tea Party activists chose to mobilise. New technologies did not fundamentally transform the social movement experience as many of the tactics used by activists can be found in prior social movements. If, in many ways, the Internet has helped increase the efficiency of some tactics, it is striking to see that in the 2018 election cycle, one of the tactics most used to get out the vote was to invite other activists over and have them write postcards to voters on behalf of a particular candidate, something Lisa McGirr's suburban warriors could also have done in the sixties.

The way the Tea Party is organised and its use of technology helped mobilise people to vote in elections. Over the past seven years, Tea Party activists have mobilised often under the radar but daily online as well as at the state Capitol or in meetings. This activity seems to show that Americans are no longer bowling alone as Robert Putnam showed in his famous work in 2000.[46] However, this increase in democratic participation and voter mobilisation has to be tempered. Indeed, one of the groups that makes up the Tea Party galaxy, the American Legal Exchange Council which is tied to the Koch brothers,[47] has also been working to pass laws that would make access to voting harder for other groups of the population such as minorities and young people. These bills got extensive support from Tea Party activists in Pennsylvania in 2012 which led to the passage of the law. Tea Party mobilisation might lead to an increase in the number of conservative voters and the regeneration of conservative activism but it is not synonymous with an overall increase in voter participation in general; in fact, it might even impede it.

Bibliography

Primary Sources

Glenn Beck's website – The 9–12 project. http://www.glennbeck.com/content/articles/article/198/21018/?utm_source=glennbeck&utm_medium=contentcopy_link
The Oathkeepers' website, https://oathkeepers.org/about/
Rick Santelli's rant on CNBC: https://www.youtube.com/watch?v=bEZB4taSEoA.

---

[46] Robert Putnam, *Bowling Alone: The Collapse and Revival of American Community* (Simon & Schuster, 2000).
[47] Tal Kopan, "Report: Think Tank tied to Kochs", politico.com, accessed November 13, 2013.

"Glenn Beck on Progressivism Part 1", youtube.com, March 20, 2010. https://www.youtube.com/watch?v=tP5epjCTW0Q.

L. John Van Til. *"Thoughtful Cal, the Founders & the Progressives."* March 30, 2010. https://www.visionandvalues.org/2010/03/2010-thoughtful-cal-the-founders-and-the-progressives/.

Armey, Dick, and Matt Kibbe. *Give Us Liberty: A Tea Party Manifesto.* William Morrow, 2010.

Secondary Sources

Allen, Mike, and Kenneth Vogel. "Inside the Koch data mine." Politico.com, December 8, 2014.

Deckman, Melissa. *School Board Battles: The Christian Right and Local Politics.* Georgetown: University Press, 2004.

Earl, Jennifer, and Katrina Kimport. *Digitally Enabled Social Change: Activism in the Internet Age.* The MIT Press, 2011.

Fetner, Tina, and Brayden King. "Three-Layer Movements, Resources and the Tea Party." In *Understanding the Tea Party Movement*, edited by Nella Van Dyke and David Meyer. Ashgate, 2014.

Gould, Deborah. *Moving Politics: Emotions and ACT UP's Fight against AIDS.* University of Chicago Press, 2009.

Hochschild, Arlie. *The Managed Heart: Commercialization of Human Feeling.* University of California Press, 1983.

Hochschild, Arlie. *Strangers in Their Own Land: Anger and Mourning on the American Right.* The New Press, 2016.

Jasper, James. "Emotions and Social Movements: Twenty Years of Theory and Research." *Annual Review of Sociology* 37 (2011): 285–303.

Kabaservice, Geoffrey. *Rule and Ruin: The Downfall of Moderation and the Destruction of the Republican Party, From Eisenhower to the Tea Party.* Oxford University Press, 2013.

Karpf, David. "Slacktivism as optical illusion." Oxford University Press' Blog, November 19, 2014. http://blog.oup.com/2014/11/slacktivism-optical-illusion-political-activism/.

Kopan, Tal. "Report: Think Tank tied to Kochs." Politico.com, November 13, 2013.

Kreiss, Daniel. *Prototype Politics: Technology-Intensive Campaigning and the Data of Democracy.* Oxford University Press, 2016.

Mayer, Jane. "Covert operations." *The New Yorker*, August 23, 2010.

McGirr, Lisa. *Suburban Warriors, The Origins of the New American Right.* Princeton University Press, 2001.

Meyer, David. *The Politics of Protest: Social Movements in America.* 2nd edition. Oxford University Press, 2015.

Parker, Christopher, and Matt Barretto. *Change They Can't Believe In: The Tea Party and Reactionary Politics in America.* Princeton University Press, 2013.

Putman, Robert. *Bowling Alone: The Collapse and Revival of American Community.* Simon & Schuster International, 2001.

Rohlinger, Deana A., and Jesse Klein. "From Fervor to Fear: ICT and Emotions in the Tea Party Movement." In *Understanding the Tea Party Movement*, edited by Nella Van Dyke and David Meyer, 125–147. Ashgate, 2014.

Schradie, Jen. *The Revolution that Wasn't: How Digital Activism Favors Conservatives*. Harvard University Press, 2019.

Skocpol, Theda, and Vanessa Williamson. *The Tea Party and the Remaking of Republican Conservatism*. Oxford University Press, 2013.

Sparks, Holloway. "Mama Grizzlies and Guardians of the Republic: The Democratic and Intersectional Politics of Anger in the Tea Party Movement." *New Political Science* 37 (2015): 25–47.

Tilly, Charles. "Getting It Together in Burgandy." *Theory and Society* 4: 479–504.

Wilcox, Clyde. *Onwards Christian Soldiers? The Religious Right in American Politics*. Westview Press, 2010.

Zernike, Kate. *Boiling Mad: Inside Tea Party America*. Times Books, 2010.

Part 4: **When Grassroots and Party Mobilisation Interact: the Case of the Republican Party in the Twentieth Century**

Robert Mason
8 The Republican Minority and Voter Mobilisation

The Pursuit of Grassroots Activism and the Politics of Conservatism and Moderation in the United States, 1933–1964

Introduction

The Republican Party's descent to minority status in the American two-party system as a result of the Great Depression and the New Deal unleashed an intensely contested debate among activists and politicians about its future. Rooted in a search for a solution to the electoral puzzle that the success of the Democrats' new coalition posed, most prominently the debate involved ideology and policy—how Republicans should respond to the programmatic activism of New Deal liberalism, the source of the coalition's popular vitality. These responses varied between the more moderate—the more supportive of accommodation with "big government" in search of solutions to socioeconomic problems—and the more conservative, which challenged more fundamentally the expansion of the federal government's role.

From the start, the policy prescriptions associated with these responses connected with electoral calculations about how best to mobilise a majority at the polls. In his 1936 book *You and I—and Roosevelt*, Charles P. Taft, a lawyer active in Cincinnati politics, outlined an argument that the party's electoral success depended on the mobilisation of moderates and thus on a moderate agenda. "If the bitter enders win out and manufacture a platform from a miscellaneous assortment of political lumber glued together by the spittle of hate," Taft wrote, "the Republicans are beaten before they begin."[1] The counter-argument would inform the title of a book written by Republican activist Phyllis Schlafly—later to gain still greater fame at the forefront of the campaign against the Equal Rights Amendment in the 1970s—in support of Barry Goldwater's presidential candidacy in 1964, *A Choice Not an Echo*. But not long after the Republicans' landslide defeat of 1936, which confirmed the arrival of the party's minority status, former

---

[1] Charles P. Taft, *You and I—and Roosevelt* (New York: Farrar & Rinehart, 1936), 109.

secretary of the Treasury Ogden L. Mills gave a series of lectures, published as *The Seventeen Million*, which offered a similar thesis—arguing that the defence of the individual against what he called the collectivism of the New Deal offered a route to electoral revitalisation for his party.[2]

As this chapter explores, the debate among Republicans about how to solve their party's minority problem did not involve connections between policy and strategy alone, however. Instead, believing that the work of party activists in mobilising voters was a crucial element in electoral success, Republicans also looked for ways to boost this work. Ostensibly neutral, perhaps, with regard to the intra-party debate about policy direction, these projects were actually linked closely to an ideological preference among their advocates, whether conservative or moderate. Seeking to recreate how Republicans analysed their party's problems in pursuit of remedying them through projects that intended to find organisational initiatives to mobilise voters more effectively, the chapter makes use of manuscript collections of leading figures involved in such efforts. Its starting point is the moment when Republicans lost control of the presidency, at the start of 1933, following the victory of Franklin D. Roosevelt; its end point involves the Goldwater candidacy, another loss for Republicans but a turning point that marked conservative victory in the intra-party debate.[3]

Scholarship on the Republican Party and on Voter Mobilisation

Exploring the debate between conservative Republicans and moderate Republicans has been at the heart of scholarly engagement with the party's history during this period.[4] The aspect of politics beyond such questions of ideology and

---

[2] Phyllis Schlafly, *A Choice Not an Echo* (Alton, Ill.: Pere Marquette, 1964); Ogden L. Mills, *The Seventeen Million* (New York: Macmillan, 1937).
[3] Because of new campaign-connected technologies and because of new patterns of activism (exemplified by the rise of single-issue groups in the 1970s), the Goldwater candidacy probably also marked a turning point in the history of voter mobilisation in the United States.
[4] Lewis L. Gould, *Grand Old Party: A History of the Republicans* (New York: Random House, 2003); Heather Cox Richardson, *To Make Men Free: A History of the Republican Party* (New York: Basic, 2014). Works that focus on Republican conservatives are Donald T. Critchlow, *The Conservative Ascendancy: How the GOP Right Made Political History* (Cambridge, Mass.: Harvard University Press, 2007); and David W. Reinhard, *The Republican Right since 1945* (Lexington: University Press of Kentucky, 1983). Geoffrey Kabaservice, *Rule and Ruin: The Downfall of Moderation*

strategy that has gained attention from historians, focusing on conservatism more broadly than on the Republican Party in particular, is grassroots activism—most notably exemplified by Lisa McGirr's study of "suburban warriors" in Orange County.[5] In general, the chronological interest of this literature involves the resurgence of conservatism and of the Republican Party that largely defined politics in the United States from the late 1960s onwards, even if the search for the origins of this transformation has encouraged historians to investigate much earlier developments.[6] There is a strong connection between much of this literature and the concept of voter mobilisation, because it has a central interest in why, and how, many voters switched from support for the Democratic Party to support for the Republican Party.[7]

And yet usually the understanding among historians of voter mobilisation is starkly different from that in political science. As Kenneth M. Goldstein and Matthew Holleque note, an expanded definition of political mobilisation is "the process by which candidates, parties, activists, and groups induce other people to participate, which includes *any* activities that increase the likelihood of someone participating," but political scientists have tended to employ a more limited definition, "focusing on what we call the canvass, meaning the direct contacts between political organisations and their representatives and citizens (e. g., face-to-face contacts, phone banks, and direct mailings)." Consequently, Goldstein and Holleque observe, political scientists have concentrated on "the medium of mobilization but not the message of mobilization."[8] It is an observation

---

and the Destruction of the Republican Party, from Eisenhower to the Tea Party (New York: Oxford University Press, 2012) is a study of moderate Republicans.

5 Lisa McGirr, *Suburban Warriors: The Origins of the New American Right* (Princeton, N.J.: Princeton University Press, 2001). Elizabeth Tandy Shermer, in *Sunbelt Capitalism: Phoenix and the Transformation of American Politics* (Philadelphia: University of Pennsylvania Press, 2013), analyses the significance of a "grasstops" level in politics—between grassroots activists and political actors belonging to high-level elites.

6 The long-term roots of "backlash" that fostered disillusionment with liberalism and that fed the conservative upsurge are explored, for example, in Thomas J. Sugrue, *The Origins of the Urban Crisis: Race and Inequality in Postwar Detroit* (Princeton, N.J.: Princeton University Press, 1996).

7 There are, however, some significant exceptions. For example, in studying activism within the Republican party, Catherine E. Rymph, in *Republican Women: Feminism and Conservatism from Suffrage through the Rise of the New Right* (Chapel Hill: University of North Carolina Press, 2006), is interested not only in how antifeminism became stronger than feminism at the time of the conservative resurgence, but also more globally in the implications of women's engagement in the party.

8 Kenneth M. Goldstein and Matthew Holleque, "Getting up off the Canvass: Rethinking the Study of Mobilization," in *The Oxford Handbook of American Elections and Political Behavior*,

that underscores the differences between research in the social sciences and the research of historians, who, by contrast, have explored the message much more than the medium.[9] (The term has been used in a different way by scholars seeking to explain electoral change—most notably that which involved the Republicans' decline and the Democrats' ascendancy at the time of the Great Depression—who have debated the role of mobilisation, involving voters new to electoral participation, in these transformations, as opposed to the role of conversion, involving voters switching from one party to the other.[10])

The Depression-era ascendancy of the Democratic Party, at the expense of the Republicans' electoral fortunes, involved the emergence of New Deal liberalism as centrally salient to electoral coalitions, disadvantageously for the Republicans—but the structures of voter mobilisation underwent change with regard to the medium as well as the message. As political scientist Sidney Milkis shows, Franklin Roosevelt's project of programmatic activism to tackle the Depression, in expanding the powers of the federal government and in particular the executive, pursued its goals via "the transcendence of partisan politics."[11] Furthermore, interest-group pluralism naturally complemented New Deal liberalism, with organised labour foremost among the Democratic Party's allies.

Because the new politics that Roosevelt shaped at the time of the Depression involved organisational as well as ideological change, it is logical that the Republicans' debate about their minority problem was not characterised by the

---

ed. Jan E. Leighley (New York: Oxford University Press, 2010), 578. In his study of "presidential party building," Daniel Galvin identifies voter mobilisation as one of six elements (which also include the provision of campaign services, the development of human capital, the recruitment of candidates, the financing of party activities and support for internal organisation). Although Galvin is attentive to the policy goals underlying "party building," his emphasis remains on "organisational capacity"; Daniel Galvin, *Presidential Party Building: Dwight D. Eisenhower to George W. Bush* (Princeton, N.J.: Princeton University Press, 2010), 5–6.

9 Among the exceptions is one for which the medium is the news media: Nicole Hemmer, *Messengers of the Right: Conservative Media and the Transformation of American Politics* (Philadelphia: University of Pennsylvania Press, 2016).

10 See, for example, Kristi Andersen, *The Creation of a Democratic Majority, 1928–1996* (Chicago: University of Chicago Press, 1979); Robert S. Erikson and Kent L. Tedin, "The 1928–1936 Partisan Realignment: The Case for the Conversion Hypothesis," *American Political Science Review* 75 (1981): 951–962; James E. Campbell, "Sources of the New Deal Realignment: The Contributions of Conversion and Mobilization to Partisan Change," *Western Political Quarterly* 38 (1985): 357–376.

11 Sidney M. Milkis, "Franklin D. Roosevelt and the Transcendence of Partisan Politics," *Political Science Quarterly* 100 (1985): 479–504; Sidney M. Milkis, *The President and the Parties: The Transformation of the American Party System since the New Deal* (New York: Oxford University Press, 1993).

moderate-conservative clash about policy alone, but also by a search for organisational initiatives to improve voter mobilisation. And yet projects in practice remained part of the larger battle between the competing visions of conservatives and moderates.

Projects of Party Revitalisation as a Response to the New Deal's Ascendancy

The connection between ideology and organisation was visible within the first responses of Republicans to their loss of electoral support in the 1932 elections, at the height of the Depression. Fresh from the campaign trail in support of Herbert Hoover's losing cause, Ogden Mills joined with other former administration officials to create Republican Federal Associates, "to supplement the work of the regular party organisations in promoting Republican principles of government." Alongside Mills in a leadership role for the new organisation was the former postmaster general Walter Folger Brown, and others who had worked at the Post Office Department under Hoover took on organisational responsibilities.[12] Republican Federal Associates' institutional roots in the Post Office Department revealed an interest in reimagining the structures of American politics in seeking to revitalise the Republican Party; lacking a permanent framework at the national level (with the exception of the national committee, a loose collection of state parties that organised the four-yearly national convention as well as smaller-scale meetings between conventions to discuss developments in politics), a party in control of the White House relied on political appointments to forge an organisational network, of which local postmasters formed the grassroots foundations. In the absence of such patronage, the "out-party" faced a formidable challenge as a presidential election approached—to set up the organisational infrastructure to take on such a task. As the Democrats' national chair during the Hoover years, mindful of this problem because of difficulties he had encountered in running their presidential campaign in 1928, John J. Raskob had reinvented the Democratic National Committee (DNC) as a permanent participant in American politics, with a Washington headquarters and a professional staff. Alongside Raskob was Charles Michelson, in charge of publicity for the DNC, who

---

12 "Hoover Men Unite to Restore Party for Victory in '34," *New York Times* [hereafter *NYT*], April 24, 1933, 1, 6 (quotation, 1).

had successfully waged an ongoing effort to demonise Hoover as the face of the nation's economic crisis.[13]

If some contemporaries saw Associates as a Republican version of the Raskob project, the implications for grassroots organisation of the plans pursued by Mills and his colleagues possessed distinctiveness.[14] Its roots in the Hoover administration also demonstrated an effort to maintain the political influence of the defeated president and his ideas, and this immersion in factional conflict about party control ignited controversy and fomented the initiative's speedy demise.[15] Having aimed first to assist voter mobilisation in the 1934 midterms, Associates did not survive long enough to pursue such an effort.

Persistent in exploring ways to revitalise his party, Mills was already part of another project, Republican Builders, initially based in New York (and animated by concern about the electoral prospects of the state party in particular) but with ambitions to achieve a national presence. The target of Republican Builders involved, as Mills put it, "thousands of men and women who under existing conditions are unwilling to associate themselves directly with the regular Party organisation"; the organisation sought to "arouse great public interest and tend to develop new leaders and a new and militant spirit, both of which are essential if the Republican Party is to survive."[16] Like Associates, Builders took an assertively conservative view of the New Deal. "The program, if made permanent," Mills told a Builders supporter, "would put in the hands of the Government in Washington the absolute power to regiment all business and direct the lives of 120,000,000 individuals."[17] For William Allen White, a Kansas newspaper editor and longtime critic of conservatism within his party, the agenda of leading figures in Builders—"a bunch of frozen faces"—was counterproductive.[18] But Mills disagreed with that perspective on the relationship between ideology and voter mobilisation. Although an anti–New Deal principle drove those in-

---

[13] David Farber, *Everybody Ought to Be Rich: The Life and Times of John J. Raskob, Capitalist* (New York: Oxford University Press, 2013), 253–255.
[14] "The R. F. A.," *NYT*, April 25, 1933, 16.
[15] Thomas M. Slopnick, "In the Shadow of Herbert Hoover: The Republican Party and the Politics of Defeat, 1932–1936" (Ph.D. dissertation, University of Connecticut, 2006), 130–147.
[16] Letter, Ogden L. Mills to Robert A. Taft, June 10, 1934, folder "Correspondence Re. Rep. Builders (A-Z) 1934–35," box 80-A, Ogden Livingston Mills Papers, Manuscript Division, Library of Congress, Washington, D.C.
[17] Letter, Ogden L. Mills to Walter E. Frew, May 10, 1934, folder "Correspondence Re. Rep. Builders (A-Z) 1934–35," box 80-A, Mills Papers.
[18] Letter, William Allen White to David Hinshaw, March 9, 1934, folder "Hinshaw, David 1934," box C215, William Allen White Papers, Manuscript Division, Library of Congress, Washington, D.C.

volved in Builders, Mills also believed that a focus on opposition to the Democrats was likelier to catalyse engagement with the organisation, observing, "it is much easier to get people to attack something than it is to unite them on a constructive and affirmative program."[19]

In an era when women had little presence of any visibility in politics (even if in Washington a "women's network" was achieving influence in shaping the New Deal), Republican Builders, with its mission to increase political engagement beyond existing Republican activists, possessed a gender profile of more diversity. The inspirational force for its creation was May Davie, chair of the New York party's finance committee, who found that women ("much less busy and almost always available for Organisation work," she noted) were likelier than men to be responsive to her efforts in support of Builders. "I am completely exhausted," she told Mills about six months after the launch of Builders, "with trying to make busy and tired men (who by the time I see them usually have had the extra cocktail that entirely dulls their brains) work for the Builders."[20] In her work for Builders, Davie encouraged women who had been "far too ladylike, far too genteel and far too nice to get into politics" to take on a political role as significant as that of men, or more so.[21]

But if efforts among Republicans to achieve organisational revitalisation depended on the contribution of women (rather like the role of McGirr's "suburban warriors" in the conservative upsurge of the 1960s), then their opponents in the Democratic Party were already being innovative in fostering the political involvement of women via the Women's Division of the Democratic National Committee, under Molly Dewson.[22] Dewson's work is just one example of diverse and multifaceted initiatives among Democrats to mobilise voters in support of the New Deal, in the end outflanking the pursuit of mobilisation among Republicans as a way to rescue their party from its Depression-era collapse. Dewson worked at the heart of the party, but especially as the 1936 campaign approached, other organisational initiatives—including the Good Neighbor League and the Commit-

---

19 Letter, Ogden L. Mills to H. Alexander Smith, May 29, 1934, folder "Correspondence Re. Rep. Builders (A-Z) 1934–35," box 80-A, Mills Papers.
20 "Republicans Form New State Group," *NYT*, September 29, 1933, 3; letter, May Davie to Ogden L. Mills, March 15, 1934, folder "Correspondence Re. Rep. Builders (A-Z) 1934–35," box 80-A, Mills Papers. Davie stepped down as finance chair to concentrate on Builders, especially to pursue its national ambitions. "Mrs. Preston Davie Resigns Party Post," *NYT*, March 2, 1934, 28.
21 "Republican Builders Plan New Deal Fight," *NYT*, October 2, 1934, 3.
22 John Thomas McGuire, "Beginning an 'Extraordinary Opportunity': Eleanor Roosevelt, Molly Dewson, and the Expansion of Women's Boundaries in the Democratic Party, 1924–1934," *Women's History Review* 23 (2014): 922–937.

tee of One—were extra-party and candidate-centred, further examples of Franklin Roosevelt's transcendence of party at a time when Ogden Mills, by contrast, saw the revitalisation of party-oriented organisations as key to successful mobilisation of voters. Even while Associates and Builders revealed a faith in voter mobilisation of this kind, Franklin Roosevelt and his aides were pioneering a new understanding of how to achieve this goal, which Mary Stuckey argues contributed to the Democrats' electoral success of the 1930s and to the emergence of the New Deal coalition.[23]

Nevertheless, an approach that placed relatively greater emphasis on the party, as opposed to the candidate, would continue to be a characteristic of Republicans. In his study of "presidential party building" from Dwight D. Eisenhower to George W. Bush, Daniel Galvin shows that Republican presidents differed from their Democratic counterparts in consistently demonstrating greater engagement in building their party's organisational capacity. Although the minority status of the Republican Party accounts in part for the difference, this is not the only explanation. "Party building bred more party building," writes Galvin, "if only because the existence of party-building operations created incentives for their further use."[24] If Mills' efforts to mobilise voters via party-connected structures did little to challenge the Republican Party's decline, then, they contributed to the institutionalisation of an intra-party difference with regard to politician-party interactions.

John D. M. Hamilton, Activism, and the Model of the UK Party System

The organisational focus of both Builders and Associates was in New York (despite bolder ambitions), but a politician with a similar belief in the importance of organisational innovation as a means of party revitalisation—John D. M. Hamilton—pursued his vision at the national level. Hamilton encountered this opportunity in particular because of his connection with fellow Kansan Alfred M. Landon, the party's 1936 presidential nominee. Hamilton, who represented his state on the Republican National Committee (RNC), revealed an interest in organisational innovation in 1934 by advocating outreach to young people and de-

---

23 Mary E. Stuckey, *Voting Deliberatively: FDR and the 1936 Presidential Campaign* (University Park: Penn State University Press, 2015).
24 Galvin, *Presidential Party Building*, 26.

veloping a network of Republican clubs for them.[25] In 1935 he then worked with fellow RNC members from the Midwest in convening a "grassroots conference" in Springfield, Illinois—a location deeply reminiscent of the party's Lincolnian heyday.[26] Following the success of the campaign he led to capture the nomination for Landon, Hamilton became national chair, with key responsibility for running the campaign against Franklin Roosevelt.[27] Underpinning his work in this capacity was a belief in the importance of strong organisation at the local level —precinct by precinct—in order to mobilise support for the party at the polls.[28] "The cornerstone of practical politics is work and more of it," Hamilton said. "I never knew the time when a group of volunteer political workers couldn't make a bunch of paid workers look like chumps."[29]

Although the Landon campaign gained a reputation for what became known as a "me too" brand of Republican moderation, Hamilton stressed a stauncher conservatism.[30] Hamilton asserted a connection between the New Deal and communism; "preserving the American form of government," he said, was at stake in the campaign.[31] On a visit to Texas, he said that the Roosevelt administration had "all the makings of a dictatorship," condemning its New Deal initiatives that "keep us goose stepping toward the Administration's promised land of a completely planned economy."[32] Such rhetoric reflected an outlook on the New Deal that differed from Landon. But it also revealed an approach to voter mobilisation distinctive from that of Charles P. Taft, whom Landon had recruited as a policy advisor. Whereas Taft was convinced that moderation was necessary

---

[25] Henry Wesley Morris, "The Republicans in a Minority Role" (Ph.D. dissertation, State University of Iowa, 1960), 72–73.
[26] "Memorandum of Conference Held at Kansas City, Feb. 17, 1935," folder "The Grassroots Republican Conference," box 1, John D. M. Hamilton Papers, Manuscript Division, Library of Congress, Washington, D.C.
[27] "GOP: Kansans Capture the Convention, Rout the Old Guard, Nominate Two Bull Moosers, and Adopt a States' Rights Platform," *News-Week*, June 20, 1936, 10–11.
[28] "Hamilton Plans To Visit Every State in Union," *Washington Post* [hereafter *WP*], June 18, 1936, 2; "Main Fight in West, Hamilton Asserts," *NYT*, August 21, 1936, 8. "With party organisations in every State, with 6,000 county and 138,000 precinct committeemen and workers all eager and ready," he said in August, after a tour of western states, "there isn't anything under the sun we fear."
[29] "Hamilton Maps 'Precinct' Fight Of Republicans," *WP*, September 15, 1936, X9.
[30] "Campaign: 'Me Too' Is Battle Cry as Nominees bid for Farm Vote; Landon Urges Own Security Plan," *News-Week*, October 3, 1936, 15–17.
[31] "Hamilton Warns of Reds," *NYT*, September 30, 1936, 19.
[32] Leland Stowe, "Hamilton Takes Fight to Texas and Oklahoma," *New York Herald Tribune* clipping, August 19, 1936, folder "Hamilton, John [3]" box 147, Raymond Clapper Papers, Manuscript Division, Library of Congress, Washington, D.C.

for an appeal to "independent" voters in the political middle (neither as conservative as loyal Republicans, nor as liberal as loyal Democrats), Hamilton's stress on organisational strength as the building block of voter mobilisation encouraged him, by contrast, to prefer a stress on conservative principle. This, he believed, unlocked activist energies that were crucial to voter mobilisation.[33] At the height of the campaign, Wilma D. Hoyal, the head of the RNC Women's Division, told reporters that the issue of communism was yet more effective than other attacks on the Democrats in mobilising women; whether with hyperbole, from propagandistic intent, or with a spirit of impassioned advocacy, Hoyal claimed that almost one million women were working in support of the Landon campaign.[34]

On suffering defeat by a landslide, Landon acknowledged "mistakes" in his campaign, adding that "possibly we made a few more mistakes because of the disorganized condition of the Republican party in so many states as the result of the elections of two and four years ago."[35] (Because the parties, lacking much institutional infrastructure, relied on the presence of elected officials, and on patronage connected to office-holding, for organisational support, the Republican Party's electoral losses of the Depression deepened the organisational problems it faced.) Retaining confidence in an avowedly conservative message, Hamilton, as national chair, looked for ways to tackle the problem of disorganisation between campaigns. A visit to the Conservative Party in the United Kingdom in 1937 provided him with inspiration. Over the years that followed, Hamilton's study of British politics informed the creation of *The Republican Reporter*, a publication targeted at those who spoke for the party, and modeled on the Conservatives' *Hints for Speakers*, and his support for the establishment in 1938 of the National Federation of Republican Women (because the organisational effectiveness of the Conservative Party's separate institutional structures for women and men had impressed him). This work was guided more profoundly by the belief that the more permanent, more centralised, and more bureaucratised institutions of the Conservative Party were more effective in fostering activist energies than the looseness and impermanence of the Republicans' campaign operations. By contrast with a counterpart in the United States, the political engagement of a Conservative activist, Hamilton observed, was deeper—connected with a culture of political activism that facilitated voter mobilisa-

---

[33] Robert Mason, *The Republican Party and American Politics from Hoover to Reagan* (New York: Cambridge University Press, 2012), 62.
[34] "Says G.O.P. Musters a Million Women," *NYT*, October 18, 1936, N2.
[35] "Landon Sums Up Race," *Kansas City Times* clipping, November 13, 1936, folder "Offer Resignation," box 1, Hamilton Papers.

tion.³⁶ "It is recognized that the maintenance of this group of volunteers is dependent upon their continued interest in the Party and its affairs and there is further recognition that sometimes and, indeed, often the dry and uninteresting field of politics will not attain that goal," Hamilton wrote. "The result is a very definite trend to the social side."³⁷

Hamilton's admiration for the Conservatives—who offered a strong example of a mass-membership party—was indicative of a different vision for political organisation from that successfully pursued by Franklin Roosevelt, who mobilised the New Deal coalition through the transcendence of party. Despite Hamilton's organisational initiatives of the late 1930s, and despite Hamilton's success as a fundraiser, that vision experienced eclipse within the Republican Party in 1940 with the emergence of Wendell Willkie as its presidential nominee. Affiliated with the Democratic Party until late 1939, Willkie achieved success among Republicans not so much because of his charisma and his effectiveness, as a corporate executive, in attacking "big government," but especially because the arrival of World War II in Europe made obsolete the anti-interventionist approach to foreign policy that the leading contenders for the nomination had advocated. On Willkie's nomination, Hamilton lost his job as national chair.³⁸ It was by no means unusual for a new presidential nominee to select a new national chair, but for Hamilton this was a signal that his project of organisational transformation had failed—because it challenged the institutional permanence that he had sought for the national committee.³⁹

"Amateurism" and the Pursuit of Independent Voters

No less than the Hamilton project, the Willkie candidacy was informed by a belief that Republican success depended on organisational revitalisation. By deep contrast with that project, however, this belief saw extra-party activism as cru-

---

36 Robert Mason, "Transatlantic Dimensions of Electoral Strategy: Republican Party Interpretations of UK Politics, 1936–c. 1960," in *Postwar Conservatism, a Transnational Investigation: Britain, France, and the United States, 1930–1990*, edited by Clarisse Berthezène and Jean-Christian Vinel (Cham, Switzerland: Palgrave Macmillan, 2017), 220–223.
37 John Hamilton, "Memorandum on English Conservative Party Organisation," June 1937, folder "Chairman's Speaking Schedules 1937," box 2, Hamilton Papers.
38 Elliot A. Rosen, *The Republican Party in the Age of Roosevelt: Sources of Anti-Government Conservatism in the United States* (Charlottesville: University of Virginia Press, 2014), 107–108.
39 Mason, "Transatlantic Dimensions," 224.

cial. A network of clubs first organised support for Willkie's nomination and then formed part of the fall campaign against Franklin Roosevelt, with responsibility for mobilising voters who were independent of party affiliation (about one in five of the electorate) or disaffected Democrats. Boosting Willkie's prospects in the South formed a strand of the clubs' mission; because memories of the Civil War and Reconstruction were long, the Republican Party remained anathema to most white southerners, but club activists believed that many were sympathetic to Willkie and open to mobilisation.[40]

Making use of the clubs alongside the party was in alignment with the argument that effective mobilisation of independent voters alongside Republican loyalists was the way to achieve a majority at the polls. But if such a bifurcation of responsibility represented promise, it encountered difficulties in practice. Rivalry and jealousy obstructed harmonious cooperation. The "professionals" believed that club activists lacked experience, whereas the "amateurs"—described by one Republican as "starry eyed enthusiasts who have just discovered civic consciousness"—saw the conservatism of party activists as hostile to effective outreach.[41] A Massachusetts journalist not only observed that "the enthusiasm of the volunteer Willkie workers was far ahead of the effectiveness of their efforts," but also saw tensions embedded in different visions of political activity. "Another aspect of the campaign which hurt ... was the faintly superior attitude which too many of the volunteers adopted with respect to the party faithful, who have been working for Republican gains for the past 10 lean years," he wrote not long after election day. "Granted the G.O.P. organisation is cluttered with hacks and incompetents; their ruffled feelings nonetheless lost votes."[42] Although the purported promise of the Willkie clubs was to reach voters usually sceptical of the Republican Party—those less socioeconomically advantaged than its habitual supporters, alongside white southerners—campaigners experienced difficulty in realising this promise. (That this outreach was a key goal for the clubs was a recognition of the principal shortcoming within the Republican coalition, but paradoxically their origins were grounded in an elite. Oren Root Jr., a young lawyer who worked for a leading firm, initiated his pro-Willkie odyssey

---

[40] Letter, Richard M. Egan to Jennings C. Wise, July 27, 1940, folder "Club Corres. Virginia: Charlottesville Wise, Jennings C.," box 15, Willkie Clubs Papers, Lilly Library, Indiana University, Bloomington, Indiana.

[41] Letter, David Hinshaw to Raymond L. Buell, September 11, 1940, folder "Miscellaneous 1," box 46, Raymond Leslie Buell Papers, Manuscript Division, Library of Congress, Washington, D.C.

[42] Letter, Walter T. Bonney to Raymond L. Buell, November 11, 1940, folder "Bonney, Walter T," box 2, Buell Papers.

by seeking to mobilise people who had graduated from Ivy League colleges in 1924 and 1925.⁴³) "I have heard a number of criticisms from the so-called common people about too much Ritz in this campaign," an Oregon activist advised Root.⁴⁴

Even if not only the enduring strength of the New Deal coalition but also the climate of international crisis assisted Franklin Roosevelt in his successful pursuit of a precedent-breaking third term in the White House, leaders of the Willkie campaign identified organisational deficiencies as an additional factor that explained their candidate's failure.⁴⁵ For longer-established Republicans, the Willkie clubs had not helped. "From what I have heard from over the country I believe the Willkie Clubs did more damage than they did good," wrote Alf Landon. "That is, the way they were handled."⁴⁶ But Club activists saw things differently. Believing that the organisational infrastructure that their energies had created could still revitalise the Republican Party, Club activists planned to sustain their operations "to encourage the exercise of good citizenship ... and to encourage competent men and women to seek public office." But the institutionalisation of such a candidate-centered initiative proved difficult to achieve, and the Willkie clubs had closed by the end of 1941.⁴⁷

Citizens for Eisenhower as a Response to the Political Role of Organised Labour

Over time concern among Republicans about their party's organisational capacity did not alleviate but rather intensified. Initially, a dominant explanation within the party for the success of their Democratic rivals in mobilising the New Deal coalition was the significance of the "bought vote"—support for the Democrats

---

43 David Levering Lewis, *The Improbable Wendell Willkie: The Businessman Who Saved the Republican Party and His Country, and Conceived a New World Order* (New York: Liveright, 2018), 128–129.
44 Letter, Kenneth L. Cooper to Oren Root Jr., August 24, 1940, folder "Club Corres. Oregon: Portland Cooper, Kenneth C.," box 14, Willkie Clubs Papers.
45 "Buell Predicts Willkie Will Be Two-Term Leader," *Berkshire Eagle* clipping, December 4, 1940, folder "Miscellaneous 1," box 46, Buell Papers.
46 Letter, Alfred M. Landon to Raymond Clapper, November 30, 1940, folder 11, box 101, Alfred M. Landon Papers, Kansas State Historical Society, Topeka, Kansas.
47 Donald Bruce Johnson, *The Republican Party and Wendell Willkie* (Urbana: University of Illinois Press, 1960), 169.

among the direct beneficiaries of federal spending.[48] As the Great Depression faded away, and as the programs of the New Deal thus dissipated, many Republicans instead concentrated on the interest-group pluralism of New Deal liberalism as an explanation for their woes at the polls. Unions in particular, Republicans believed, provided the organisational muscle that ensured the success of Democratic efforts in voter mobilisation. Crystallising this belief was the emergence in electoral politics of the Political Action Committee of the Congress of Industrial Organisations (CIO), created in 1943 and already in the following year identified as a crucial factor in assisting Roosevelt to achieve his fourth presidential victory.[49] Against this backdrop, no less than his predecessor John Hamilton, Herbert Brownell, who ran the party's presidential campaign in 1944 and acted as national chair from 1944 to 1946, identified an imperative for organisational transformation and in particular institutional permanence. "Our party organisation nationally must be put upon a full-time basis," he said in early 1945. "Its primary job, to educate the voters in the principles of the Republican Party, must be carried on constantly. Its publicity and research facilities must be strengthened. Its machinery of getting out the vote must be modernized."[50]

Questions of the connection between organisation and voter mobilisation took a new turn at the start of the 1950s, in parallel with a new turn in the party debate between moderates and conservatives. The electoral argument in favour of an assertively conservative alternative to the Democrats' liberalism had gained strength especially in the aftermath of Thomas E. Dewey's unexpected loss to Harry Truman in the 1948 presidential election. "The result of the election was a tragedy, largely because it was entirely unnecessary," commented Senator Robert A. Taft of Ohio, an unsuccessful challenger to Dewey for the party's nomination, and emerging as the figurehead of conservatives (and thus with a political outlook quite different from that of Charles P. Taft, his brother). "Dewey could have won, and we could have elected a Republican Congress if the right kind of campaign had been put on."[51] Especially after he apparently demonstrated his vote-getting qualities in resisting a labour-supported challenge to his Senate re-election in 1950, Taft seemed certain to become the party's presidential

---

48 Mason, *Republican Party*, 49–52.
49 "Bloc Votes Tipped the Balance in Closest Election Since 1916," *Newsweek*, November 20, 1944, 27–28.
50 Herbert Brownell, "The Republicans' Future Role," January 21, 1945, folder 13, box 38, series 2, Thomas E. Dewey Papers, University of Rochester Libraries, Rochester, New York.
51 Letter, Robert A. Taft to Billie Noojin, January 17, 1949, folder "Mrs. B. L. Noojin (Billie)," box 34, Robert A. Taft Papers, Manuscript Division, Library of Congress, Washington, D.C.

nominee in 1952—as the first flagbearer of Republican conservatism, in the eyes of his "Taftite" supporters, since the arrival of the New Deal. But the entry in party politics of Dwight D. Eisenhower, hero of World War II, reignited the fortunes of "Deweyite" moderates. Just as Eisenhower transformed the ideological battlefield, defeating Taft for the nomination and creating a new opportunity for a moderate Republican alternative to New Deal liberalism, his charismatic appeal as a candidate inspired an organisation that promised to offer a powerful alternative to labour unions as a vehicle for voter mobilisation.

Launched as the organisational framework for Eisenhower's quest for the presidential nomination, Citizens for Eisenhower achieved unusual success—claiming a membership of some 250,000 activists at the height of the campaign against Taft. Unsympathetic Republicans not uncommonly saw parallels with the Willkie clubs of 1940—parallels that led RNC officials to resist the creation of a role for Citizens in the fall campaign. This resistance was unsuccessful, however, and Citizens secured a similar organisational role in the campaign against Adlai Stevenson, charged with voter mobilisation among independents and disaffected Democrats (while the party concentrated on Republican loyalists), then reaching a claimed membership of some two million Americans. The stress of Citizens, in providing organisational infrastructure for voter outreach, was on grassroots activism, but it also offered a framework for expert assistance to the Eisenhower campaign—for the contributions in particular of advertising executives and television professionals. Eisenhower as a candidate and then as president successfully made pioneering use of television, rapidly achieving dominance as a medium of political communication. If, until this historical moment, success in voter mobilisation had depended overwhelmingly on activism, now television possessed a central role in the relationship between politicians and voters.[52]

Yet mastery of television did not alleviate concerns among Republicans about what they perceived as their party's organisational inadequacies. Leonard Hall, the party's national chair between 1953 and 1957, remained sure that "there is no substitute for doorbell-ringing and shoe leather," and thus that the role of

---

[52] "Fast Start," *NYT*, August 10, 1952, E1; W.H. Lawrence, "Aide of Eisenhower Spurns Reports of Mississippians' Third Party Proposal," *NYT*, August 3, 1952, 50; Robert Mason, "Citizens for Eisenhower and the Republican Party, 1951–1965," *Historical Journal* 56 (2013), 513, 520; Craig Allen, *Eisenhower and the Mass Media: Peace, Prosperity, and Prime-time TV* (Chapel Hill: University of North Carolina Press, 1993); David Haven Blake, *Liking Ike: Eisenhower, Advertising, and the Rise of Celebrity Politics* (New York: Oxford University Press, 2016).

party workers remained crucial in mobilising voters.[53] Reflecting on the disappointing results of the 1954 midterms, when Republicans lost control of Capitol Hill (which they would not recover for decades), Robert Humphreys of the RNC observed that the party "was out-maneuvered, out-manned and out-financed"—especially because of organised labour.[54] The 1955 merger between the CIO and the American Federation of Labor, to form the AFL–CIO as a single umbrella organisation for unions, further boosted this concern.[55]

The success of Citizens in 1952 encouraged its reactivation in subsequent campaigns—not only Eisenhower's bid for re-election in 1956 but also the midterms contests of 1954 and 1958 (when the organisation stressed the need for congressional support of Eisenhower). There was even an effort to resuscitate the organisation in 1962, after Eisenhower had left the White House, as the National Republican Citizens Committee. Even in 1956, however, the organisation lacked some of the energy associated with the initial mobilisation in support of Eisenhower, which had prompted many to identify it as a "Crusade."[56]

That Citizens achieved a degree of longer-term institutionalisation is indicative of this candidate-centred organisation's power as a vehicle for voter mobilisation, but it also reveals the failure of a larger goal—to achieve the ideological and organisational transformation of the Republican Party. The revitalisation of the party was an important project for the Eisenhower administration.[57] Among its strands was an effort to integrate Citizens into the party. Soon after the 1952 election, Walter Williams, a leader of Citizens, urged members to keep alive the "spirit" of their movement "by infusion of that 'spirit' in the form of people—live, pulsating, forward-looking Citizens—into the Republican Party."[58]

As Williams' words suggest, this idea did not involve a straightforward effort to improve the party's organisational capacity. A belief in the democracy-enhancing impact of expanded engagement in political activism underpinned Citizens, but more centrally this aspiration for Citizens activists to become active in the party connected with the administration's promotion of "Modern Republi-

---

53 Leonard Hall, "An Old Pro Describes How Politics in U.S. Has Changed," *Life*, April 25, 1960, 127.
54 Harold Lavine, *Smoke-Filled Rooms* (Englewood Cliffs, N.J.: Prentice-Hall, 1970), 135.
55 Mason, *Republican Party*, 169.
56 See, for example, "The General's 'Crusade,'" *Commonweal*, July 25, 1952, 379–380.
57 Cornelius P. Cotter, "Eisenhower as Party Leader," *Political Science Quarterly* 98 (1983): 255–283; Galvin, *Presidential Party Building*, 41–69.
58 Letter, Walter Williams to Citizens members, December 31, 1952, folder "Williams, Walter," box 822, series 320, Pre-Presidential Papers of Richard M. Nixon, Richard Nixon Presidential Library, Yorba Linda, California.

canism"—a label that Eisenhower adopted for his agenda, involving a moderate alternative to the Democrats' New Deal liberalism. He was sure that a stress on conservatism was electorally counterproductive. "Should any political party attempt to abolish Social Security, unemployment insurance, and eliminate labor laws and farm programs," Eisenhower observed in 1954, "you would not hear of that party again in our political history."[59] Thus the recruitment to the party of Citizens activists not only would improve the Republicans' capacity to mobilise voters, but their inclination to a moderate perspective on politics would support the embrace of Eisenhower's Modern Republicanism. "Within the party organisation itself, the indefatigable worker is rarely to be denied, especially when there are enough of them to support each other," Jacob K. Javits, a New York Republican, advised Eisenhower in late 1954. "Therefore, independents and young people who are for the President's policy should be encouraged by Citizens for Eisenhower to join the political organisation itself and exercise their strength and influence within the political organisation in adequate numbers."[60] There was, however, a significant exception to the connection between Citizens and the politics of moderation—in the South, where the organisation operated as a way to achieve outreach to whites for whom the Republican Party remained anathema. Instead, not only the defense of states' rights but even support for segregationism infected the message of Citizens campaigners.[61]

According to studies of public opinion, the quest for Modern Republicanism had limited success in modifying perceptions of the Republican Party; although the Eisenhower administration's record encouraged fewer Americans to see the party as a threat to the achievements of the New Deal, there was not equal success in challenging its disadvantageous image as aligned with the interests of a socioeconomic elite.[62] Furthermore, the call-to-arms issued by Walter Williams to Citizens activists at campaign's end in 1952 failed to initiate an organisational transformation of the party. In the 1960, at the close of the Eisenhower years,

---

59 Letter, Dwight D. Eisenhower to Edgar Eisenhower, November 8, 1954, folder "DDE Diary—November 1954 (2)," box 8, DDE Diary Series, Dwight D. Eisenhower Papers as President, Dwight D. Eisenhower Presidential Library, Abilene, Kansas.
60 Memo, Jacob K. Javits to Dwight D. Eisenhower, December 27, 1954, folder "Presidential Campaign – 1952 [iii]," box 3, subseries 2, series 5, Jacob K. Javits Collection, Frank Melville Jr. Memorial Library, Stony Brook University, Stony Brook, New York.
61 Julian M. Pleasants, "'Call Your Next Case': H. F. 'Chub' Seawell Jr., the Gubernatorial Election of 1952, and the Rise of the Republican Party in North Carolina," *North Carolina Historical Review* 76 (1999), 88; G. Wayne Dowdy, *Crusades for Freedom: Memphis and the Political Transformation of the American South* (Jackson: University Press of Mississippi, 2010), 56.
62 Angus Campbell, Philip E. Converse, Warren E. Miller and Donald E. Stokes, *The American Voter* (New York: Wiley, 1960), 47.

Walter N. Thayer, another Citizens leader, observed that "the Republican Party, for whatever reason, during the past eight years has not found the way to avail itself of the energy and enthusiasm these people have to offer." There had been missteps within the administration in formulating an effective strategy to foster the integration of Citizens into the party, and at local level factional jealousies sometimes hindered the harmoniousness on which integration depended. But more profoundly the candidate-centred political interest that informed Citizens activism was not necessarily similar to the party-oriented motivation that sustained Republican activism. Furthermore, an impulse to participate in a campaign was not necessarily similar to an ongoing commitment to political work. Valley Knudsen and Henriette Cowgill, two leaders in Citizens, noted that activists in their organisation were ready to "come in on a crusade for a Candidate or on an issue and work hard for a short time but wanted to be relieved of any Party organisation responsibility."[63]

"A Choice Not an Echo" and the Conservative Ascendancy

Not only did the twofold project of Citizens for Eisenhower and Modern Republicanism fail to achieve lasting success for a moderate alternative to New Deal liberalism, but the 1950s even witnessed the revitalisation instead of conservative Republicanism. Within the party the leader of this new conservatism was Senator Barry Goldwater of Arizona, whose 1960 book *The Conscience of a Conservative* was scarcely less angry in criticising the moderate Republican agenda of Dwight Eisenhower than the Democratic opposition's liberalism.[64] Buoying Goldwater's advocacy of conservatism was a challenge to the argument that moderation possessed electoral promise. Like John Hamilton in the 1930s, Goldwater saw conservatism as necessary to motivate activism, which in turn he saw as necessary for success in voter mobilisation. He told Javits, by then his Senate colleague, "that we can elect individual governors or presidents on a personal, popular basis; but this in itself, unless the candidate stands on a philosophical ground acceptable to the majority of Republican workers, will not enhance the Republican Party's position." The defeats of Willkie and Dewey, Goldwater claimed, led to the loss of House seats gained in off-year elections; because

---

[63] Mason, "Citizens for Eisenhower," 524–527 (quotations, 525).
[64] Barry Goldwater, *The Conscience of a Conservative* (Shepardsville, Ky.: Victor, 1960).

"Me-too-ism" characterised the presidential candidacies, "the Republican workers would not buy their philosophy, and they didn't work and we did not win."[65]

Informed by the paradigm for voter mobilisation of "a choice not an echo"—at fundamental odds with the electoral assumptions behind the Eisenhower project—Goldwater enthusiasm swept the party in 1964. Indeed, the pro-Goldwater movement drew benefit from that project's shortcomings because the party's continuing grassroots weakness allowed Goldwater enthusiasts to take control of local Republican committees.[66] This impetus was carefully led by a central campaign operation that emphasised organisational might as the foundation of success in the battle for the Republican nomination. "Precinct organisation means political power," wrote Peter O'Donnell Jr. to his fellow leaders of the Goldwater campaign.[67] "There are only 1,308 individuals who nominate the candidate," said one of them, F. Clifton White, soon after the convention. "I learned to count and count accurately."[68] This focus on enthusiasm-impelled organisation helped to secure the nomination for Barry Goldwater, though relative disarray among anti-Goldwater Republicans was a factor, too.[69]

Paradoxically, what had been strong during the nomination campaign was weak instead during the fall campaign against Lyndon B. Johnson; it was, one Republican said, "the most poorly run campaign I've ever seen." Furthermore, relations between the new Goldwater activists and longer-established Republicans were often tense, even though Goldwater had rationalised his conservatism as in harmony with party workers.[70]

Although the issue context was anyway not favourable to the Goldwater candidacy, the campaign also demonstrated the hollowness of its underlying paradigm of voter mobilisation. As he had outlined to Javits, Goldwater believed that a stress on conservatism would unlock activist enthusiasms necessary to success in voter mobilisation. But the "choice not an echo" thesis also now posited a problem of non-mobilisation on the grounds that the Republican alternative to the Democrats' liberalism was inadequately distinctive to encourage conserva-

---

[65] Letter, Barry Goldwater to Jacob K. Javits, May 25, 1960, folder "Barry Goldwater 1960," box 9, subseries 2, series 5, Javits Collection.
[66] Jack L. Walker, "The Republican Party and the Birth Rate," *Antioch Review* 25 (1965), 299.
[67] Peter O'Donnell Jr., "Progress Report #4," n.d., folder 7, box 155, William A. Rusher Papers, Manuscript Division, Library of Congress, Washington, D.C.
[68] "'Let's Grow Up, Conservatives!'" *Newsweek*, July 27, 1964, 28.
[69] Contingency was significant, too; Goldwater narrowly won the critically significant California primary shortly after news of a baby for key rival Nelson Rockefeller, reminding voters of Rockefeller's divorce and remarriage, then widely considered scandalous.
[70] "After the Fall: To the Mainstream?" *Newsweek*, November 9, 1964, 31–32 (quotation, 31).

tive voters to participate in elections. During the summer and fall of 1964 the idea of a "hidden" or "silent" vote, open to mobilisation by Goldwater conservatism, gained currency especially because of the increased salience of civil rights issues; there was much talk of "backlash" against civil rights that would boost Republican support.[71] On election day, however, not only did a hidden vote in support of Goldwater fail to appear, but "frontlash"—of habitual Republican voters who preferred Lyndon Johnson's record of action on civil rights—seemed more significant than backlash. The argument about voter mobilisation that has been powerful enough to inflame the Goldwater candidacy was, the returns suggested, a myth.[72]

Conclusion

Concern about Republicans about their party's organisational deficiencies were persistent, and so was the belief that these deficiencies accounted for inadequacies in voter mobilisation—and perhaps critically so. In studying the Republican Party during this period, historians have tended to overlook the significance of this belief and the ways in which, for political actors of the era, the secret to success at the polls by no means entirely involved the right set of policies; questions of organisation and campaign technique were important too. The issues explored by scholars in political science interested in voter mobilisation deserve attention among historians, too.

Distinctive at first sight from the ongoing debate over policy between conservatives and moderates, ideas about voter mobilisation were actually in close connection with that debate. In a political era characterised by Franklin Roosevelt's success in building an electoral coalition through the transcendence of party, these initiatives often revealed a confidence in the revitalisation of party organisation as a route to the restoration of the Republican Party's electoral fortunes. But although Republicans of this era possessed this confidence in organisational enhancements, from the 1930s to the 1960s such innovation in pursuit of voter mobilisation did not uncover a solution to the Republicans' minority problem.

---

71 John Chamberlain, "These Days: The Silent Vote," *WP*, October 14, 1964, A13; Earl Mazo, "The Silent Vote," *NYT*, October 23, 1964, 27; Tom Wicker, "Election Trends Please Both Sides," *NYT*, October 27, 1964, 31; "VPA: The Making of an Avalanche—1964," *Newsweek*, November 9, 1964, 28–29.
72 Philip E. Converse, Aage R. Clausen and Warren E. Miller, "Electoral Myth and Reality: The 1964 Election," *American Political Science Review* 59 (1965): 321–336.

Bibliography

Primary Sources

Manuscript Sources

Abilene, Kans.: Dwight D. Eisenhower Presidential Library.
    Dwight D. Eisenhower Papers as President.
Bloomington, Ind.: Lilly Library, Indiana University.
    Willkie Clubs Papers.
Rochester, N.Y.: University of Rochester Libraries.
    Thomas E. Dewey Papers.
Stony Brook, N.Y.: Frank Melville Jr. Memorial Library, Stony Brook University.
    Jacob K. Javits Collection.
Topeka, Kans.: Kansas State Historical Society
    Alfred M. Landon Papers.
Washington, D.C.: Manuscript Division, Library of Congress.
    Raymond Leslie Buell Papers; Raymond Clapper Papers; John D.M. Hamilton Papers; Ogden Livingston Mills Papers; William A. Rusher Papers; Robert A. Taft Papers; William Allen White Papers.
Yorba Linda, Calif.: Richard Nixon Presidential Library.
    Pre-Presidential Papers of Richard M. Nixon.

Newspapers and Magazines

Commonweal.
Life.
New York Times.
Newsweek.
Washington Post.

Books

Campbell, Angus, Philip E. Converse, Warren E. Miller and Donald E. Stokes. *The American Voter.* New York: Wiley, 1960.
Goldwater, Barry. *The Conscience of a Conservative.* Shepardsville, Ky.: Victor, 1960.
Lavine, Harold. *Smoke-Filled Rooms.* Englewood Cliffs, N.J.: Prentice-Hall, 1970.
Schlafly, Phyllis. *A Choice Not an Echo.* Alton, Ill.: Pere Marquette, 1964.
Taft, Charles P. *You and I—and Roosevelt.* New York: Farrar & Rinehart, 1936.

Secondary Sources

Journal Articles and Book Chapters

Campbell, James E. "Sources of the New Deal Realignment: The Contributions of Conversion and Mobilization to Political Change." *Western Political Quarterly* 38 (1985): 357–376.

Converse, Philip E., Aage R. Clausen, and Warren E. Miller. "Electoral Myth and Reality: The 1964 Election." *American Political Science Review* 59 (1965): 321–336.

Cotter, Cornelius P. "Eisenhower as Party Leader." *Political Science Quarterly* 98 (1983): 255–283.

Erikson, Robert S., and Kent L. Tedin, "The 1928–1936 Partisan Realignment: The Case for the Conversion Hypothesis." *American Political Science Review* 75 (1981): 951–962.

Goldstein, Kenneth M., and Matthew Holleque. "Getting up off the Canvass: Rethinking the Study of Mobilization." In *The Oxford Handbook of American Elections and Political Behavior*, edited by Jan E. Leighley, 577–594. New York: Oxford University Press, 2010.

McGuire, John Thomas. "Beginning an 'Extraordinary Opportunity': Eleanor Roosevelt, Molly Dewson, and the Expansion of Women's Boundaries in the Democratic Party, 1924–1934." *Women's History Review* 23 (2014): 922–937.

Mason, Robert. "Citizens for Eisenhower and the Republican Party, 1951–1965." *Historical Journal* 56 (2013): 513–536.

Mason, Robert. "Transatlantic Dimensions of Electoral Strategy: Republican Party Interpretations of UK Politics, 1936–c. 1960." In *Postwar Conservatism, a Transnational Investigation: Britain, France, and the United States, 1930–1990*, edited by Clarisse Berthezène and Jean-Christian Vinel, 215–242. Cham, Switzerland: Palgrave Macmillan, 2017.

Milkis, Sidney M. "Franklin D. Roosevelt and the Transcendence of Partisan Politics." *Political Science Quarterly* 100 (1985): 479–504.

Pleasants, Julian M. "'Call Your Next Case': H. F. 'Chub' Seawell Jr., the Gubernatorial Election of 1952, and the Rise of the Republican Party in North Carolina." *North Carolina Historical Review* 76 (1999): 66–101.

Walker, Jack L. "The Republican Party and the Birth Rate." *Antioch Review* 25 (1965): 297–308.

Books

Allen, Craig. *Eisenhower and the Mass Media: Peace, Prosperity, and Prime-time TV*. Chapel Hill: University of North Carolina Press, 1993.

Andersen, Kristi. *The Creation of a Democratic Majority, 1928–1996*. Chicago: University of Chicago Press, 1979.

Blake, David Haven. *Liking Ike: Eisenhower, Advertising, and the Rise of Celebrity Politics*. New York: Oxford University Press, 2016.

Critchlow, Donald T. *The Conservative Ascendancy: How the GOP Right Made Political History*. Cambridge, Mass.: Harvard University Press, 2007.

Dowdy, G. Wayne. *Crusades for Freedom: Memphis and the Political Transformation of the American South*. Jackson: University Press of Mississippi, 2010.

Farber, David. *Everybody Ought to Be Rich: The Life and Times of John J. Raskob, Capitalist.* New York: Oxford University Press, 2013.

Galvin, Daniel J. *Presidential Party-Building: Dwight D. Eisenhower to George W. Bush.* Princeton, N.J.: Princeton University Press, 2010.

Gould, Lewis L. *Grand Old Party: A History of the Republicans.* New York: Random House, 2003.

Hemmer, Nicole. *Messengers of the Right: Conservative Media and the Transformation of American Politics.* Philadelphia: University of Pennsylvania Press, 2016.

Johnson, Donald Bruce. *The Republican Party and Wendell Willkie.* Urbana: University of Illinois Press, 1960.

Kabaservice, Geoffrey. *Rule and Ruin: The Downfall of Moderation and the Destruction of the Republican Party, from Eisenhower to the Tea Party.* New York: Oxford University Press, 2012.

Lewis, David Levering. *The Improbable Wendell Willkie: The Businessman Who Saved the Republican Party and His Country, and Conceived a New World Order.* New York: Liveright, 2018.

McGirr, Lisa. *Suburban Warriors: The Origins of the New American Right.* Princeton, N.J.: Princeton University Press, 2001.

Mason, Robert. *The Republican Party and American Politics from Hoover to Reagan.* New York: Cambridge University Press, 2012.

Milkis, Sidney M. *The President and the Parties: The Transformation of the American Party System since the New Deal.* New York: Oxford University Press, 1993.

Reinhard, David W. *The Republican Right since 1945.* Lexington: University Press of Kentucky, 1983.

Richardson, Heather Cox. *To Make Men Free: A History of the Republican Party.* New York: Basic, 2014.

Rosen, Elliot A. *The Republican Party in the Age of Roosevelt: Sources of Anti-Government Conservatism in the United States.* Charlottesville: University of Virginia Press, 2014.

Rymph, Catherine E. *Republican Women: Feminism and Conservatism from Suffrage through the Rise of the New Right.* Chapel Hill: University of North Carolina Press, 2006.

Shermer, Elizabeth Tandy. *Sunbelt Capitalism: Phoenix and the Transformation of American Politics.* Philadelphia: University of Pennsylvania Press, 2013.

Stuckey, Mary E. *Voting Deliberatively: FDR and the 1936 Presidential Campaign.* University Park: Penn State University Press, 2015.

Sugrue, Thomas J. *The Origins of the Urban Crisis: Race and Inequality in Postwar Detroit.* Princeton, N.J.: Princeton University Press, 1996.

Dissertations

Morris, Henry Wesley. "The Republicans in a Minority Role." Ph.D. dissertation, State University of Iowa, 1960.

Slopnick, Thomas M. "In the Shadow of Herbert Hoover: The Republican Party and the Politics of Defeat, 1932–1936." Ph.D. dissertation, University of Connecticut, 2006.

List of contributors

Sharon Baptiste is a senior lecturer at the Université Sorbonne Paris Nord in France. Her research interests include the presence of black peoples in Britain and their contributions to and impact on British history and society. Her work focuses more particularly on the social, political and cultural representations of the African Caribbean diaspora. Her most recent publications in this domain include a book chapter, „The Children of the Windrush Generation" in a collective work published by Routledge in January 2020 entitled Windrush (1948), Rivers of Blood (1968): Legacy and Assessment and an article, „The Evolution of the Black Cultural Archives 1981–2015, published in *Colonial Extensions, Postcolonial Decentrings: Cultures and Discourses on the Edge* (2017), in the Peter Lang Collection Comparatism and Society.

Gregory Benedetti is an associate Professor in American civilisation at Grenoble Alpes University and member of the research center ILCEA 4. His research focuses on contemporary African-American history through political and cultural studies.In 2014, he defended his PhD dissertation entitled: „L'émergence d'une classe politique noire post-raciale, 2000–2012. He is the author of several articles, among which „Barack Obama's Popularization of Science: a Political Strategy?" in *Using and Abusing Science: Science and Political Discourse from Burke's „French Revolution" to Obama's Science Fair* (CSP, 2016).

Geraldine Castel, is an assistant professor in British civilisation at Grenoble Alpes University in France. She belongs to the PDI (Politics, Discourse and Innovation) team of the ILCEA4 lab. After working on strategic and communication issues related to the main British political parties from a historical perspective, she then moved to their more contemporary manifestations through the impact of the introduction of ICTs in that field. This has led her in turn to start exploring the field of the digital humanities.

Marion Douzou is an assistant professor at the Université Lumière Lyon 2 and a member of the research unit Triangle (UMR 5206). She defended her dissertation on the Tea Party movement in Pennsylvania in December 2017. Her fieldwork was made possible by a scholarship from the Lurcy Foundation.

John A. Kirk is the George W. Donaghey Distinguished Professor of History at the University of Arkansas at Little Rock. He is author or editor of nine books including the award-winning *Redefining the Color Line: Black Activism in Little Rock, Arkansas, 1940–1970* (Gainesville: University Press of Florida, 2002), *Martin Luther King, Jr.* (London and New York: Pearson Longman, 2005), ed. *Race and Ethnicity in Arkansas: New Perspectives* (Fayetteville: University of Arkansas Press, 2014), and ed. *The Civil Rights Movement: A Documentary Reader* (Hoboken, NJ: Wiley Blackwell, 2020).

Jean-Louis Marin-Lamellet received his PhD in American studies from Université Lumière-Lyon 2, France, in 2016. His research focuses on the interplay between print culture and protest movements at the turn of the twentieth century, the representations and receptions of Populism and Progressivism, and the long history of anti-monopoly. He teaches at Université Savoie-Mont Blanc, Chambéry (France) and in high school.

List of contributors

Robert Mason is a Professor of History at the University of Edinburgh in Scotland. He is the author of *Richard Nixon and the Quest for a New Majority* (Chapel Hill: University of North Carolina Press, 2004) and *The Republican Party and American Politics from Hoover to Reagan* (New York: Cambridge University Press, 2012). With Alix Meyer and François Vergniolle de Chantal, he is coauthor of *Réactions en Chaîne : Les Républicains, de Dwight D. Eisenhower à George W. Bush (1952–2008)* (Paris: Éditions Fahrenheit, 2015). He is coeditor, with Iwan Morgan, of *Seeking a New Majority: The Republican Party and American Politics, 1960–1980* (Nashville, TN: Vanderbilt University Press, 2013) and *The Liberal Consensus Reconsidered: American Politics and Society in the Postwar Era* (Gainesville: University Press of Florida, 2017).

Véronique Molinari is a Professor of British Studies at Grenoble Alpes University, France. Her research focuses on the women's movement in Edwardian and interwar Britain and on women's participation in politics. She is among others the author of *Citoyennes, et après ? Le droit de vote des femmes et ses conséquences en Grande-Bretagne, 1918–1939*, (Bern : Peter Lang, 2008) and co-editor of several books, including *Women and Science, 17th Century to Present: Pioneers, Activists and Protagonists*, with Donna Andreolle (CSP, 2011) and *Using and Abusing Science: Science and Political Discourse from Burke's „French Revolution" to Obama's Science Fair* with Cyril Besson (CSP, 2016).

Olivier Richomme is an assistant professor of U.S. history at the University of Lyon, France. His field of research is race and politics in the U.S.. He wrote extensively on the history of ethnoracial statistics and anti-discrimination policies. He now focuses on redistricting, election law and voting rights. His latest book is Race and Partisanship in California Redistricting: From the 1965 Voting Rights Act to the Present, Lexington, 2019.

Karine Rivière-De Franco is a senior lecturer in British civilisation at the University of Orléans, France and works on elections and political communication. Her research also focuses on parliamentary, gender and media studies. She has published *La communication électorale en Grande-Bretagne. De M. Thatcher à T. Blair* (l'Harmattan, Paris, 2008) and co-edited books on electoral strategies and the role of the media in politics (*Stratégies politiques et représentations médiatiques dans les sociétés européennes de 1945 à nos jours*, Orléans, Editions Paradigmes, 2018. *Stratégies et campagnes électorales en Grande-Bretagne et aux Etats-Unis*, Paris, L'Harmattan, 2009. *Image et communication politique. La Grande-Bretagne depuis 1980*, Paris, L'Harmattan, 2007).

Index

Adkins, Gov. Homer   65f.
African Americans   2f., 9f., 26–29 33f., 40–42, 120, 124f.
Alliance Circulating Library   117
Alliance Exchange   115
American Legal Exchange Council   196
A. Philip Randolph   56
Arkansas Negro Democratic Association (ANDA)   53
Astor, Nancy   131, 137

Barack Obama   17, 167, 181, 185
Beck, Glenn   181, 185, 188f.
Black Lives Matter   2, 7
Blair, Tony   17, 81, 83, 132, 135, 147, 155, 157, 159, 168
Breitbart.com   188f.
Brexit   1, 14, 142f., 146, 164, 166, 174
British Election Survey   78
British Transport Workers   114
Brown v. Board of Education   49
Bryan, William Jennings   126

Cable, Vince   158
Cameron, David   16, 89, 131, 133, 137, 142, 145, 147f., 157–159, 163, 167, 167
Campbell, Alastair   168
Carpool Momentum   161
Chancellor Frank H. Dodge   54
Churchill, Randolph   136
Civil Rights   1f., 4, 9f., 25, 27f., 48–50, 52–56, 58, 61f., 65, 69, 72, 125, 220
Clegg, Nick   89, 159
Clinton, Hillary   5
Committee on Negro Organizations (CNO)   48, 59, 61
Community Empowerment Roadshows   91f.
Conjoined polarization   10, 27f., 38, 40
Conservative, Conservative Party   4, 6, 9, 13–15, 17f., 27, 32, 72, 81–85, 89, 94f., 99–101, 132–140, 142–148, 157–165, 167–169, 174, 182–190, 192f., 195f., 201–207, 210f., 214, 218–220

Conservative Women's Organisation   137
Conservative Women's Policy Group   148
Cooperatives   112, 115f., 119, 125
Corbyn, Jeremy   143, 145, 161, 163, 167, 169–171
Covid-19   1

Dealignment   3–5, 7
Democratic Party   10f., 26f., 40, 42, 47, 50, 53–56, 62, 64f., 72, 126, 203f., 207, 211
Democratic Party of Arkansas (DPA)   48
Demos   175
Dennis Prager   189
Descriptive representation   13, 26, 34f., 42, 78, 92, 132, 136, 147
Dialogue   31, 83, 88, 161
Dom Giordano   185
Dr. John Marshall Robinson   48, 52f., 59, 62, 72
Du Bois, W.E.B.   2, 9

Eisenhower, Dwight D.   4, 10, 50, 180, 201f., 208, 213, 215–217
Emmet Till   49
Enfranchisement   2f., 9f., 11, 13, 25, 28
Ethnic Minority British Election Survey   78
Excalibur   17, 155, 164
eXpress campaign bus   90f., 97

Facebook   16f., 154, 158f., 162–167, 169, 171, 174, 183, 188–191, 193
Fair Employment Practice Committee (FEPC)   56
Farmers' Alliances   12, 109–112, 114, 119–126
Fawcett Society   2, 14, 131, 134, 144
Flower, Benjamin O.   113f., 119, 121f.
Flowers, William Harold   48, 55, 57–62, 69–72

Gender gap   13, 135
Gerrymandering   3, 9, 37–42
Google   16, 115, 159, 163, 167

Granny Voter 2
Greenback party 120

Harman, Harriet 144f., 146

ICTs 153f., 158, 166, 169
Instagram 16, 159, 167

John Birch Society 185
Jones, Scipio Africanus 48, 52f., 59, 72
Judge Richard M. Mann 54

Kellie, Luna 120f.
King, Martin Luther 49, 61
Knights of Labor 112, 114

Labour, Labour Party 3f., 6., 15, 49, 81–85, 94f., 97, 100, 132–137, 140f., 143–145, 147, 157–165, 167f., 170f.
Lawrence, Stephen 83, 110
League of Women Voters 2, 12
Lease, Mary Elizabeth 121f.
Legal Defense and Educational Fund, Inc. 58
Liberal Democrats 4, 157–159, 161, 163
Little Rock 10, 48–50, 52–54, 57, 61–65, 67f.

Major, John 81, 83
Marshall, Thurgood 58, 63–65, 76
May, Theresa 13f., 90, 101, 104, 131–13, 137, 142–148, 157f, 160, 179
McDonald-Valesh, Eva 121, 127f
Meetup 183, 188
Membersnet 160f., 169
Merlin 164, 169
Miliband, Ed 157
Moms4Bush 2
Moms4Trump 2
MP Shadowing Scheme 89, 93–95, 101
Mujeres Latinas en Accion 2

National Association for the Advancement of Colored People (NAACP) 2, 52–55, 57–59, 61, 65–70, 73
National Association of Latino Elected Officials (NALEO) 33, 45

National Council for La Raza 2
National Organization for Women 2
National Union of Students 86
Nation Builder 161, 164f.
New Deal 18, 48, 55, 57, 60, 76, 201f., 204–209, 211, 213–215, 217f., 222f.

Obama, Barak 5, 16f., 161, 167, 182, 185
Operation Black Vote 2, 11, 77–105

Parliamentary Shadowing Scheme 92–94
People's Party, Populist Party 110, 117, 123, 129
Perot, Ross 153, 155, 173, 178
Pickles, Eric 167, 178
Political representation 11, 19, 25f., 28, 40, 42, 47–53, 71f., 77, 86, 92, 101, 147
Populism 12, 110–112, 116–118, 120, 123–126, 128–130
Primrose League 136

Quinn, Jim 185

Racial polarization 26f.
Reagan, Ronald 4f., 210, 223
Realignment 3–5, 7, 20f, 26f., 43, 45, 204, 222
Redistricting 3, 9, 25–28, 32–37, 39–45, 70
Representation of the People Act 1928 12
Representation of the People Act in 1918 11, 131
Republican Party of Arkansas (RPA) 48, 51, 53, 70
Roosevelt, Franklin Delano 4, 18, 26, 55f., 74, 192, 201–204, 208f., 211–214, 220–223

Santelli, Rick 187, 196
Segregation 26, 47f., 51, 55, 58, 60, 64, 72, 125
Smith v. Allwright 64f., 76
Snapchat 16, 159f., 228
Straw, Jack 83
Student Nonviolent Coordinating Committee (SNCC) 69, 229

Substantive representation   13, 26, 34, 36
  78, 92, 103, 132, 136, 147
Swing voters   19, 163

Tea Party   17, 180–198, 203, 223
Tennent, Rose   185
13th Amendment   9,
15th Amendment   3, 9, 25
19th Amendment   11 f.
Thatcher, Margaret   5, 13, 20, 83, 131 f., 136–143, 146–149
The Commonwealth Foundation   185
The Daily caller   188 f.
The Enterprise Institute   189
The Heritage Foundation   185
Thornberry, Emily   168
Trump, Donald   1, 5–7, 27, 42, 166
Twitter   16 f., 101, 154, 158, 165, 167, 169 f., 183, 190 f.

UKIP, United Kingdom Independence Party   6, 164, 168 f.
Understanding Power   86 f.

Violence Against Women and Girls   145
Votesource   164
Voting Rights Act   9, 25–30, 32, 35–37, 40–46, 68–70, 73
Voto Latino   2

Weaver, James   125
WhatsApp   162, 169
Who runs my City?   87–90
Wilson, Woodrow   126
Woman's Christian Temperance Union   119
Women2win   145

Young Women's Christian Association England and Wales   14
Youtube   16 f., 158, 163, 174, 179, 183, 187, 189, 196 f.

Zuckerberg, Mark   159

www.ingramcontent.com/pod-product-compliance
Lightning Source LLC
Chambersburg PA
CBHW020229170426
43201CB00007B/365